IGCSE
Information and Communication Technology

Endorsed by
University of Cambridge
International Examinations

IGCSE

Information and Communication Technology

Graham Brown
and David Watson

HODDER
EDUCATION
AN HACHETTE UK COMPANY

Acknowledgements

The authors would like to thank the following for their assistance, patience, understanding and proofreading: Tracy Brown, Philippa Brown, Laura Brown, Jenna Brown, Karla Brown, John Reeves, Brian Sargent and Stuart Morris. Images: SnowAngel – © Graham Brown, Snowball.jpg – © Graham Brown, Trees.jpg – © Graham Brown. Chapter 10 page 125: Snowman – © Karla Brown, Six trees – © Graham Brown.

p. 1 *tr* ©iStockphoto.com/Dennys Bisogno, *tl* © istockphoto.com/Nicholas Monu, *br* © iStockphoto.com/bluestocking/Uyen Le, *bl* © Ronen/iStockphoto.com; **p. 3** *tr* © iStockphoto.com/Dennys Bisogno, *tl* © istockphoto.com/Nicholas Monu, *l* © Godfried Edelman/istockphoto.com; **p. 5** Photodisc/Getty Images; **p. 6** *t* Photodisc/Getty Images, *c* © Sirin Buse/istockphoto.com, *b* © iStockphoto.com/bluestocking/Uyen Le; **p. 7** DreamPictures/The Image Bank/Getty Images; **p. 8** *t* Ingram Publishing, *b* © Dmitriy Melnikov – Fotolia.com; **p. 9** *t* © Cindy England/istockphoto.com, *c* © George Clerk/istockphoto.com, *b* www.purestockx.com; **p. 10** © Dmitry Vinogradov/istockphoto.com; **p. 11** *t* © Mariano Ruiz/istockphoto.com, *b* ©kmit – Fotolia.com; **p. 12** *t* © jerges/istockphoto.com, *b* Thinkstock/Jupiterimages/Getty Images; **p. 13** *t* Brand X/Getty Images, *c* Photodisc/Getty Images, *b* ©lauriek/istockphoto.com; **p. 14** *t* © Jostein Hauge/istockphoto.com, *b* Martin Firus/istockphoto.com; **p. 15** *t* © Royalty-Free/Corbis, *b* © thumb/istockphoto.com; **p. 16** *t* Reproduced by permission of Scantron Corporation. Copyright © Scantron Corporation. All rights reserved, *b* Access IS, UK; **p. 17** *tl* Access IS, UK, *tr* Beaconstox/Alamy, *cl* © 216Photo/iStockphoto.com, *bl* © Juanmonino/istockphoto.com, *tr* Beaconstox/Alamy; **p. 18** *t* © Michal Mrozek/istockphoto.com, *b* Photodisc/Getty Images; **p. 19** © BMPix/istockphoto.com; **p. 20** *t* © fotoIE/istockphoto.com, *b* ©asterix0597/istockphoto.com; **p. 21** Ingram Publishing; **p. 22** *t* © LoopAll – Fotolia.com, *b* © Konstantin Shevtsov – Fotolia.com; **p. 23** *t* © Murat BAYSAN – Fotolia.com, *bl & r* ©Z Corporation; **p. 24** Ted Foxx/Alamy; **p. 25** *t* © Mike McCune/istockphoto.com, *c* © Ronen/iStockphoto.com, *b* © Andrey Turchaninov/istockphoto.com; **p. 26** ©Tomasz Zachariasz/istockphoto.com; **p. 27** *t* Andrew Lambert Photography/Science Photo Library, *c* © Yury Kosourov/istockphoto.com, *b* Oliver Leedham/Alamy; **p. 30** *t* © rocksunderwater/istockphoto.com, *b* © Long Ha/istockphoto.com; **p. 31** © fotoIE/istockphoto.com; **p. 32** © brentmelissa/iStockphoto.com; **p. 33** © peregrina/istockphoto.com; **p. 34** imagebroker/Alamy; **p. 35** © Tatiana Popova/istockphoto.com; **p. 36** ©scubabartek/istockphoto.com; **p. 41** © sambrogio/istockphoto.com; **p. 42** *t* Thinkstock/Jupiterimages/Getty Images, *c* © Dino Ablakovic/istockphoto.com, *b* © Norman Chan/istockphoto.com; **p. 58** *l* © Tootles – Fotolia.com, photodisc/Getty Images, *r* photodisc/Getty Images; **p. 87** David R. Frazier Photolibrary, Inc/Alamy

t = top, *b* = bottom, *l* = left, *r* = right, *c* = centre

Although every effort has been made to ensure that website addresses are correct at time of going to press, Hodder Education cannot be held responsible for the content of any website mentioned in this book. It is sometimes possible to find a relocated web page by typing in the address of the home page for a website in the URL window of your browser.

Hachette UK's policy is to use papers that are natural, renewable and recyclable products and made from wood grown in sustainable forests. The logging and manufacturing processes are expected to conform to the environmental regulations of the country of origin.

Orders: please contact Bookpoint Ltd, 130 Milton Park, Abingdon, Oxon OX14 4SB. Telephone: (44) 01235 827720. Fax: (44) 01235 400454. Lines are open 9.00–5.00, Monday to Saturday, with a 24-hour message answering service. Visit our website at http://www.hoddereducation.co.uk.

Cover photo © Digital Vision
Illustrations by Barking Dog Art
Typeset in 11pt Galliard by Pantek Arts Ltd
Printed in Italy
A catalogue record for this title is available from the British Library
ISBN 978 0 340 983829

Contents

Introduction

Aims

This book has been written to provide the knowledge, understanding and practical skills that you need for the Cambridge IGCSE in Information and Communication Technology. This book, together with the accompanying CD and image for scanning, provides:

- practice examination questions for the theory elements of the course
- practice tasks which offer guidance on how to answer questions for the practical parts of the course
- activities which allow students practice in answering questions for the practical parts of the course
- source data files for the tasks and activities
- hints and tips for the practical papers
- suggestions for possible teaching methods.

Although it has been written with the CIE syllabus in mind, it can also be used as a useful reference text for other practical ICT qualifications at GCSE and other equivalent Level 2 courses.

Using the book

The text is in 16 chapters. Although it is possible that some elements of the practical chapters may be examined in the theory question papers, and vice versa, the sections for the theory work are in Chapters 1–8 and the sections for the practical work in Chapters 9–16.

Examination questions

For the theory section, there are examination-style questions on the CD, together with model answers, all in portable document format (.pdf). For the practical section, the examination-style questions appear as activities in the book, with the model answers on the CD. Two practice examination papers also appear on the CD.

Colour codes and symbols used

Throughout the book there are a number of colours and symbols used. Key presses are shown as <Enter>, but be careful with Chapter 15, where html codes are also shown in angled brackets, like this <html>. Different sections of text are in the following styles.

Tasks

These are examination-style questions in the practical section (which often include the use of source files from the CD for the practical tasks) that are answered within the chapter. The text demonstrates the techniques used to solve the task and gives some example answers. These provide easy-to-follow step-by-step instructions, so that practical skills are developed alongside the knowledge and understanding.

Activities

These are examination-style questions in the practical section, usually at the end of a chapter or section for the students to answer. These often include the use of source files from the CD. Model answers for each activity are available in portable document format (.pdf) on the CD.

Exercises

In the theory section, these are short exercises for the students to complete in order to confirm their understanding of the concepts covered in a section or chapter.

Hints

These give hints, tips, shortcuts and advice on examination techniques.

```
HTML markup
All html markup appears in a blue,
proportionally spaced font.

Cascading stylesheets
All cascading stylesheet markup
appears in a red proportionally
spaced font.
```

Text colours

Some words or phrases within the text are printed in **red**. Definitions of these terms can be found in the glossary.

In the practical section, words that appear in **blue** indicate an action or location found within the software package, for example 'Select the **Home** tab.'

In the database sections of the book, words in **orange** show field names.

Words in **green** show the functions or formulae entered into the cell of a spreadsheet, for example a cell may contain the function **=SUM(B2:B12)**.

■ Hardware and software used

The practical elements of the examinations can be undertaken on any hardware platform and using any appropriate software packages. For the purposes of this book, we have needed to choose specific software packages, but the functionality of many other packages is very similar. Many of the skills demonstrated in Chapters 9 to 16 are transferable and can be adapted for other hardware and software platforms.

All the tasks and activities within the practical chapters have therefore been created using a PC platform with *Microsoft Windows Vista* operating system and include the use of *Notepad*. Independent packages used for the practical sections include packages from *Microsoft Office Professional Edition 2007*, including *Word, Excel, Access* and *PowerPoint*. *Internet Explorer* has been used as the web browser and *Windows Live Mail* as a web-based email editor.

For the website authoring section of the book (Chapter 15), all work has been produced in html code without the use of a WYSIWYG package. Although you may have a WYSIWYG package available and may wish to allow students to use this, it is important to realise that they are expected to have knowledge of underlying HTML and cascading stylesheet code. All html written within this chapter is written in HTML version 4.01 strict, and are W3C validated (although the Doctype statements have been removed so as to avoid confusing students). All cascading stylesheets used have been W3C validated.

■ Using the source image

You have been provided with a source image which can be scanned when attempting Activity 10b in Chapter 10. This can be found at the very end of the book, after the index.

■ Using source files

Source files can be found on the CD and will need to be copied onto your local machine or network

drive in order to use them. Copy them and give them read/write access. This is essential to ensure that you can use some of the file types included on the CD. For example, you cannot create queries or reports in *Access* when working from the CD. The CD will contain all source files in a series of sub-folders, one for each of the practical chapters.

PC users

From the **Start** button, select the **Computer** option and locate the CD drive, which may be called drive D: or E:. For the purposes of this section, we will assume that it is called drive E:. If your machine has a different drive for the CD letter, adapt these instructions accordingly. Locate the **Chapter source files** folder, which can be found at **E:\Resources\Chapter source files**. To locate an individual file, such as the image SNOWBALL.JPG used in Chapter 10, use the path **E:\Resources\Chapter source files\Chapter 10\Snowball.jpg**.

It may be better to copy the contents of this folder into a new folder on your local machine or network drive. Open each file as you wish to use it. Select the **Office** button, and then **Save As...** to save a new copy with an amended filename. You may need to change the file permissions of these files to read/write to enable you work on them; however, check with your network administrator before attempting to make these changes.

MAC users

Double click on the CD icon on the desktop. Use *Finder* to navigate to the location for the new folder, then create a new folder (<Apple>+<Shift>+<N>). With *Finder*, choose the CD and select all files (<Apple>+<A>) and copy them (<Apple>+<C>). Go to the new folder using *Finder* and paste the files (<Apple>+<V>).

Changing the source files to match your regional settings

Before attempting any of these processes, back up all source files. The source .csv (comma separated value) files supplied on the CD have commas as separators between fields and full stops within currency values. If your regional settings for these values are different to these (for example, if you use commas within currency values rather than full stops and your software settings require you to use semicolons for separators between fields), then the source data files will need to be edited for use with the regional settings for your software. This process may be required to convert the source data files before the start of the practical examinations. You can do this process in many packages, but the easiest (at this level) is *Word*. Open the .csv file in *Word* using the **Office** button and **Open**. Select the file from the list and click on [Open ▾]. This will open the file, which will look similar to this.

```
Who manufactured the car?,Model,Colour,Price that we bought the car
for,Price that we will sell the car for,Year,Extras,Does the car need
cleaning?
TVR,Tuscan,Black,18000,20305,2006,Alloy Wheels   Air Conditioning,N
Mercedes,C200,Silver,4995,5995,2003,Air Conditioning,N
Toyota,MR2 roadster,Electric blue,13995,15895,2005,Leather Seats   Air
Conditioning,N
```

Select the **Home** tab, then the **Editing** section followed by the **Replace** icon. Enter a , (comma) into the **Find what:** box and a ; (semicolon) into the **Replace with:** box, then click on [Replace All].

Repeat this process, replacing a . (full stop) with a , (comma). All the characters will have been replaced within the file like this.

```
Who manufactured the car?;Model;Colour;Price that we bought the car
for;Price that we will sell the car for;Year;Extras;Does the car need
cleaning?
TVR;Tuscan;Black;18000;20305;2006;Alloy Wheels   Air Conditioning;N
Mercedes;C200;Silver;4995;5995;2003;Air Conditioning;N
Toyota;MR2 roadster;Electric blue;13995;15895;2005;Leather Seats   Air
Conditioning;N
```

Save the file with the same file name using the **Office** button and **Save**. This will ensure that the file is saved in .csv format.

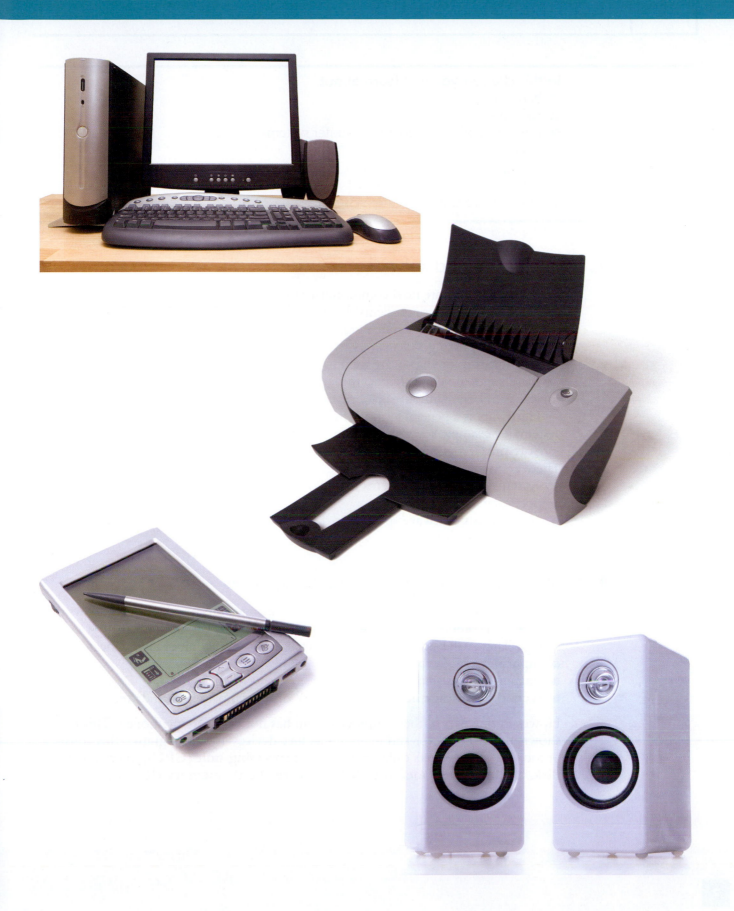

Part 1

Types and components of computer systems

In this chapter you will learn about:
- hardware
- software
- the main components of a computer system
- operating systems:
  - graphical user interface (GUI)
  - command line interface (CLI)
- different types of computer systems.

1.1 Hardware and software

Computer systems are now commonplace in every part of our daily life. This chapter introduces the basic components that make up these computer systems; most of these will be described in much greater depth in later chapters. Comparing books with computers is a good analogy: the actual pages and the ink used on the pages are equivalent to the hardware used to make up these computers; the words written on these pages are equivalent to the software. Without the words, the book is useless. Similarly, without software, computers would be of little use to any of us.

Hardware is a general term for the physical components that make up a computer system, for example keyboard, mouse, monitor, processor, circuit board and so on.

Software is a general term for the programs that control the computer system. There are two types of software:

- **systems software**: programs that allow the hardware to run properly, e.g. operating systems
- **applications software**: programs that allow the user to do specific tasks, e.g. spreadsheets.

1.2 Main components of computer systems

A typical computer system is made up of hardware and software. Figure 1.1 shows an example of a computer system consisting of input devices, output devices and secondary storage. These will be discussed in more detail in Chapter 2, but examples include:

- **input devices**: keyboard, mouse
- **output devices**: monitor, printer
- **secondary storage devices**: DVD R/W drive, removable hard drive.

However, one part of the computer system has not yet been mentioned. This is shown as the 'Processor and internal memory devices' in the diagram – this consists of four key components called the **central processing unit (CPU)**, internal **hard disk**, **random access memory (RAM)** and **read only memory (ROM)**.

Figure 1.1 A typical computer system

The central processing unit (CPU) is the part of the computer which interprets and executes the commands from the computer hardware and software. CPUs used to be made up of discrete components and numerous small integrated circuits, which were combined together on one or more circuit board/s. However, due to modern manufacturing techniques, the term **microprocessor** is now used instead of CPU. This is a single integrated circuit (see Figure 1.2) which is at the heart of most PCs and is also found in many household devices and equipment where some control or monitoring is needed (e.g. the engine management system in a car).

The internal hard drive is the computer's main memory; this is where the **applications software**, disk **operating system** and **data files** are stored. The main advantage of these memories is the fast data transfer/access times and their large capacity to store data (this is discussed further in Chapter 3).

Random access memory (RAM) is an internal chip where data is temporarily stored when running applications. This memory can be written to and read from. Since its contents are lost when power to the computer is turned off, it is often referred to as a 'volatile' or 'temporary' memory.

Read only memory (ROM) is a memory used to store information that needs to be permanent. It is often used to contain, for example, configuration data for a computer system. These chips cannot be altered and can only be read from (hence their name). One of the main advantages is that the information stored on the ROM chip is not lost even when power is turned off to the computer. They are often referred to as 'non-volatile' memories.

Figure 1.2 Typical microprocessor

It is worth noting that ROM also contains some coding known as the boot file. This code tells the computer what to do when it first starts up; it is often referred to as the **BIOS (basic input/output system)**. When the computer is turned on, the BIOS carries out a hardware check to find out if all the devices are present and whether they are functional. Then it loads the operating system into the RAM. The BIOS stores the date, time and system configuration in a non-volatile chip called a **CMOS (complementary metal oxide semiconductor)**, which is usually battery powered.

1.3 Operating systems

Reference to operating systems has already been made earlier in this chapter.

To enable users to communicate with computer systems, special software, known as operating systems, have been developed. The general tasks for a typical operating system include:

- controlling the operation of the input, output and backing storage devices
- supervising the loading, running and storage of applications programs

- dealing with errors that occur in applications programs
- maintaining security of the whole computer system
- maintaining a computer log (which contains details of computer usage)
- allowing communication between user and the computer system (user interface).

Computer users need to be able to communicate with the operating system – this is called the 'user interface'. There are two main types of user interfaces: **command line interfaces (CLIs)** and **graphical user interfaces (GUIs)**.

Command line interfaces

CLIs require a user to type in instructions in order to choose options from menus, open software etc. There are often a number of commands that need to be typed in, for example, to save or load a file. The user therefore has to learn a number of commands just to carry out basic operations. It is also slow having to key in these commands every time an operation has to be carried out. However, the advantage of CLI is that the user is in direct communication with the computer and is not restricted to a number of pre-determined options.

For example, Figure 1.3 shows the CLI code required for importing data into a table called B.

```
1. SQLPrepare(hStmt,
2. ?              (SQLCHAR *) "INSERT INTO tableB SELECT * FROM
                   tableA",
3. ?              SQL_NTS):
4. ? SQLExecute(hStmt);
```

Figure 1.3 Example of CLI code

The above statements show how complex it is just to carry out a fairly straightforward operation using CLI.

Graphical user interfaces

GUIs allow the user to interact with a computer (or MP3 player, gaming device, mobile phone, etc.) using pictures or symbols (**icons**) rather than having to type in a number of commands. For example, the whole of the CLI code shown in Figure 1.3 could have been replaced by a single icon:  (table update). Simply selecting this icon would automatically execute all of the steps shown in Figure 1.3 without the need to type them in each time.

GUIs use various technologies and devices to provide the user interface. One of the most common is **windows icons menu and pointing device (WIMP)** which was developed for use on **personal computers (PCs)**. This uses a mouse to control a cursor, which then selects icons to open/run windows. Each window contains an application and modern computer systems allow several windows to be open at the same time. In the example shown in Figure 1.4, a number of icons can be seen on the left-hand side and on the bottom right; three windows are open and these are shown as grey rectangles at the bottom of the screen.

A windows manager looks after the interaction between windows, the applications and the windowing system (which handles the pointing devices and the cursor's position).

Figure 1.4 A typical GUI

In recent years, devices such as **touch screen** phones use **post-WIMP** interaction, where fingers are in contact with the screen. This allows actions such as **pinching** and rotating, which would be difficult to do using a single pointer and device such as a mouse.

1.4 Types of computers

There are many types of computer systems in existence. This section summarises some of the more common types currently available.

PC/desktop computers

PC/**desktop** usually refers to a general purpose computer which is made up of separate monitor, keyboard, mouse and processor unit (see Figure 1.1). The term PC (personal computer) usually refers to computer systems which are IBM-compatible, thus distinguishing them from, for example, Macintosh systems.

It is worth making a comparison here with laptop computers:

Advantages

- Spare parts and connections tend to be standardised, which usually results in low costs.
- Desktops tend to have a better specification (e.g. faster processor) for a given price (often due to size and construction constraints in laptops).
- The large casing allows good dissipation of any heat build-up.

Disadvantages

- Desktops are not particularly portable since they are made up of separate components.
- All the components need to be hooked up by wiring, which can be quite complex and clutters up the desk space.
- Because they are not particularly portable, it is necessary to copy files, etc. when you want to do some work elsewhere (e.g. at home).

Laptop computers

Laptop (or notebook) refers to a type of computer where the monitor, keyboard, pointing device and processor are all together in one single unit. This makes them extremely portable systems.

The key features you would expect to find in a laptop are:
- low weight (to aid portability)
- low power consumption (and also long battery life)
- a processor that does not generate too much heat (cooling is very important).

Advantages

- They are very portable, since the monitor, pointing device, keyboard, processor and backing store units are all together in one single box.
- There are no trailing wires, etc. because everything is in one single unit.
- They can take full advantage of **WiFi** (see discussion in Chapter 4).
- Since they are portable, they can link into any multimedia system.

Disadvantages

- Since they are portable, they are easy to steal!
- They have limited battery life so the user may need to carry a heavy adaptor.
- The keyboards and pointing devices can sometimes be awkward to use.
- Heat dissipation is more difficult due to the structure of the laptop computers.

Netbooks

Netbook is a term used to describe a computer that can almost fit onto a hand and is a smaller version of a laptop. These used to be known as **palmtop** computers, but this term now generally applies to much smaller devices which use touch screens and often a stylus to key in data (see below).

Advantages

Netbook computers have many of the features of laptops and therefore have similar advantages and disadvantages.

Disadvantages

In addition to the disadvantages listed above for laptops:
- netbooks don't have optical drives
- the keyboards are only about 80 per cent the size of laptop keyboards
- they lack some of the features found in larger machines, principally due to the size constraints and to the fact that they are cheaper to purchase.

Personal digital assistants

Personal digital assistants (PDAs) are small handheld computers that usually come with a touch screen that is activated using a stylus. Data (e.g. text) is entered by using a keyboard that appears on the touch screen. Originally, these devices were used as personal organisers but their use has expanded somewhat to include new generation mobile phones, **data loggers**, satellite navigation systems, etc. Many PDAs now have basic database, **word-processing** and **spreadsheet** facilities.

Advantages

- They can be used anywhere because of their size.
- They are very lightweight and are more portable than laptop computers.

Disadvantages

- It is difficult to enter text quickly.
- They have very limited capabilities due to the software and the operating system used.

Mainframe computers

Mainframe computer is a term used for a large, very powerful, computer system. The name comes from the days when the individual components were housed in large (often room-sized) frames.

Uses

Their main purpose is to run commercial applications, such as banking and insurance, where huge amounts of data need to be processed each day.

The main features of main frame computers are as follows.

- They can have several CPUs.
- They have very fast processor speeds.
- They can support multiple operating systems.
- They have huge amounts of storage capacity.
- They have huge internal memories (e.g. several hundred Gbyte of RAM).
- They often operate using time sharing or batch processing (see Chapter 7).

Advantages

- Due to the features listed above, they can be used to do very large jobs which require large memories and very fast processor time.
- They are used in time-sharing systems to allow users to be given a time slice of the very powerful facilities afforded by a mainframe system.
- They are capable of very large number crunching, and so can deal with very complex mathematical functions (e.g. fractals) which would be very time consuming using, for example, a PC.

Disadvantages

- Mainframe computers need to be permanently housed in a large room, so cannot be moved around.
- They are very expensive to operate and maintain.

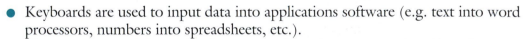

Input and output devices

In this chapter you will learn about:

- input devices:
  - the uses of each device
  - the advantages of each device
  - the disadvantages of each device
- output devices:
  - the uses of each device
  - the advantages of each device
  - the disadvantages of each device
- control applications and the uses of each device.

2.1 Input devices

As the name suggests, input devices are hardware devices that allow data to be input into a computer. Many such devices exist, ranging from the more common ones, such as the keyboard, through to the more specialist devices, such as barcode readers. A number are described in this section.

Keyboards

These are the most common input devices and are used to input text, numbers and instructions into the computer. Most use the **QWERTY** layout (this name comes from the keys on the top row, which spell out 'QWERTY').

Ergonomic keyboards have also been developed recently. These are designed to reduce health-related problems associated with the standard keyboard (e.g. carpal tunnel syndrome or repetitive strain injury (RSI) – see Section 6.7).

Uses

- Keyboards are used to input data into applications software (e.g. text into word processors, numbers into spreadsheets, etc.).
- They are also used for typing in commands to the computer (e.g. Prnt Scrn, Ctrl+P to print out, etc.)

Advantages

- Keyboards enable fast entry of new text into a document.
- They are a well-tried technology and a well-known method of entry.
- Most people find them easy to use.
- It is easy to do **verification** checks as data is entered, as it appears on the screen simultaneously.

Disadvantages

- Users with limited arm/wrist use can find keyboards hard to use.
- Entering data using a keyboard is slow when compared to direct data entry (e.g. **optical mark recognition**).
- Keyboards are fairly large devices that use up valuable desk space.

The **concept keyboard** uses icons or phrases instead of standard letters. These are often used in, for example, fast food restaurants, offices and shops, where a single key represents an item. For example, the symbol shown in the photo represents 'add tax'. The person using the keyboard only needs to touch this key to calculate the tax on an invoice.

Advantages

- Concept keyboards enable fast data entry, as there is no need to type in whole commands.
- They are waterproof, which is useful in a restaurant environment.
- These keyboards are tamper proof and so are useful in certain applications (e.g. at unmanned airport information kiosks), preventing people from keying in information which could potentially corrupt the computer system.

Numeric keypads

A **numeric keypad** is used to enter numbers only (although some have a function key to allow input of alphabetic characters).

Uses

- Numeric keypads are used in **automatic teller machines (ATMs)**, where customers can key in their **personal identification number (PIN)**, an amount of money, etc.
- Telephones have numeric keypads to allow phone numbers, etc. to be keyed in.
- **Electronic point of sale (EPOS) terminals** have numeric keypads in case the barcode reader fails to read the barcode and the number has to be keyed in manually by the operator.
- Chip and PIN devices have numeric keypads for entry of PIN, amount of money, etc.
- They are used to enable fast entry of numeric data into a spreadsheet.

Advantages

- Numeric keypads are faster than standard keyboards for entry of numeric data.
- Since many are small devices (e.g. mobile phones), they are very easy to carry around.

Disadvantages

- They can be difficult to use, due to very small keys.
- It is difficult to use them for entering text.
- Sometimes the order of the numbers on the keypad isn't intuitive.

Mice

The **mouse** is an example of a **pointing device**. A ball is used underneath the mouse to detect movement, so by moving the mouse around the user can control the position of a pointer on the screen. There are usually two buttons, which have different functions: very often the left button is used to select something by double clicking it and the right button brings up drop-down menus (see Figure 2.1).

Many mice also have a scroll button, which speeds up the process of moving through a document.

Figure 2.1 Example of a drop-down menu

Recent developments have produced the **optical mouse** (where movement is detected by reflected light rather than the position of a moving ball) and the **cordless mouse** (which is an example of a wireless device). The advantage of an optical mouse is it has no moving parts and it also doesn't pick up any dirt. This makes it more robust and improves its performance, since the older type of mouse can 'skid' on certain surfaces reducing the control of the pointer.

Uses

- Mice can be used for opening, closing and minimising software.
- They can be used for grouping, moving and deleting files.
- They are very useful when editing images, for example controlling the size and position of a drawing pasted into a document.
- Mice are used for controlling the position of a pointer on the screen to allow selection from a menu or selecting an icon and for scrolling up and down/left to right.

Advantages

- It can be faster to select an option using a mouse rather than a keyboard.
- Mice enable rapid navigation through applications and the internet.
- Mice are small and so take up little area.

Disadvantages

- People with restricted hand/wrist movement can find it hard to operate a mouse.
- Mice are easily damaged and the older type of mouse also quickly becomes clogged up with dirt.
- They are difficult to use if there is no flat surface readily available (e.g. on an aeroplane).

Touchpads

Touchpads are used in many laptop computers as a pointing device. The pointer is controlled by the user moving their finger on the touchpad and then gently tapping it to simulate the left hand button of a mouse (i.e. selection). They also have buttons under the touchpad which serve the same function as the left and right buttons on a mouse.

Uses

The uses of a touchpad are the same as those of a mouse.

Advantages

- It can be faster to select an option using a touchpad rather than a keyboard.
- Touchpads enable rapid navigation through applications and the internet.
- Since the touchpad is integrated into the laptop computer, there is no need for a separate mouse, aiding portability.
- They can be used even when there are no flat surfaces available.

Disadvantages

- People with limited hand/wrist movement find touchpads difficult to use.
- It can be more difficult to control the pointer when compared with a mouse.
- They are more difficult to use when doing certain operations such as 'drag and drop'.

Trackerballs

Trackerballs are similar to a mouse, except that the ball is on the top of the device and the user controls the pointer on the screen by rotating the ball with the hand. Some trackerballs have two buttons which have the same function as the left- and right-hand mouse buttons. If they have a third button, this is equivalent to a double click.

Uses

- They have the same pointing/cursor control capability as a mouse.
- They are used in applications where the user has a disability (such as RSI).
- They are used in a control room environment, where it is faster than a mouse to navigate through process screens and is more robust than a mouse.

Advantages

- Trackerballs do not need the same fine control as a mouse.
- People with limited hand/wrist movement find it easier to use than a mouse.
- The pointer can be positioned more accurately on the screen than with a mouse.
- They take up less desk space than mice since they are stationary.

Disadvantages

- Trackerballs are not supplied with the computer as standard, so they are more expensive.
- User may need training since they are not standard equipment.

Remote controls

A **remote control** is used to control the operation of other devices remotely by using infra red signals. The buttons on the keypad are used to select options (such as television stations, sound levels on a hifi, timings on a DVD recorder, etc.).

Uses

- Most home entertainment devices such as a television, satellite system, DVD player/recorder, hifi systems, etc. have remote controls.
- Remote controls are also used to control multimedia systems.
- They are used in industrial applications to remotely control processes, stop and start machinery, etc.

Advantages

- Remote controls enable devices to be operated from any distance, which is particularly useful for people with disabilities.
- Some chemical processes are hazardous, so it is safer to operate equipment from a distance.

Disadvantages

- People with limited hand/wrist movement can find them hard to use.
- The signal between the control and the device can be easily blocked.

Joysticks

Joysticks have similar functions to mice and trackerballs. By gripping the stick, a pointer on the screen can be controlled and buttons are used to make selections. Often they have another button on the top of the stick that is used for gaming purposes, e.g. to fire a weapon.

Uses

- Video/computer games are often controlled by joysticks.
- They are used in **simulators** (e.g. flight simulators) to mimic actual controls.

Advantages

- It is easier to navigate round a screen using a joystick rather than a keyboard.
- Control is in three dimensions.

Disadvantages

- It is more difficult to control the on-screen pointer with a joystick than with other devices, such as a mouse.

Touch screens

With this system the user can choose an option by simply touching the button/icon on the screen. The selection is automatically made without the need for any pointing device.

Uses

- Touch screens are used for self-service tills, e.g. petrol stations, where the user just touches the screen to select the fuel grade and payment method.
- Touch screens are used where selections are made on screen, for example ATMs, point of sale terminals (e.g. at restaurants), public information systems at airports, railway stations, tourist offices.
- Personal digital assistants (PDAs), mobile phones and satellite navigation systems use touch screens.
- Interactive white boards used for education are large touch screens.
- Touch screens are used in computer base training (CBT) where selections are made in answering on screen testing.

Advantages

- Touch screens enable faster entry of options than using a keyboard or a mouse.
- It is very easy to choose options.
- It is a user friendly method for inputting data, so no training is necessary.
- Touch screens are tamper proof, preventing people from keying in information which could potentially corrupt the computer system (e.g. at unmanned ticket collection kiosks).

Disadvantages

- There is a limited number of options available.
- Using touch screens frequently can lead to health problems (e.g. straining of arm muscles, RSI, etc.).
- The screen can get very dirty with constant touching.

Magnetic stripe readers

These are used to read information on the **magnetic stripe** found, for example, on the back of a credit card (see Figure 2.2). The stripe contains useful information, such as the account number, sort code, expiry date and start date.

Uses

- Credit and debit cards have magnetic stripes that are used by ATMs or EFTPOS (electronic funds transfer point of sale) terminals.
- Security cards for entry to buildings, hotel rooms, etc. use magnetic stripes.
- Travel systems (e.g. train and underground tickets) use magnetic stripes.

Magnetic strip

Figure 2.2 The magnetic stripe on a credit card

Advantages

- Data entry is faster compared with keying in using a keyboard or keypad.
- The system is error free, since no typing is involved.
- The information held on the magnetic stripe is secure: because it cannot be read directly by a person; and, since there is no typing, there is not the risk of somebody observing your key strokes.
- They can prevent access to restricted/secure areas.
- Magnetic stripes are unaffected by oil, water, moisture, etc.
- There are no moving parts, so they are physically very robust.

Disadvantages

- If the magnetic stripe gets damaged (e.g. due to exposure to a strong magnetic field or excessive use) the data is lost.
- The card needs to be in close contact with the reader, so magnetic stripe readers don't work at a distance.
- Since the information is not human readable, this can be a disadvantage in some applications (e.g. hotel room numbers are not printed on the card, so there needs to be another way of showing the information for the customer).

Smart card readers

Smart cards contain chips (see Figure 2.3) and are similar to magnetic stripe cards. With these cards the information is stored on the chip (e.g. PIN and personal data). The data stored on the chip can be updated (e.g. on loyalty cards). For example, certain oil companies use these cards: when a customer buys fuel at a filling station, the loyalty card is swiped and 'points' are added to the card; these points can be used for air miles, money off next purchases, and so on. The storage capacity of the chip is much greater than a magnetic stripe, so more information (such as customer details) can be stored.

Uses

- Loyalty cards, ID cards and public transport passes use smart cards.
- Smart cards can be used to track customer/passenger movements (e.g. on a metro system).
- They are used with satellite systems to decode program signals.
- Smart cards are used for electronic passports and driving licences.

Figure 2.3 The chip on a smart card

Advantages

- Some smart cards (e.g. transport tickets) are used instead of money, reducing the need to carry cash.
- The chip on the card does not need to be in contact with reader, so there is less damage compared with a magnetic stripe reader.
- Data is more secure, since it is easier to copy information on a magnetic stripe than it is to copy information on a chip.

Disadvantages

If the card is lost, information stored on the chip could be used in identity theft.

Chip and PIN readers

Chip and PIN readers are similar to smart card readers, but are used at EFTPOS terminals. The device has a slot into which the card is placed and the chip is read. The PIN is entered using the keypad. A small screen is also part of the reader, which gives instructions to the operator.

Uses

- Chip and PIN readers are used where payments are made using cards (restaurants, supermarkets, travel agents, etc.).

Advantages

- Chip and PIN readers provide a more secure payment system than requiring a signature or using a magnetic stripe, since the PIN typed in must match up with PIN stored on chip.
- Chip and PIN readers provide a more robust system than magnetic stripe readers, since the chip does not need to be in contact with the reader.

Disadvantages

- Since the customer types in the PIN, they need to be careful that it isn't read by somebody else, thus giving an opportunity for fraud.

Scanners

Scanners are used to enter information on hard copy (e.g. text documents, photographs) into a computer. The most common type is the flat bed (as shown here) which is made up of a glass panel and lid. The hard copy document or photo is scanned by a light source and produces a computer-readable image.

The subsequent image can then be manipulated using a drawing package. Images can also be used with optical character recognition (OCR) software to allow the information to used in a word processor, desktop publishing, presentation software, etc. Specialist scanners exist which are designed to carry out a specific task, e.g. barcode scanners (discussed later in this section).

Uses

- Scanners are used to scan in documents and convert them into a format for use in various software packages.
- Old and valuable documents and books can be scanned, thus protecting the originals from damage through handling and also producing records in case the paper copies are lost or destroyed.
- Non-digital photographs need to be scanned if they are to be stored on computer.

Advantages

- Images can be stored for editing at a later date (paper documents cannot be edited unless they are scanned first).
- Scanners are much faster and more accurate (i.e. no typing errors) than typing in documents again.
- It is possible to recover damaged documents and photographs by scanning them and then using appropriate software to produce an acceptable copy.

Disadvantages

- The quality can be limited, depending on how good the scanner resolution is.

Barcode readers

Barcode readers are used to read information in the form of a bar code (illustrated in Figure 2.4). The readers are usually in the form of a barcode scanner and are often built into POS terminals in supermarkets. *Handheld scanners or wands* (as shown here) are also very common for reading barcodes if portability is required (e.g. if the barcodes are on large or fixed objects).

Figure 2.4 A barcode

Uses

- Barcode scanners are used in supermarkets and other shops where the goods are marked with a barcode; the barcodes are used to give information about the product, which enables automatic stock control, itemised billing, etc. to take place.
- They are used in libraries, to scan both users' library cards and barcodes on books, in order to keep track of books on loan.
- They are used as a safety function in many companies to ensure that electrical equipment is checked on a regular basis. Barcodes are placed on an item to identify it and a database holds all the information related to that barcode so it is possible to interrogate the system as part of a safety audit.

Advantages

- Scanning barcodes is much faster than keying in data manually and fewer mistakes are made.
- When barcodes are used as a way of recording data, they can improve safety.
- Barcodes enable automatic stock control.
- Barcode scanning is a tried and trusted technology.
- When an item price is changed, only the central database needs to be updated. There is no need to change the prices individually on each item.

Disadvantages

- Barcode scanning is a relatively expensive system to administer since every item in the shop needs a barcode and every barcode needs to be entered on to the central database. Also, there is a need to invest in the computer technology together with staff training, which can all be very expensive.
- The system is not foolproof – barcodes can be swapped around on items!

OMR devices

Optical mark recognition (OMR) is a system which can read marks written in pen or pencil. The places where the pen or pencil marks can be made are clearly shown on the form, for example:

1 ●—● 2 ● ● 3 ● ●

In this example, a pencil mark has been made between the dots on answer 1. The position of the mark is stored in the computer's memory after being read by the OMR device.

Uses

- OMR devices are used to read questionnaires, multiple-choice examination papers and many other types of form where responses are registered in the form of lines or shaded areas.

Advantages

- It is a very fast way of inputting the results of a survey, etc. – the documents are fed in automatically and there is no user input.
- Since there is no typing, it is more accurate than keying in the data.
- OMR is more accurate than OCR (discussed later in this section).

Disadvantages

- The forms need to be carefully designed to make sure that the marks/shading are correctly positioned to gather accurate information.
- There can be problems if the forms haven't been filled in correctly and sometimes they have to be manually checked before being read by the OMR device – this is both time consuming and expensive.

OCR readers

Optical character recognition (OCR) is the name given to software that takes scanned text and converts it into a computer readable form. The text can then be used in various application packages such as word processors, desktop publishers and presentation software.

Uses

- One of the most recent uses is in the processing of passports and identity cards.
- OCR is used when scanning in documents so that they can be modified using a word processor or desktop publisher package.

Advantages

- It is a much faster data entry system than manually keying in data.
- Since no manual data entry, the number of errors is also reduced.

Disadvantages

- The system still has difficulty reading handwriting.
- It is still not a very accurate technique.

MICR devices

Magnetic ink character recognition (MICR) is a system which can read characters printed in a special ink (containing iron particles). Only certain characters written in a standard font can be read, for example the characters at the bottom of a bank cheque (see Figure 2.5). These characters are converted into a form that the computer can understand and then stored in a computer file.

Characters read by MICR

Figure 2.5 A bank cheque

Uses

● It is primarily used to process cheques in banking operations. When a cheque is presented its value is then printed on the cheque in the special ink. The cheques are all gathered together (either at the end of the day or after some specified period) and then read using a **batch processing** method (see Section 7.9).

Advantages

● MICR offers greater security than OCR since the printed characters cannot be altered.
● There is no manual input, thus errors are reduced.
● Even if somebody writes over the magnetic ink characters (e.g. with a signature) they can still be read.

Disadvantages

● Only certain characters can be read and the number of different characters is very limited.
● It is a more expensive method than other methods used in direct data entry.

Digital cameras

Digital cameras are rapidly replacing traditional, film-based cameras. Once photographs are stored in memory, they are easily transferred to a computer using a **universal serial bus (USB)** connection (see Figure 2.6). Once saved, the images can be manipulated (e.g. cropped, re-sized, contrast altered, etc.).

Uses

● Digital cameras produce photographs for transfer to a computer directly or to print out by connecting directly to a printer.
● Many digital cameras also allow short video clips to be produced.
● Photographs can be uploaded directly into applications software such as word processors, desktop publishers, etc.

Figure 2.6 USB connectors

Advantages

● It is easier to produce better quality photographs than with a traditional camera.
● It is easier and faster to upload photographs to a computer rather than having to scan in hard copies when using traditional methods.
● There is no need to develop film and print out photographs any more – this saves money and is also environmentally more acceptable (saves paper and no longer need the chemicals used in developing the films).
● It is easy just to delete an image from memory if it is not satisfactory and take the photograph again.
● The memory cards can store several hundred photographs. A traditional camera was limited by the number of photographs that could be taken on a roll of film.

17

Disadvantages

- The camera user needs to be computer literate to use the cameras properly; also the transferring, storing and manipulating of the images via a computer requires some understanding of how computers work.
- There is some artistry lost since clever software now corrects errors in the photographs (e.g. incorrect exposure, removal of red eye, etc.).
- The resolution is not yet as good as traditional cameras, although this is improving all the time. The quality of photographs depends on the number of **pixels** (many cameras now offer more than 10 mega pixels per image), quality of lens, etc.
- Images often need to be compressed to reduce the amount of memory used (a single image can use more than 2 Mbytes of memory, for example).
- It is possible to fill up computer memory very quickly with several photographs of the same subject in an attempt to find the 'perfect' snap shot.

Webcams

Webcams are similar to digital video cameras; however, they are connected directly to the computer (through a USB port) and they do not have a memory. The information that the webcam picks up is transmitted directly to the computer. Many computer systems now have webcams built into the top of their monitors as standard equipment.

Uses

- While chatting online, many people use webcams as a more personal way of having a conversation.
- They are used to enable video conferencing to take place (discussed in Chapter 4).

Advantages

- Webcams can be left on constantly, only being activated as required.
- They allow people to keep in contact with each other without the need to travel, so they are particularly useful for elderly or disabled people.

Disadvantages

- Webcams have very limited features and the picture is often of poor quality.
- They need to be connected to the computer, although this is less of an issue with laptop computers when the webcam is built into the monitor lid.

Microphones

Microphones can be connected directly to a computer. Sounds can be inputted and then manipulated. The input sound is converted to an analogue signal and then converted into a digital signal. The computer's sound card usually does this automatically (i.e. it acts as an **analogue to digital converter (ADC)**.

Uses

- Microphones are used to input speech/sounds to be used in various applications, e.g. presentations, sampling (in films, music, etc.), special effects (films).
- They are used in voice recognition software, which can have a number of purposes, for example:
  - conversion of speech into text that can be used in, for example, a word processor
  - recognition of commands (e.g. some cars now have voice-activated systems to switch on the lights, turn up the radio volume, etc.).

Advantages

- It is faster to read in text than to type it in using a keyboard.
- Using special software, it is possible to manipulate sound in real time rather than working on a recording done at some earlier stage.
- If used in a voice activation system, this has the advantage of improving safety since, for example, car drivers don't need to take their hands off the wheel to operate a switch or alter the radio station etc.

Disadvantages

- Sound files can use up a lot of computer memory.
- Voice recognition software isn't as accurate as typing in manually (for example, the software can't distinguish the difference between 'their' and 'there').

Sensors

This section deals with **analogue sensors**. A sensor is a device which inputs data to a computer, where the data is a measurement of some physical quantity which is continuously changing (e.g. temperature, light, moisture, etc.). These physical quantities are analogue in nature. Since computers only understand digital data (i.e. 1s and 0s), the information from the sensors needs to be converted into a digital form. This is done using an analogue to digital converter (ADC).

Uses

Sensors are used in monitoring and control applications – the type of sensor depends on the application (see Table 2.1). When monitoring, the data sent to the computer is often transferred directly to a spreadsheet package (e.g. taking measurements in a scientific experiment, measuring atmospheric pollution, etc.).

Type of sensor	Applications
Temperature	Automatic washing machines, central heating systems, automatic greenhouses, ovens
Pressure	Burglar alarm systems, washing machines, robotics, environmental monitoring
Light	Automatic greenhouses, automatic doors, burglar alarm systems, street lighting control
Sound	Burglar alarm systems, monitoring liquid and powder flow in pipes
Humidity/moisture	Automatic greenhouses, environmental monitoring, factories where moisture levels are crucial (e.g. manufacture of microchips, paint spraying)
pH	Automatic greenhouses, chemical processes, environmental monitoring

Table 2.1 Applications of different types of sensors

Advantages

- Readings taken using sensors are generally more accurate that those taken by human operators.
- Readings are continuous, so there is no break in the monitoring.
- Because it is a continuous process, any necessary action (control system) or warning (monitoring system) will be initiated immediately.
- The system can be automatic, removing the need for human intervention. This is particularly important if the process is hazardous or needs precise control/monitoring.

Disadvantages

- Faulty sensors can give spurious results (e.g. if the sensors on the rear bumper of a car which monitor for obstacles become dirty, they may either not identify an obstacle or give a continuous alarm).

Graphics tablets

A **graphics tablet** is used with a stylus to produce freehand drawings for example. The images produced can then be stored in a file on a computer.

Uses

- Graphics tablets are used to produce drawings, computer graphics, etc.
- In countries where characters are complex (e.g. China, Japan), they are used as a form of input since it is faster than typing in the characters using a keyboard.
- They are used in **computer aided design (CAD)** work.

Advantages

- It is possible to modify drawings before they are input.
- They offer a very accurate method of drawing, which is better than using a mouse or trackerball.

Disadvantages

- They are more expensive than other pointing devices, such as a mouse.

Light pens

Light pens contain sensors that send signals to a computer whenever light changes are detected. At the moment, the devices only work with **cathode ray tube (CRT) monitors** (see Section 2.1) because they rely on the screen image being built up row by row by an electron beam. The screen is refreshed 50 times every second, so the computer is able to determine the pen's position by noting exactly when the light pen detected the electron beam passing its tip. Systems to operate with **thin film transistor (TFT) monitors** are still at the development stage.

Uses

- Light pens are used for selecting objects on CRT screens.
- They are also used for drawing on screen (e.g. with CAD packages).

Advantages

- Light pens are more accurate than touch screens.
- They are small, so can be used where space is an issue.
- They are easy to use.

Disadvantages

- There are problems with lag when drawing on screen.
- At the moment, they only work with CRT monitors.
- They are not very accurate when drawing.

2.2 Output devices

As the name suggests, output devices are hardware devices that allow data to be output from a computer. Some devices hold the data temporarily (such as a printer) whereas other devices produce permanent output in the form of a hard copy (such as a printer producing output on paper). There is a third type of output device which is used to control processes in conjunction with sensor input devices. These are covered separately in Section 1.3.

CRT monitors

CRT monitors are the least expensive type of monitor, although they are becoming increasingly rare as TFT monitors are now taking over. They come in various sizes. They use an electron gun to fire against a phosphor screen, which creates a picture that is made up of tiny dots. Each dot is coloured red, green or blue – the intensity of each coloured dot makes up the vast range of colours interpreted by the eye.

Uses

- CRT monitors are used as the primary output device for computers so the user can see immediately what they are typing in.
- They are used with light pens, for example to allow designs to be created on screen.

Advantages

- CRT monitors still produce a higher quality image than TFT monitors.
- The angle of viewing is still better than with a TFT monitor.
- They work with light pens in computer-aided design and computer-aided manufacturing (CAD/CAM) applications.

Disadvantages

- CRT monitors tend to be rather heavy and are a weight hazard if not supported properly.
- They run very hot and can cause fires if left unattended (especially as they get older).
- They consume considerably more power than the modern TFT monitors.
- They can flicker, which can lead to headaches and eyesight problems with prolonged use.

TFT monitors

TFT monitors are taking over from CRT monitors as the main output device. One of the reasons for the rapid development of laptop computers can be attributed to the advancements made in TFT technology. The screen is made up of thousands of tiny pixels, which are made up of transistors controlled by a microprocessor. Each pixel has three transistors, coloured red, green or blue; the intensity of each governs the effective colour of the pixel seen by the eye.

Uses

- TFT monitors are used as the primary output device for computers so the user can see immediately what they are typing in.
- They are an integral part of laptop computers.

Advantages

- TFT monitors are lightweight, so do not pose the same risks as CRT monitors.
- They produce less glare than CRT monitors and also emit less radiation.
- They consume much less power and do not generate as much heat as a CRT monitor.

Disadvantages

- The angle of viewing a TFT monitor is fairly critical, with the image appearing unclear when viewed slightly from the side. This can be an issue if several people are looking at a screen at the same time.
- The definition is sometimes not as good as CRT monitors.
- TFT monitors cannot yet be used with light pens, so these monitors cannot be used in CAD if light pens are used to create and edit drawings.

Laser printers

Laser printers produce very high-quality hard copy output. The print rate per page is very quick if a large number of pages are being printed. They rely on large buffer memories, where the data for the whole document is stored before the pages can be printed out.

Uses

- Laser printers are used where noise levels need to be kept low (e.g. in an office).
- They are the best option for fast high quality high volume printing.

Advantages

- Printing is fast for high volumes. If only a few pages are to be printed they are little faster than inkjet printers.
- They can handle very large print jobs.
- The quality is consistently high.
- Toner cartridges last for a long time, so laser printers can be a cost effective option, particularly if colour outputs are not required.

Disadvantages

- Laser printers are expensive to buy.
- They are only really fast if several copies are being made.
- Colour laser printers tend to be expensive to run, since four cartridges (three colours plus black) are needed as well as diffuser kits, etc.
- They produce ozone and volatile organic compounds because of their method of printing and type of toner/ink used. These have been linked to health hazards in the office.

Inkjet printers

Inkjet printers are used to produce good quality hard copies. Although the quality is not quite as good as that from laser printers, it is far better than that from dot matrix printers. Unlike laser printers, inkjet printers do not have large buffers, so printing is done a bit at a time. This is why printing is sometimes paused, since the whole page can't be stored in the buffer and it has to wait for the computer to send more data.

Uses

- Inkjet printers are used where low output volumes are required.
- If high-quality printing is required for single pages (or only a small print job) then these printers are ideal, for example they are very good at producing photo quality printouts.
- 3D inkjet printers are now being used in industry to produce prototypes (see below).

Advantages

- The output is of high quality.
- Inkjet printers are cheaper to buy than laser printers.
- They are very lightweight and have a small footprint (i.e. take up little space).
- They do not produce ozone and volatile organic compounds, unlike laser printers.

Disadvantages

- The output is slow if several copies needed, as there is little buffer capacity to store the pages.
- The ink cartridges run out too quickly to be used for large print jobs.
- Printing can 'smudge' if the user is not careful.
- Inkjet printers can be expensive to run if they are used a lot, since original ink cartridges are expensive.

3D inkjet printers

These are a new type of printer that produce solid 3D models using modified inkjet technology. In this technology, known as 'tomography', thin layers of fine powder (plaster, resin and starch) are bonded together as a 3D model is slowly built up (each layer is only about 0.25 mm thick). Figure 2.7 shows some items produced on a **3D inkjet printer** – these are known as prototypes.

Figure 2.7 A prototype produced on a 3D inkjet printer

Uses

- Inkjet printers are used to produce prototypes which actually work from CAD packages, photograph images, stored drawings, etc.
- Scale models are produced in colour before the real thing is manufactured.
- The ultimate objective is to produce organic objects (such as replacement human organs) using this layering technology.

Advantages

- 3D inkjet printers save a lot of money, since making prototypes by other methods is very time consuming and expensive.
- Physical scale models are produced with working parts, which gives a better idea of how the end product will look.
- The powders used can often be ground up and re-used.

Disadvantages

- 3D inkjet printers are expensive to buy.
- They are slow at producing their output.
- The end product can sometimes be a little rough and often needs further work to be done on it.

Dot matrix printers

Dot matrix printers are a type of impact printer, where a printhead (made up of a matrix of pins) presses against an inked ribbon. They tend to be slow, noisy and the output is not good quality. They are still useful, however, where multi-part or continuous stationery (e.g. long reams of perforated paper) is being used.

Uses

- They can be used in noisy environments (e.g. garage workshops) and in applications where print quality is not very important.

Advantages

- Dot matrix printers can be used in environments which would be a problem for laser or inkjet printers (e.g. dusty, dirty or moist atmospheres).
- Carbon copies or multi-part outputs can be produced.
- They are very cheap to run and maintain.
- They are easy to use if continuous stationery is required (e.g. long print jobs such as wages slips).

Disadvantages

- They are very noisy and so not good in an office environment.
- They cost more than an inkjet printer to buy.
- They are very slow and the printing is of poor quality.

Plotters

Plotters (also known as graph plotters) are devices that produce hard copies, but operate in a different way to printers. They are not limited to normal printer paper size and are capable of producing highly accurate, very large drawings and posters. The most common types are pen plotters (which use coloured pens to draw), electrostatic (similar method to laser printers) and inkjet plotters. With pen plotters the coloured pens are controlled by a computer and the paper can move backwards and forwards to allow accurate shapes to be drawn.

Uses

- Plotters are used to produce large drawings (e.g. blueprints of buildings, factories, etc.) and are often used with CAD applications.
- They are used to produce large pictures for use on billboards or giant posters. They can also print on plastic-coated paper.
- If the pens are replaced with cutting tools, it is also possible to make large signs.

Advantages

- They can produce huge printouts.
- The print quality is extremely high.

Disadvantages

- They are slow in operation.
- They are expensive, both to buy and to maintain.

Speakers

Speakers can be connected directly to a computer or are built into the monitor or casing (as in a laptop computer). Digital data from the computer is converted into analogue form, using a digital to analogue converter (DAC). The signal is then amplified through the speakers.

Uses

- Speakers are used to output sound from multimedia presentations.
- They are used in home entertainment centres.
- They can help blind people (together with speech generation software) through audio output of text on the screen.
- They are used to play downloaded sound files.

Multimedia projectors

Multimedia projectors receive signals that can be either analogue or digital, although most modern projectors only work with digital inputs. The signal source is usually from a computer, television or DVD player. The image from the source is magnified and projected onto a large screen. The devices usually work with a remote control, but can also use virtual mouse technology which actually becomes a cordless PC mouse with the same features as a mouse. It is then possible to direct the computer presentation without being tied to the computer. Another feature of the virtual mouse is the laser pointer. Most multimedia projectors take input from various types of video format such as NTSC, PAL or SECAM.

Uses

- Multimedia projectors are used for training presentations (to allow the whole audience to see the images from a computer).
- They are also used for advertising presentations (large images showing product features of, for example, a new car, can be shown at exhibitions, shopping malls, etc.).
- Home cinema systems (projecting the images from a DVD or television) use multimedia projectors.

Advantages

- They enable many people to see a presentation rather than all of them crowding round a small computer screen.
- They avoid the need for several networked computers. For example, when looking at a video clip on an internet site, everybody can see the video on the large screen rather than logging on to a number of computers.

Disadvantages

- Images can sometimes be fuzzy.
- Multimedia projectors are expensive to buy.
- Setting up projectors can be a little difficult.

2.3 Control devices

Control devices are another type of output device. They are used to control processes in conjunction with sensor input devices. This section gives an overview of actuators and the devices that they operate, but the use of sensors and actuators are covered in more depth in Section 7.7.

Actuators

Actuators are **transducers** and are used to take signals from a computer and convert them into some form of motion, for example operating motors, pumps, switches and valves. As part of the control process, digital signals are sent from the computer to an actuator to operate a device. Usually, conversion of the digital signal to analogue is required first (using a DAC).

Motors

The motor is turned on or off by the actuator.

Uses

- Motors are used in many domestic appliances, such as automatic washing machines (to make the drum rotate), cookers (to switch on fans), water pumps in central heating systems and automatic greenhouses to open windows and switch on fans.
- In industry, they are used to control robot arms.
- In computers, they operate fans, disk drives and DVD drives.

Buzzers

The buzzers are switched on or off by the actuator.

Uses

- Buzzers are used in cookers and microwave ovens to tell the operator when the cooking process is complete.
- They are used in burglar alarm systems to warn if intruders are present.

Lights

The actuator is connected to the switch that turns the lights on or off.

Uses

- They are used for security lights.
- Lights are used in greenhouses to control the lighting conditions.

Heaters

Actuators are connected to switches which turn the heater on or off.

Uses

- Heaters are used in automatic washing machines, cookers and central heating systems.
- Heaters are used in automatic greenhouses to control the temperature.

Storage devices and media

In this chapter you will learn about:
■ back-up storage
■ why it is necessary to back up data and files
■ the types of access used by the backing stores
■ the types of internal and external backing storage devices:
  ● magnetic
  ● optical
  ● solid state.

3.1 Backing up data

The first two sections in this chapter consider the need for backing up data and the different ways of storing and accessing data. Section 3.3 then discusses many forms of **backing storage** and compares the advantages and disadvantages of each type. The comparative performance and main uses for each type of store are also discussed in some depth.

What is backing up of data?

Backing up refers to the copying of files and data to a different medium (disk, tape, flash drive, etc.) in case of a problem with the main storage device. Backing up files and data on a regular basis is seen as good computing practice and many computer systems can be set to back up files automatically on a regular basis.

The backups are often stored in a different place to the main storage. This is in case of fire or some other situation which could lead to irretrievable loss of key data and files.

Why back up data?

There are various reasons why backups are made. Some of the more common reasons are considered below:
● Data could be lost due to failure of the original storage device. This could be due to hardware failure (e.g. head crash on a hard drive unit), problems caused by files being over-written accidentally (or otherwise) or possible corruption of files (e.g. caused by power surges).
● Hackers could be responsible for the corruption or even loss of data. This may not be their intention (they may only want to gain access to the information for other purposes, e.g. to find personal information such as bank account details). However, the very act of hacking into files could cause problems such as corruption or data loss.
● Backups are also made in case the files need to be used elsewhere. The original files are then protected against possible corruption or loss.

However, backups do not necessarily guard against the effect of a virus. The virus could attach itself to the files which could mean that the backups were also affected. If the computer was 'cleaned' of the virus and then the backup files were re-loaded there would remain the risk that the same virus could infect the computer system again. The best protection is not to get a virus in the first place (discussed in Chapter 6).

3.2 Types of access

The way data is stored and read by different backing storage devices varies considerably. This section briefly describes the two main methods of accessing data.

Serial access

With this system, to access data it is necessary to start at the beginning and then access each piece of data in turn until the required information is found.

It is primarily used on magnetic tape systems and is a very slow form of access. It is used in applications where speed of access or where the order in which the data is accessed is not important, for example in utility billing, clearing bank cheques or producing pay slips.

When a magnetic tape needs **updating**, an additional tape is required so that the old information can be **merged** with the new data (itself often on another tape, but the new data could be stored in various ways) to produce the updated tape (see Figure 3.1).

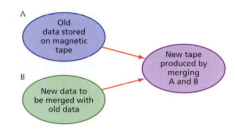

Figure 3.1 Updating the data on a magnetic tape

Direct access

This method is used with magnetic disks and with optical media (such as CDs and DVDs). The computer uses a key field to calculate where data has been stored. It is then able to access the data directly from the calculated position. Consequently, access is much faster than with serial access.

It is used in applications where access speed is vital (e.g. in **real-time process control** systems such as controlling a chemical plant or **online** systems such as booking air tickets or automatic stock control).

When updating media which uses direct access, the new data is written to the next available location and its position is calculated using the built-in algorithm.

3.3 Backing storage media

Dating back to the development of the personal computer, all computer systems have come equipped with some form of backing storage. When a user types data into a computer, the information is stored temporarily on the **RAM** – however, this information would be lost as soon as the computer was turned off. Backing storage devices ensure that data is stored permanently and can be used at a later date. This section will be considering various types of backing storage and the media used.

Backing storage devices are either internal or external (i.e. plug-in devices) to the computer, and are one of three types:
- magnetic
- optical
- solid state.

Fixed hard disk

Fixed hard disk drives are available on all computers and are the main method used for data storage. On a PC this is usually a fixed hard disk with read/write heads allowing data to be written to or read from the disk surface. The disk surface is coated in a magnetic film which allows data to be stored by altering the magnetic properties to represent binary 1s or 0s (the fundamental units of computer memories). The hard drive disks usually store the **disk operating system (DOS)** and other important software and files. Applications software (e.g. spreadsheets and word processors) need a hard drive to allow them to quickly retrieve and save data.

Uses

- Fixed hard drives are used to store the operating system and working data.
- They are used for storing applications software that needs fast retrieval and storage of data.
- Real-time systems (e.g. robots, control of a chemical plant) and online systems (e.g. booking airline tickets, automatic stock control (using EPOS)) used fixed hard drives.
- They are used in file servers for computer networks.

Advantages

- They have a very fast data transfer rate and fast access times to data.
- They have very large memory capacities.

Disadvantages

- They can be fairly easily damaged (e.g. if the correct shut-down procedure on a laptop computer has not been correctly carried out and the computer is then moved).
- They lack portability unless a portable hard disk drive is used (see next sub-section).

Portable hard disk drives

These devices work in much the same way as fixed hard disk drives but are usually connected to the computer via a **universal serial bus (USB)** port and can be disconnected and used on different computers. The disks are generally capable of storing more data than the equivalent optical disk (CD, DVD and so on).

Uses

- Portable hard disks can be used as back-up systems to prevent loss of data.
- They can be used to transfer data, files and software between computers.

Advantages

- The data access time and data transfer rate is very fast.
- They have large memory capacities.
- They can be used as a method of transferring information between computers.

Disadvantages

- As with fixed drives, a portable hard disk can be easily damaged if the user accidentally drops it or does not shut it down correctly after use.

Floppy disk drives

Floppy disks are still used on some computer systems. They consist of a thin disk of plastic which is housed in a plastic case with a window where the disk can be accessed. As the disk rotates, a read/write head is used to add or read data stored on the surface.

Uses

- They are still used where small files need to be transferred/stored (e.g. word-processed documents).
- Some older computer systems still make use of this method of storage.

Advantages

- Using a CD to store a small file (e.g. a word-processed document) is often regarded as wasteful – especially if CD-R is used.
- It is a very simple technology. Floppy disk drives are also extremely low cost items to buy.

Disadvantages

- Floppy disks have a very low memory capacity when compared to CD/DVDs, for example.
- Very few modern computers have floppy disk drives.
- The data transfer rate is slow compared to more modern data storage devices.
- Floppy disks are not very robust.

Magnetic tapes

A **magnetic tape** is a very thin strip of plastic which is coated in a magnetic layer. They are read and written to by a read/write head. The data is stored in magnetic areas which represent 1s and 0s. Data is written to and read from the tape in sequence (i.e. in order) – for example, if five records A, B, C, D and E were stored they would be in the order E D C B A on the tape; so if record **B** was to be read it would be necessary to read E, D and C first *before* getting to the required record. This is known as **serial access**. This type of storage is useless in a real-time or online application (due to the very slow access speeds) and is best suited to offline or batch processing.

Uses

- Magnetic tapes are used in applications where batch processing is used, for example in clearing bank cheques, utility billing (gas, electricity, water) and producing pay slips. In these applications, there is no need for any specific processing order and speed of data access is not important).
- They are used as a back-up media since all the data needs to be stored.

Advantages

- They are generally less expensive than the equivalent-capacity hard disk.
- It is a very robust technology.
- The data transfer rate is fast.

Disadvantages

- Access time is very slow.
- When updating, another tape is needed (i.e. original tape + tape with the changes produces an updated tape).

Optical storage media

Optical storage devices, such as CD and DVD, all use optical (i.e. light) read/write methods, unlike tapes and floppy/hard drive disks which are magnetic media. A laser beam is used to write to and read from the optical media.

The CDs and DVDs are manufactured either from a single polycarbonate disk or from two polycarbonate disks bonded together. A very thin layer of metal or organic dye is used as the recording media. The big advantage of these storage media is that they are portable and can store large data files (e.g. films, music or multimedia files) which would be too large for a floppy disk.

CD-ROM and DVD-ROM

CD-ROMs and DVD-ROMs are read only memory (ROM), which means they cannot be written over and can only be read. The data is stored as a series of **pits** (equivalent to a binary value of 1) and **lands** (equivalent to the binary value of 0) in the metallic optical layer. The pits are formed by a laser beam etching the surface at the manufacturing stage. Only a single track exists which spirals out from the centre of the disk.

The pits and lands are read by a low-powered laser beam which follows the data stream and reads from the centre outwards in a spiral. The light reflects differently off a pit than it does off a land and this is interpreted as 1s and 0s (i.e. data) – hence the term digital media.

Uses

- CD-ROMs are used by manufacturers to store music files and software, computer games and reference software (such as an encyclopedia).
- DVD-ROMs have much larger storage capacity than CD-ROMs and are used to store films. They are now increasingly used to store computer data and ever-more sophisticated computer and arcade games.

Advantages

- They hold far more data than floppy disks, so one CD/DVD could replace several floppy disks in some applications.
- They are less expensive than hard disk drive systems.

Disadvantages

- The data transfer rate and data access time are slower than for hard disks.

CD-R and DVD-R

The letter 'R' here means the disk is recordable *once* only and then it becomes a CD-ROM or DVD-ROM. These use a thin layer of an organic dye as the recording media; DVDs also use an additional silver alloy or gold reflector. A laser beam produces **heated spots** and **unheated spots**. On reading the disk, a laser beam is capable of distinguishing between the two types of spots and effectively reads the data stream from the centre outwards in a spiral action. This data is then interpreted as 1s and 0s.

Uses

- They are used for home recordings of music (CD-Rs) and films (DVD-Rs).
- They are used to store data to be kept for later use or to be transferred to another computer.
- They are used in applications where it is necessary to prevent the deletion or over-writing of important data).

Advantages

- CD-Rs and DVD-Rs are cheaper than RW disks.
- Once burned (and **finalised**), they are like ROM disks.

Disadvantages

- They can only be recorded once, so if an error occurs then the disk has to be thrown away.
- Not all CD/DVD players can read CD-R/DVD-R.

CD-RW and DVD-RW

The 'RW' means that these disks are a re-writable media and can be written over several times. Unlike CD-R/DVD-R, they don't become ROMs. The recording layer uses a special phase-changing metal alloy. The alloy can switch between crystalline and amorphous (non-crystalline) phases, thus changing its reflectivity to light, depending on the laser beam power. **Spots** are produced which can be read by a laser and then interpreted as 1s and 0s. The system allows data to be written, erased and re-written many times.

Uses

- CD-RWs and DVD-RWs are used to record radio and television programmes, but can be recorded over time and time again.
- They are used in closed circuit television (CCTV) systems.

Advantages

- CD-RWs and DVD-RWs can be re-used many times.
- They can use different file formats each time they are used.
- The RW format is not as wasteful as the R format since files or data can be added at a later stage.

Disadvantages

- CD-RWs and DVD-RWs can be relatively expensive media.
- It is possible to accidentally overwrite data.

DVD-RAM

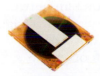

DVD-RAM is a recent addition to the optical media group. Unlike other CD and DVD formats, DVD-RAMs have several discrete concentric tracks rather than a single spiral track. This gives them the advantage that writing and reading can occur at the same time. This makes it possible to watch an already recorded television programme at the same time as a different programme is being recorded. DVD-RAMs can be written to many times.

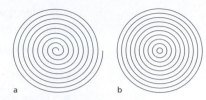

Figure 3.2 compares the single spiral track found on normal CDs and DVDs with the discrete single tracks found on a DVD-RAM.

Figure 3.2 a Spiral tracks on a normal CD or DVD **b** Discrete tracks on a DVD-RAM

The recording layer is made from a similar phase-changing material to that used in RW technology. When writing, a laser heats the phase-changing alloy on the disk to about 500–700°C, changing the reflective properties from shiny to dull (i.e. pits). If the disk needs to be erased, a laser heats the surface to about 200°C to return the disk to its original shiny state. A low power laser is used to read the written marks on the surface. The shiny and dull (pits) marks represent data to a computer where they are interpreted.

Uses

- DVD-RAMs are used in recording devices such as satellite receivers to allow simultaneous recording and playback.
- They are used in camcorders to store films.

Advantages

- DVD-RAMs have a long life – minimum life is estimated to be 30 years.
- It is possible to do a re-write operation over 100,000 times, compared with the RW format which only allows about 1,000 re-writes.
- Writing on DVD-RAMs is very reliable, as they have in-built verification software to ensure the accuracy of the data.
- Access is very fast if the files are fairly small.
- There is no need to finalise the disk.
- They have a very large capacity (about 10 Gbyte if double-sided format is used).
- They offer the ability to read data at the same time as data is being written.

Disadvantages

- DVD-RAMs are not as compatible as R or RW format, as many systems will not recognise their format.
- They are relatively expensive, costing about 4 times as much as a DVD-RW disk.

Blu-ray disks

Blu-ray disks have the largest capacity of all the optical media available and go up to 100 Gbyte (at the present time). The laser beam used is at the blue/violet end of the spectrum, rather than red which is the colour of the lasers used in other optical media. Consequently, the light used has a shorter wavelength, allowing more data to be stored/read on the disk.

Uses

- Blu-ray disks are used in home video consoles.
- They are used for storing and playing back films: 1 high-definition film of two hours duration uses 25 Gbyte of memory.
- PCs can use this technology for data storage or backing up hard drives.
- Camcorders can use this media (in cartridge form) to store film footage.

Advantages

- They have a very large storage capacity, and so are ideal for storing high definition films.
- The data transfer rate is very fast.
- The data access speed is also greater than with other optical media.

Disadvantages

- The disks are relatively expensive .
- At the time of writing, blu-ray systems still have encryption problems (which are used to stop piracy) when used to store video.

Solid state backing store

Solid state technology is being developed to the point where solid state drives will soon replace hard disk drives in laptop computers. This is due to their inherent thinness, their much faster data access time and the fact that they are extremely robust.

They are similar to magnetic and optical media in that data is still stored as 1s and 0s. However, instead of changing the magnetic properties on the thin film surface of a rotating disk, these solid state systems control the movement of electrons within a microchip. The 1s and 0s are stored in millions of miniature transistors within the microchip: if the transistor conducts a current, this is equivalent to a 1, otherwise it is a 0.

They consequently have no moving parts, consume much less power and are extremely robust.

They are used primarily as removable storage devices and are collectively known as flash memory. The most common examples are memory sticks/pen drives and memory cards.

Memory sticks/pen drives

Memory sticks/pen drives can store several Gbytes of data and use the solid state technology described above. They are usually connected to a computer through the USB port and power to operate them is drawn from the host computer. They are extremely small and very portable. Most operating systems recognise these storage media, which means that no additional software is needed to operate them.

Some expensive software increasingly use these storage methods (sometimes referred to as portable flash drives) as a form of security. They plug into the computer using the USB port and are known as **dongles**. The software installed on a computer sends out a request (in encrypted form) to the dongle asking for an encrypted validation key. Thus a person trying to commit **software piracy** would have to crack the code on the dongle first before they could use the software. Some systems go one stage further and have key bits of software stored on the dongle in encrypted form. The software looks for these pieces of encrypted code to enable it to run. This gives an added security benefit to the software.

Uses

- Memory sticks and pen drives are used for transporting files between computers or as a back-up store.
- They are used as a security device – a dongle – to prevent software piracy.

Advantages

- They are very compact and portable media.
- They are very robust.

Disadvantages

- It is not possible to write protect the data and files.
- Their small physical size means that they are easy to lose.

Flash memory cards

These are a form of **electrically erasable programmable read only memory (EEPROM)** and are another example of solid state memories.

Uses

- Flash memory cards are used to store photos on digital cameras.
- Mobile phones use them as memory cards.
- They are used in **MP3** players to store music files.
- They are used as a back-up store in handheld computer devices.

Advantages

- Flash memory cards are very compact, so they can be easily removed and used in another device or used for transferring photos directly to a computer or printer.
- Since they are solid state memories, they are very robust.

Disadvantages

- They are expensive per Gbyte of memory when compared to hard drive disks.
- They have a finite life in terms of the number of times they can be read from or written to.
- They have a lower storage capacity than hard disks.

Computer networks

In this chapter you will learn about:

■ types of networks:
  - ring, bus, star and tree
  - local area networks (LANs), wide area networks (WANs) and wireless LANs (WLANs)
■ network devices – modems, hubs and switches, routers and bridges
■ the internet – web browsers and internet services providers (ISPs)
■ intranets
■ network security – user IDs, passwords, encryption and authentication techniques
■ communications – fax, email, video conferencing and voice over internet protocol (VOIP).

4.1 Introduction

Most computer systems are now connected together in some way to form what is known as a **network**. This ranges from the basic school/home network of only a few computers (often set up to share resources such as printers or software) to large networks such as the **internet** which effectively allows any computer connected to it to communicate with any other computer similarly connected.

This chapter considers the types of networks that exist and the many features that are available because of networking.

4.2 Common types of network

Most networks are controlled by the use of **servers**. There are different types of servers, for example:

● **file servers**, which allow users to save and load data/files
● **applications servers**, which deal with the distribution of applications software to each computer
● **printer servers**, which ensure printing from devices on the network is done in a queue, for example
● **proxy servers**, which are used as a buffer between WANs (discussed at the end of this section) and LANs (discussed in Section 4.3).

This section will now describe a number of different types of networks.

Local area networks

A **local area network (LAN)** is usually within one building or certainly not over a large geographical area. A typical LAN will consist of a number of computers and devices (e.g. printers) which will be connected to **hubs** or **switches**. One of the hubs or switches will usually be connected to a **router** and **modem** (usually **broadband**) to allow the LAN to connect to the internet; in doing so it then becomes part of a **wide area network (WAN)**.

There are advantages of networking computers together using LANs:
- the sharing of resources (such as expensive peripherals and applications software)
- communication between users
- a network administrator to control and monitor all aspects of the network (e.g. changing passwords, monitoring internet use and so on).

However, there are also disadvantages:
- easier spread of viruses throughout the whole network
- the development of printer queues, which can be frustrating
- slower access to external networks, such as the internet
- increased security risk when compared to stand-alone computers
- the fact that if the main server breaks down, in most cases the network will no longer function.

There are four common types of LAN network **topologies**: ring, bus, star and tree networks.

Ring networks

Ring networks, shown in Figure 4.1, are becoming less popular. Every computer in the network is connected in a ring, including the server. Data is transmitted around the ring and each computer only removes the data which is relevant to it. This allows each computer to send and receive data since they all have a unique identification/address.

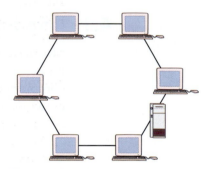

Figure 4.1 A ring network

Advantages

- Ring networks work well under heavy loading.
- It is possible to create very large networks using this topology.

Disadvantages

- If there is a fault in the wiring between two computers then the whole network will fail.
- Adding a new device or computer to the network can be difficult since it has to be placed between two existing devices.

Bus networks

In a **bus network**, illustrated in Figure 4.2, each computer or device is connected to a common central line. Data travels along this central line until it reaches the computer or device that requires it. The ends of the line have terminators to prevent, for example, signal bounce, which would cause data interference.

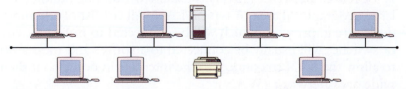

Figure 4.2 A bus network

Advantages

- It is easy to add a new computer or device to the network.
- If one device or computer fails, it does not affect the rest of the network.
- This type of network doesn't need a hub or a switch and also requires less cabling than, for example, a star network. It therefore also saves on costs.

Disadvantages

- It is difficult to isolate any fault on the network.
- If the central line has a fault then the whole network fails.
- This is becoming an increasingly outdated topology for network design.
- Its performance worsens noticeably as more and more devices/ computers are added.

Star networks

With a **star network**, shown in Figure 4.3, each computer or device is connected via a central hub or switch. Data is sent to the hub which then sends out data along *every* cable to every computer or device (no checking is done to see where the data should be sent).

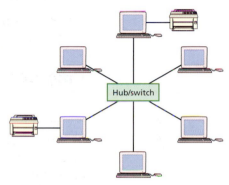

Figure 4.3 A star network

Advantages

- If one computer or device fails, then the rest of the network is unaffected.
- Problems on the network are easy to identify and work can be carried out on a faulty device without affecting the rest of the network.
- It is easy to expand the network.

Disadvantages

- If the central hub breaks down, the whole network crashes.

Tree network

A **tree network** has a central line (just like a bus network) connecting together a series of star networks, as shown in Figure 4.4. The server is also connected to this central line. Because of its flexibility, and the fact that it has the advantages of both bus and star networks, this topology is becoming increasingly popular.

The advantages and disadvantages are the same as for bus and star networks.

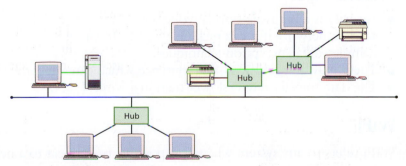

Figure 4.4 A tree network

Wireless LANs (WLANs)

WLANs are similar to LANs but there are no wires or cables. In other words, they provide wireless network communications over fairly short distances (a few metres) using radio or infrared signals instead of cables.

Devices, known as **access points (APs)**, are connected into the wired network at fixed locations (see Figure 4.5). Because of the limited range, most commercial WLANs (e.g. on a college campus or at an airport) need several APs to permit uninterrupted wireless communications. The APs use either **spread spectrum technology** (which is a wideband radio frequency with a range of about 30 to 50 metres) or **infrared** but this has a very short range (i.e. about 1 to 2 metres) and is easily blocked, so is of limited use.

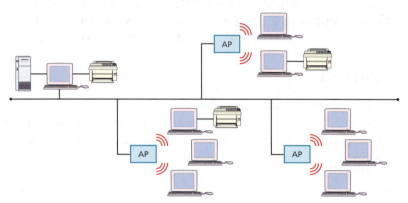

Figure 4.5 A network connecting WLANs

The AP receives and transmits data between the WLAN and the wired network structure. End users access the WLAN through WLAN adapters, which are built into the devices or are plug-in modules.

Advantages

- All computers can access the same services and resources (e.g. printers, scanners, internet access from anywhere within range of the APs).
- There is no cabling to individual computers and devices so safety is improved.
- The system is more flexible, since users can move their laptops from their desks.
- Adding new computers and devices is very easy (all that is required is a WLAN adapter, provided the device is within range of an AP) and costs are reduced since no extra cabling is needed.

Disadvantages

- Security is a big issue since anyone with a WLAN-enabled laptop computer can access a network if it can pick up a signal. It is therefore necessary to adopt complex data encryption techniques.
- There may be problems of interference which can affect the signal.
- The data transfer rate is slower than in a wired LAN.

WiFi

WiFi refers to any system where it is possible to connect to a network or to a single computer through wireless communications, for example:
- on the WLAN described above
- PDAs and other handheld devices

- laptop computers which are WiFi enabled
- peripheral devices such as printers, keyboards and mouse which can interface with the single computer when fitted with WiFi adapters.

WiFi systems rely on some form of AP, which uses radio frequency technology to enable the device to receive and send signals.

Note that WiFi is *not* short for wireless fidelity (a common misconception!). Rather, it is the trademark name for any product which is based on the **IEEE 802.11** standard.

WiFi **hotspots** are places where you can access WiFi (free or paid). They exist in public places such as airports, hotels and internet cafés. It is possible to logon to free WiFi hotspots unless they are protected by passwords. Software exists which can be loaded onto a laptop computer which then searches for non-protected WiFi systems. The practice of driving around in a car looking for these unsecured WiFi hotspots is known as **war driving** and poses a security risk to any unsecured WiFi system.

Bluetooth

Bluetooth is an example of **wireless personal area networking (WPAN)** technology. Spread spectrum transmission (radio waves) is used to provide wireless links between mobile phones, computers and other handheld devices and allow connection to the internet.

With this system, it is possible to create a small home network, for example, to allow communication between any PDA, mobile phone, computer, media player and printer. The range is, however, quite small (about 10 metres). Examples of its use include the transfer of photographs from a digital camera to a mobile phone or the transfer of phone details to a computer. It behaves like a mini-LAN.

Wide area networks

A wide area network (WAN) is basically formed by a number of LANs being connected together through either a router or a modem. Some companies will set up private WANs (usually by way of fibre optic cabling or telephone wires restricted to company use only). This is expensive but comes with the advantage of much enhanced security. It is more common to use an **internet service provider (ISP)** for connections to the internet and communicate via this network system.

The following additional hardware is needed for a WAN: routers, modems and **proxy servers** (described in Section 4.3).

4.3 Network devices

Modems

Modem means *mod*ulator *dem*odulator and is a device which converts a computer's digital signal (i.e. modulates it) into an analogue signal for transmission over an existing telephone line. It also does the reverse process, in that it converts analogue signals from a telephone line into digital signals (demodulates) to enable the computer to process the data. (Section 5.5 discusses digital and analogue data in more detail.)

Modems are used to allow computers to connect to networks (e.g the internet) over long distances using existing telephone networks.

Dial-up modems operate at transmission speeds of about 60 kilobits per second, which is quite slow by today's standards. (These are discussed in more detail in Section 4.4.) However, modern broadband or **asymmetric digital subscriber line (ADSL)** modems operate at 11,000 kilobits per second (or higher). The term 'asymmetric' means that the modem is faster at **downloading** (getting) data than it is **uploading** (sending) data.

Although the ADSL modems still use the existing telephone network, unlike dial-up modems they do not tie up the line while accessing the internet, so the land-line telephone can still be used at the same time. Furthermore, they can always be 'on' so internet access can be available 24 hours a day. ADSL modems can allow telephone conversations and internet traffic to occur at the same time because of the wide bandwidth signal used: the higher frequencies are used to carry the internet signals, so they do not interfere with normal telephone traffic. Cable modems also exist which allow cable television providers to offer internet access as well as receiving television signals.

Network hubs

Network hubs are hardware devices that can have a number of devices/computers connected to them. Its main task is to take any data received via one of the ports and then send out this data from all of the ports. Each computer/device will receive the data, whether it is relevant or not.

Switches

Switches are similar to hubs but are more efficient in the way they distribute data. A hub learns which devices are connected to which ports. Each device has a **media access control (MAC) address** which identifies it uniquely. **Data packets** sent to the switch will have a mac address giving the source and receiving device. If a device X is always sending the switch data via port 4 then it learns that X must be connected to that port; any data packet which is intended for X only is then sent through port 4 and not through any of the others. This means that the network traffic only goes to where it is needed and so a switch is more efficient than a hub, especially when the network is very busy.

Bridges

Bridges are devices that connect one LAN to another LAN that uses the same **protocol** (the rules that determine the format and transmission of data). They decide whether a message from a user is going to another user on the same LAN or to a user on a different LAN. The bridge examines each message and passes on those known to be on the same LAN and forwards messages meant for a user on a different LAN.

In networks that use bridges, workstation addresses are not specific to their location and therefore messages are actually sent out to every workstation on the network. However, only the target workstation accepts this message. Networks using bridges are interconnected LANs since sending out every message to every workstation would flood a large network with unnecessary traffic.

Routers

Since large companies often have more than one network there are occasions when the computers in one network want to communicate with the computers in one of the other networks. Routers are often used to connect the LANs together and also connect them to the internet.

Routers inspect the data packages sent to it from any computer on any of the networks connected to it. Since every computer on the same network has the same first part of an **internet protocol (IP) address,** the router is able to send the data package to the appropriate switch and it will then be delivered using the mac destination address in the data packet. If this mac address doesn't match any device on the network it passes on to another switch on the same network until the device is found.

HTTP proxy servers

This is a special type of server that acts as a buffer between a WAN (usually the internet) and a LAN. The server passes on the service requests to the internet and then passes back the requested pages. It therefore retrieves web pages and passes them on to the computer that made the request. Any page retrieved from the internet is stored on the server, which means that when a different computer requests the same page it is available immediately thus considerably speeding up the browsing process.

4.4 The internet

The internet is a worldwide collection of networks which allows a subscriber to send and receive emails, chat (using text or voice) or browse the world wide web.

The **world wide web (WWW or web)** is the part of the internet which the user can access by way of a **web browser** (e.g. Microsoft Internet Explorer). A web browser is software that allows the user to display and interact with pages and files from the web.

Websites

The web is made up of millions of these **websites** (e.g. www.hoddereducation.com) and millions of **web pages** (e.g. Hodder Education front page, shown in Figure 4.6). Web pages are documents on a computer screen which may consist of text, pictures, sounds, animation or video (i.e. multimedia). A website consists of many of these pages linked together.

Figure 4.6 Example of a web page

The website shows these **hyperlinks** to allow users to **navigate** between web pages. These hyperlinks are often shown as blue underlined text or sometimes a small hand appears 🖑 under a picture or under some text indicating the link to another page or website. The user clicks on these hyperlinks using a mouse (or other pointing device) to move to another page.

Web browsers use uniform resource locations (URLs) to retrieve files. URLs are a standard way of locating a resource on the internet; they are usually a set of four numbers, e.g. 194.106.220.19. However, as this can be difficult to remember, an alphanumeric form is usually used which has the format:

protocol://site address/path/filename

where:
- **protocol** is usually http
- **site address** consists of: host computer name, domain name, domain type and (very often) the country code:
  - **computer name** is usually www
  - **domain name** is the name of the website
  - **domain type** is commonly one of the following: .com, .org, .co, .net, .gov
  - examples of **country code** include .uk, .us, .de, .cy
- **path** is the web page
- **filename** is the item on the webpage.

Thus, a full URL could be http://www.urlexamples.co.cy/pages/example1

Accessing the internet

An ISP is a company that provides users with access to the internet, usually for a fee. When a user registers with an ISP, an account is set up and they are given **login** details, which include a **username** and a **password**. The user connects to the internet via the user account which also allows the provider to monitor usage. Most ISPs also provide an **email** account (see Figure 4.7 for an example of an email page).

Emails are an electronic way of sending documents (etc.) from one computer to another. They allow **attachments**, which can be word-processed documents, spreadsheets, data files, music files, movie files, etc. An email address contains two parts:

Figure 4.7 Example of an email page

example1@yahoo.co.uk OR example2@yahoo.com

The first part is the user name e.g. **example1** or **example2** and the second part is @ followed by host name e.g. **@yahoo.co.uk** or **@yahoo.com**.
Emails are discussed in more depth in Chapter 9.

There are three common ways of accessing the internet offered by service providers:
- dial-up internet access
- cable internet access
- digital subscriber line (DSL) (broadband) internet access.

These were discussed in Section 4.3 as part of modems and are summarised in Table 4.1.

Type of access	Description
Dial-up internet access (dial-up modem)	This is the slowest type of connection (about 60 kbps).
	The user connects to the internet via the telephone line by dialling one of the numbers supplied by the ISP. They are therefore not on all the time; ISP contracts are usually for a number of hours per month of internet access time and additional charges are incurred if this is exceeded.
	A big disadvantage is that the telephone line is tied up while a dial up modem is in operation.
Cable internet access (cable modem)	Local cable television operators give a user access to the internet through their own cable networks using a cable network modem.
Internet access via DSL (broadband modem)	The fastest download speeds can be obtained by using DSL broadband connections (at least 11,000 kbps). This is often offered with wireless interface which requires an AP and a router. ISPs usually have a download/upload limit (e.g. 20 Gbyte of data) as part of the contact. This is not a problem unless the user is often downloading music or movie files which can quickly use up the memory allocation.
	Broadband has the advantage of always being on, since it doesn't tie up the telephone line.
	The fast transfer rate allows systems such as **voice over IP (VOIP)** and online chat rooms to be used effectively.

Table 4.1 Methods of accessing the internet

4.5 Intranets

Many companies use an **intranet** as well as the internet. The simple definition of an intranet is 'a computer network based on internet technology that is designed to meet the internal needs for sharing information within a single organisation/company'. There are number of reasons for doing this.
- It is safer since there is less chance of external hacking or viruses.
- It is possible to prevent employees from accessing unwanted websites.
- Companies can ensure that the information available is specific to their needs.
- It is easier to send out *sensitive* messages that will remain only within the company.

It is now worth comparing the internet with intranets:
- The term 'internet' comes from the phrase *inter*national *net*work.
- The term 'intranet' comes from the phrase *intra*nal restricted access *net*work.
- An intranet is used to give local information relevant to the company whereas the internet covers topics of global interest.
- It is possible to block out certain internet sites using an intranet. This is much more difficult to do from the internet.
- An intranet requires password entry and can only be accessed from agreed points, whereas the internet can be accessed from anywhere provided the user has an ISP account.

- An intranet is behind a firewall, which gives some protection against **hackers** (unauthorised users), viruses and so on. This is much more difficult to do with internet access since it is more open on an international scale.
- Information used in intranets is usually stored on local servers, which makes it more secure from outside agencies.

4.6 Network security

The security problems when using networks such as the internet are well documented. There are various security threats to networks and there are many equally varied ways of combating the threat. Many of these issues are discussed in Chapter 6 but this section will concentrate on four areas:

- user ID
- password
- encryption
- authentication techniques.

User IDs

When logging on to any network system, a user will be asked to type in a **user ID**. This assigns the user privileges once the logon procedure is successful. For example, on a network, top level **privilege** would be for an **administrator**, who is able to set passwords, delete files from the server, etc., whilst a user privilege may only allow access to their own work area.

Passwords

After keying in the user ID, the user will then be requested to type in their **password**. This should be a combination of letters and numbers which would be difficult for somebody else to guess. When the password is typed in it often shows on the screen as ******** so nobody overlooking can see what the user has typed in. If the user's password doesn't match up with the user ID then access will be denied. Many systems ask for the password to be typed in twice as a **verification** check (check on input errors). To help protect the system, users are only allowed to type in their password a finite number of times – three times is usually the maximum number of tries allowed before the system locks the user out. After that, the user will be unable to logon until the system administrator has re-set their password.

When using some internet websites, if a user forgets their password they can request the password to be sent to their email address. The password is never shown on the computer screen for reasons of security.

Encryption

Encryption is the converting of data into a code by scrambling it or **encoding** it. This is done by employing encryption software (or an encryption key). Since the data is all jumbled up it appears meaningless to a hacker or anyone who illegally accesses the data. It should be stressed that this technique *does not* prevent illegal access, it only makes the data useless to somebody if they don't have the necessary decryption software (or decryption key). It is used to protect sensitive data (such as a person's banking details).

The system works like this:
- A user writes a message and the computer sending this message uses an encryption key to encode the data. For example, the message 'THIS IS AN EXAMPLE' (sent on 15 April) is encoded to '43Kr Kr T7 W04887W'.
- At the other end, the receiving computer has a decryption key which it uses to decode the message. Note that the date when the message was sent is important since this formed part of the encryption **algorithm**.

Encryption keys are much more complex than the one above, in order to prevent computers being used to crack the code. Very sophisticated algorithms are used which make the codes almost unbreakable.

Authentication techniques

As shown above, there are many ways in which a computer user can prove who they are. This is called **authentication**, and a type of authentication is used in the banking example that follows. Most systems adopt the following authentication logic:
- something you know – e.g. PIN/password
- something belonging to you – e.g. your bank card
- something unique to you – e.g. your fingerprints.

At least two of these are needed at the moment when a user has to prove who they are. For example, the following banking example uses:
- something you know – surname, reference number, PIN, date last logged on
- something belonging to you – card put into card reader to produce the 8-digit code.

In future, the third feature will be introduced (such as a fingerprint scanner attached to a computer to uniquely identify the user).

Banking example

A user belongs to H&S Bank. He wants to check the status of his account online. He logs onto the H&S Bank website using his ISP. Figure 4.8 illustrates a sophisticated set of steps taken to prevent unauthorised access.

Only once each page has been successfully navigated will the user have access to his bank account. The last stage is a final check to see if the customer's account has been illegally accessed – if they hadn't logged into the website on 15 April at 17:45 then this would trigger a security check into the customer's account. Note that the last web page makes use of what are called **radio buttons**.

Figure 4.8 The authentication process

4.7 Communication methods

Many methods of communication using networks exist. These include **fax**, email, **video conferencing** and VOIP.

Fax

The term **fax** is short for the word 'facsimile'. With this system, documents are scanned electronically and converted into a **bit map** image (a bit is a *b*inary dig*it* and is a 1 or a 0). This is then transmitted as a series of electrical signals through the telephone network. The receiving fax machine converts this electronic image and prints it out on paper.

It is also possible to generate fax signals from a computer to allow files and documents to be sent to a fax machine – this saves printing out the document first and then passing it through a fax machine. Fax/modem software in the computer converts the image into a form recognised by a fax machine. However, this is not as efficient as the email system where the electronic copy is sent and is then stored electronically thus permitting the document to be edited, for example.

Email

This is an electronic method for sending text and attachments from one computer to another over a network (see Section 4.4 for further details).

The advantages of using email include:
- the speed of sending and receiving replies using the email system
- the low cost, since stamps, paper and envelopes are not needed
- not needing to leave home to send the mail.

Disadvantages include:
- the possibility of virus threats and hacking
- the need for the email address to be completely correct
- the inability to send bulky objects via emails.

Video conferencing

This is a method of communication between people at two separate locations (e.g. in different countries). This is done in **real time** and makes use of a LAN, if internal, or through a WAN, e.g. the internet, if national or international. The system works in real time and uses additional hardware such as webcams, large monitors/television screens, microphones and speakers.

The system also uses special software such as:
- CODEC, which converts and compresses analogue data into digital data to send down digital lines
- echo cancellation software, which allows talking in real time and synchronises communications.

Delegates at one end speak into a microphone and look at a webcam. The other delegates can see them and hear them using large monitors and speakers.

There are potential problems with these systems such as time lag (the time it takes for the signal to reach its destination, which can be difficult when trying to have a conversation since there seems to be a delay). Also, sound quality and picture quality can be poor unless expensive hardware and software is used.

However, these systems are becoming increasingly popular as the cost of travelling increases and the risk of terrorist attacks becomes higher. One large company, which reduced travelling from Europe to USA and used video conferencing wherever possible to discuss product development, claims to have saved several million US dollars over a 12-month period. The savings were due to reduced travelling (mostly air fares) and to reduced overnight accommodation. Since little or no travelling is involved meetings can be held at short notice, but time differences between countries can become an issue.

VOIP

Voice over internet protocol (VOIP) is a method used to talk to people using the internet. VOIP converts sound (picked up by the computer microphone or special VOIP telephone plugged into the USB port of the computer) into discrete digital packets which can be sent to their destination via the internet. One of the big advantages is that it is either free (if the talking is done computer to computer, i.e. both computers have VOIP telephones or use their built-in/plugged-in microphones and speakers) or at a local rate to anywhere in the world (when VOIP is used to communicate with a mobile or land line telephone rather than another computer).

To work in real time this system requires a broadband ISP. The main problems are usually sound quality (echo and 'weird sounds' are both common faults). Security is also a main concern with VOIP, as it is with other internet technologies. The most prominent security issues over VOIP are:

- identity and service theft
- **viruses** and **malware** (malicious software)
- **spamming** (sending **junk mail**)
- **phishing** attacks (the act of sending an email to a user falsely claiming to be an established legitimate enterprise in an attempt to scam the user into surrendering private information that will be used for identity theft).

Data types

5.1 Introduction

Data can exist in many forms, and so there are various defined types of data that computers use. All the data that is stored on computers is digital, but lots of types of data in the real world involve physical measurements of continuously varying data. These need to be converted into digital data for storage and manipulation on a computer.

Data frequently needs to be stored in a logical sequence to allow access and/or searching to be done at some later stage. One of the most common methods of data storage is the use of databases.

5.2 Types of data

There are several data types found in most computer systems:
- logical/Boolean
- alphanumeric/text
- numeric
- date.

Logical/Boolean data

Boolean data (or logic data type) can have only two values: **true** or **false**. This works if there are only two possible responses to a question or situation, i.e. (Yes or No), (True or False) or (1 or 0).

This is made most use of when carrying out a search in a database or on the internet. In these cases, **logical operators** are used which are based on true (i.e. binary 1) or false (i.e. binary 0) logic.

The AND operator

Consider the list of seven students in Table 5.1.

Name	Sex	Height (m)
A	Male	1.6
B	Male	1.7
C	Female	1.5
D	Female	1.7
E	Male	1.4
F	Female	1.6
G	Male	1.5

Table 5.1 A small database

Suppose we now make the search:

(Sex = Male) AND (Height (m) > 1.6)

Table 5.2 shows the logic status for each part of the search query. There is only one match where the search condition is **true** for (Sex = Male) AND **true** for (Height (m) > 1.6): name B.

Name	Sex	Sex logic status	Height (m)	Height logic status
A	Male	True	1.6	False
B	Male	True	1.7	True
C	Female	False	1.5	False
D	Female	False	1.7	True
E	Male	True	1.4	False
F	Female	False	1.6	False
G	Male	True	1.5	False

Table 5.2 Logic status for search query (Sex = Male) AND (Height (m) > 1.6)

Note that the logic operator called AND looks for the situation where something is **true** in *both* groups. For example, consider two groups X and Y where X = {1, 2, 3, 4} and Y = {3, 4, 5, 6}. The statement X AND Y would be equal to {3, 4} since it is true that 3 and 4 are the only items which are common (i.e. true) to both groups (see Table 5.3).

Number	Number is in group X	Number is in group Y
1	True	False
2	True	False
3	True	True
4	True	True
5	False	True
6	False	True

Table 5.3 Logic status for statement X AND Y

In the student database only example B contains items which are true (common) to both groups (i.e Male *and* 1.7 m).

The OR operator

Now consider a different search:

(Sex = Female) OR (Height (m) < 1.6)

This gives the logic status shown in Table 5.4. There are five matches where the search condition is **true** for (Sex = Female) OR **true** for (Height (m) < 1.6): names C, D, E, F and G.

Name	Sex	Sex logic status	Height (m)	Height logic status
A	Male	False	1.6	False
B	Male	False	1.7	False
C	Female	True	1.5	True
D	Female	True	1.7	False
E	Male	False	1.4	True
F	Female	True	1.6	False
G	Male	False	1.5	True

Table 5.4 Logic status for search query (Sex = Female) OR (Height (m) < 1.6)

Note that the logic operator called OR looks for the situation where something is **true** in *either* group. For example, consider two groups X and Y where X = {1, 2, 3, 4} and Y = {3, 4, 5, 6}. The statement X OR Y would be equal to {1, 2, 3, 4, 5, 6} since it is true that all six numbers occur in either group (see Table 5.5).

Number	Number is in group X	Number is in group Y
1	True	False
2	True	False
3	True	True
4	True	True
5	False	True
6	False	True

Table 5.5 Logic status for statement X OR Y

In the student database example, C, D, E, F and G contain items which are true in either group.

Alphanumeric and text data

Looking at a standard keyboard, you see the letters A to Z, the digits 0 to 9 and other characters such as : @ & £) } etc. The letters A to Z are referred to as **text** and the letters A to Z *plus* the digits 0 to 9 are referred to as **alphanumeric** (some definitions also include the remaining keyboard characters such as @ & £) } as part of the alphanumeric character set).

For example, the password 'MARQUES' contains letters only and is therefore text. However, the password 'MIKE62' contains letters and numbers and is therefore alphanumeric. A person's name would always be text but their address, which could contain letters and numbers, would be alphanumeric.

Numeric data

Numeric data can be in two forms: **integer** (whole numbers) or **real** (containing decimals). For example, 3416 is an integer, but 34.16 is real.

Examples of integers include the number of floors in a hotel, the number of students in a class or the number of wheels on a car. Examples of real numbers include temperatures, price of an item in a shop or a person's height in metres. Numeric data also includes zero (0) and negative numbers such as – 4516 (integer) or – 30.26 (real).

Date data

Date can be written in many forms, for example:
- dd/mm/yyyy (dd = day, mm = month and yy/yyyy = year), e.g. 19/08/2009
- dd/mm/yy, e.g. 19/08/09
- dd.mm.yy, e.g. 19.08.09
- yyyy-mm-dd, e.g. 2009-08-19.

All of the above examples use a number form of the month, but it can also be written as the full word or the three-letter abbreviation:
- dd mmmm yyyy, e.g. 19 August 2009
- dd-mmm-yyyy, e.g. 19-Aug-2009.

All the above are accepted as date in most application packages (such as spreadsheets and databases) where the format is particularly important due to data manipulation (e.g. sorting) or searching.

5.3 Data structures

Data is often stored in **files**, which consist of **records**, which in turn consist of **fields**, as illustrated in Figure 5.1.

For example, a company may have set up a file to include information about their employees in the following format:

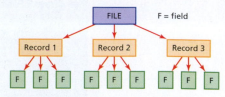

Figure 5.1 Structure of a data file

reference number/name/date started/department

Figure 5.2 shows a possible structure for the file COMPANY EMPLOYEE FILE. The information is held in one file with five records and four fields per record. In this example, the first field (the reference number) is known as the **key field** or **primary key**. Each primary key is unique and is used to locate a record in a file during a search operation.

Record 1	1416	J. Smith	30/05/2003	Sales
Record 2	1417	K. Shah	11/02/1989	Manager
Record 3	1431	R. Marques	15/10/2001	Finance
Record 4	1452	T. Rodriguez	27/09/1995	Sales
Record 5	1461	V. Schultz	09/12/2005	Graduate
	field	field	field	field

FILE

Figure 5.2 The file 'COMPANY EMPLOYEE FILE'

Also note the data types for each field:

reference number	numeric data (integer)
name	text
date	date format (dd/mm/yyyy)
department	text

In reality, COMPANY EMPLOYEE FILE would be much larger, containing all the records for all the company's employees. This type of file is often referred to as a **flat file structure**.

5.4 Databases

A **database** is a collection of information which is structured in some way to permit manipulation and searching of data.

Why are databases used?

- They promote data consistency. When data is updated on a database it is up to date for *any* application which uses the database.
- Data duplication is reduced to a minimum since only one copy of each data item needs to be kept.
- It is relatively easy to expand the database if some new application is being considered.

- Security of data is easier to monitor and maintain. Data access can be controlled by database **front ends**; the actual database will be 'invisible' to all users except the database administrator (see Figure 5.3).

Early databases were examples of flat file structures, as described in Section 5.3 and illustrated by the COMPANY EMPLOYEE FILE. The way the data is organised makes it difficult to search for a specific piece of information or to create **reports** which only contain certain information (fields) from each of the records.

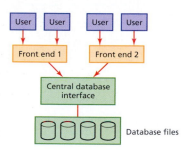

Figure 5.3 User access to data contained in a database

Relational databases

Relational databases were first introduced in 1970 following the work of F. F. Codd, a researcher at IBM.

Relational databases consist of a number of separate **tables** which are related (a table is made up of rows and columns in much the same way as a spreadsheet is structured). Each table contains a primary (key) field that is also a field in at least one other table. It is possible to combine data from different tables to produce a report which only contains the required information.

Relational databases do not need to repeat data, which is one of the problems of flat file structure (in the example that follows, three flat files would be needed containing repeated fields of key data since there would be no links connecting each file). Information is stored in separate tables only connected by the primary (key) field. Other advantages of relational databases include:

- faster data retrieval (because of links between tables)
- easy expansion of the database by adding extra data or new tables
- the need to change data in only one table – all other references to this data will then also be up to date, resulting in what is known as **data integrity**.

Tables can also contain **foreign keys** that relate tables in the database to one another. A foreign key in one table is a primary key in another.

We will now look at an example that shows the structure of tables in a relational database. In this example, there are three connected tables. It is important to note that in commercial databases there will be several tables connected together. The examples shown here contain only two or three and are being used to show the principle of relational databases.

Example

A garage sells cars and keeps a database of sales, customers and servicing, as shown in Figure 5.4 overleaf.

The primary (key) field is **Car number** and the column is shaded red).

The foreign key fields are **Invoice number** and **Engine ID** and these are shaded green.

Information from all three tables is linked together so, for example, if a car service was due then by typing in **Car number** the customer's details and servicing details are brought up on the screen. This means information can be sent to the customer as a reminder. Once the service is carried out, the servicing table will be updated which means all other references to it will also be up to date.

To help you understand these complex structures, go through the following exercise, which contains a flat data structure and a relational database.

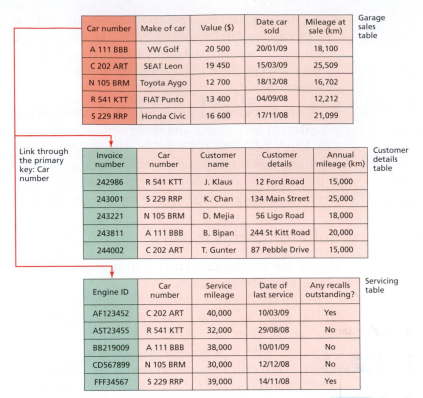

Figure 5.4 Three related tables in a relational database for a garage

Exercise 5a

Example 1
Table 5.6 shows a flat data structure.

Employee number	Name of employee	Date joined	Salary ($)	Department	Telephone number
A6121	Mr J. Bloggs	30/01/2000	18,000	Sales	151 216 009
B4142	Ms N. Kahn	19/02/2001	25,000	Accounts	153 423 111
B5041	Ms R. Spacek	04/11/2001	19,000	Sales	155 119 110
A3046	Mr K. Silva	15/12/2003	40,000	Legal	148 222 333
A5211	Mr N. Choudry	01/07/2004	25,000	Accounts	130 115 100

Table 5.6 Flat file structure for data on employees in a company

a How many records are there in this section of the database?
b How many fields are there in each record?
c Which field contains:
   i numeric data only
   ii text data only
   iii alphanumeric data only?
d What field is the primary key?
e In which field has the database been sorted?
f If the database was sorted in descending order on salary, using the Employee Number only, what would be the new order of data in the sorted database?

Example 2

The database shown in Table 5.7 contains two linked tables. The database is being used to keep a record of which customers have borrowed CDs from the music lending library.

CD stock table

Barcode	CD title	CD Artist	Year released	Number of tracks
77779287727	Seasons End	Marillion	1989	10
99969313424	Kingdom of Rust	Doves	2009	9
24354273506	Let It Go	Nada Surf	2002	11
94639624829	Our Love to Admire	Interpol	2007	9
02498669105	The Invitation	Thirteen Senses	2004	12
45099625627	Seal	Seal	1994	10

Table 5.7 Tables of data relating to CDs borrowed from a library

Customer borrowing table

Customer number	Customer name	Telephone number	CD borrowed	Date due back
M10411	Mr K. Sahz	415 003 455	02498669105	15/10/2009
M21516	Mr D. Silva	841 133 222	77779287727	14/10/2009
F18113	Mr A. Adak	614 555 211	45099625627	14/10/2009
M20004	Mr R. Choudhury	416 888 210	24354273506	12/10/2009
F16117	Ms L. Smith	416 219 000	94639624829	11/10/2009
F50316	Mr M. Egodi	841 567 228	99969313424	10/10/2009

a How many records are there in the CD stock table?
b How many fields are there in each record in the Customer borrowing table?
c What type of database is being used here?
d What is the primary key in the CD stock table?
e Which field is a foreign key?
f What data type would you use in the Date due back field?
g What data types have been used in all the other fields?

5.5 Analogue and digital data

As we have already learnt from earlier chapters, computers work with **digital data**, which is defined as discrete, fixed values in a given range.

However, in the real world, physical measurements (i.e. data) are not digital but are continuously variable, producing an infinite number of values within a given range. For example, length, weight, temperature, pressure, etc. can take any value, depending on the accuracy to which they are measured. These values are measured by an **analogue device** which represents physical measurement on a continuous analogue scale, as illustrated in Figure 5.5. The speedometer represents speed by showing the position of a pointer on a dial, while the thermometer represents temperature by the height of the liquid column.

The data is known as **analogue data**. Most control and monitoring applications use devices called **sensors** to measure these physical, analogue quantities. Examples of sensors and their use in monitoring and control applications are discussed in Chapter 7.

Figure 5.5 Examples of analogue devices

However, computers can only understand and manipulate digital data. Analogue data would not make any sense to the computer and may even cause some damage. To enable data in analogue form (often the input from a sensor) to be processed by a computer, it needs to be changed into a digital form. This is done using an **analogue to digital converter (ADC)**.

Alternatively, if the computer is being used to control a device, such as a motor or a valve, the device may need to be controlled by continuously variable voltages. There would be no use sending out a digital signal. It would first need to be changed into an analogue signal, requiring another device, known as a **digital to analogue converter (DAC)**.

Example of a control system

This example shows why there is a need to convert analogue to digital and also digital to analogue as part of control system involving a computer:

Figure 5.6 shows a computer being used to control a furnace heated by burning gas supplied from a gas source (the amount of gas is controlled by a valve which can have an infinite number of positions).

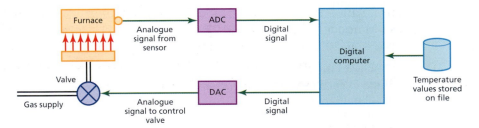

Figure 5.6 Control system for a furnace

A sensor is used to measure temperature in the furnace and it sends readings in analogue form (small electric currents/voltages). This data is converted into digital by an ADC and is fed to a computer, which compares the input temperature with the required temperature stored on a file. If any action is needed (furnace temperature is too low or too high) then a digital signal is sent out from the computer. This signal is converted into an electric current/voltage (i.e. analogue) so that the valve can be regulated (i.e. opened or closed to control the gas supply and hence the furnace temperature).

CHAPTER 6

The effects of using ICT

In this chapter you will learn about:
- software copyright rules
- viruses and hacking:
  - definitions
  - ways of protecting the system
- the effects of ICT on society:
  - employment
  - social impact
  - online shopping and banking
  - policing of the internet
  - use of microprocessors in household appliances
- information from the internet:
  - reliability of data
  - risks of undesirable websites
  - security (including phishing, pharming and spam)
- internet developments, e.g. blogs, wikis and social networking
- health and safety issues.

6.1 Introduction

The use of ICT has affected our everyday lives in many ways. These range from the effects of ICT on society in general, such as the changes in types and styles of employment, to the convenience that it offers the individual, through services such as online shopping and banking. However, in addition to providing new opportunities, ICT has introduced its own problem, such as issues relating to copyright, security of both companies and individuals, and health and safety. This chapter discusses many of these effects.

6.2 Software copyright

Software is protected by copyright laws in much the same way as music CDs, film DVDs and articles from magazines and books are protected.

When software is supplied on CD or DVD there are certain rules that must be obeyed.
- It is not legal to make a software copy and then sell it or give it away to a friend or colleague.
- Software cannot be used on a network or used in multiple computers unless a licence has been acquired to allow this to happen.
- It is not legal to use coding from the copyright software in your own software and then pass this software on or sell it as your own without the permission of the copyright holders.
- Renting out a software package without permission to do so is illegal.
- It is illegal to use the name of copyrighted software on other software without agreement to do so.

Software **piracy** (illegal copies of software) is a big issue amongst software companies. They take many steps to stop the illegal copying of software and to stop illegal copies being used once they have been sold. The following list shows a number of ways in which software is protected, both by making the installer agree to certain conditions and also by methods which require the original software to be present for it to work.

- When software is being installed, the user will be asked to key in a unique reference number (a string of letters and numbers) which was supplied with the original copy of the software.
- The user will be asked to click 'OK' or 'I agree' to the licence agreement before the software continues to install.
- The original software packaging often comes with a sticker informing the purchaser that it is illegal to make copies of the software; the label is often in the form of a **hologram**, which indicates that this is a genuine copy.
- Some software will only run if the CD-ROM or DVD-ROM is actually in the drive. This stops illegal multiple use and network use of the software.
- Some software will only run if a **dongle** is plugged into one of the USB ports (dongles were discussed in Section 3.3).

6.3 Viruses and hacking

A **virus** is a program that replicates (copies) itself and is designed to cause harm to a computer system. It often causes damage by attaching itself to files, leading to one or more of the following effects:

- causing the computer to **crash** (i.e. to stop functioning normally, lock up or stop responding to other software)
- loss of files – sometimes system files are lost which leads to a computer malfunction
- corruption of the data stored on files.

Viruses infect computers through email attachments and through illegal software or downloading of files from the internet that are infected. The following list shows ways of protecting systems against viruses.

- Use up-to-date **anti-virus** software. This detects viruses and then removes or quarantines (i.e. isolates) any file/attachment which has been infected.
- Do not allow illegal software to be loaded onto a computer and do not use any CD/DVD in the computer which comes from an unknown source.
- Only download software and files from the internet if they are from a reputable site.
- Use **firewalls** (discussed below) on networks to protect against viruses.

Note that backing up files on a regular basis does not necessarily guarantee the prevention of viruses spreading. If a file is already infected and it is then backed up, when the file is re-loaded into the 'cleaned' computer the virus may actually be re-installed!

Hacking is the act of gaining access to a computer system or network without legal authorisation. Although some **hackers** do this as a form of intellectual challenge, many do it with the sole intention of causing harm (e.g. editing/deleting files, installing harmful software, executing files in a user's directory or even committing fraud).

Some large companies actually employ hackers to test out their security systems. Although the only foolproof way of stopping a networked computer from being hacked into is to disconnect it from the internet, this is clearly not a practical or desirable solution. Similarly, the only certain way to prevent a stand-alone computer from being hacked into is to keep it in a locked room when not in use; again, this is not always practical.

However, there are a number of ways to minimise the risk of hacking:

- use of **firewalls**: these are used on networked computers. They provide a detailed log of incoming and outgoing traffic and can control this traffic. They are able to stop malicious traffic getting to a user's computer and can also prevent a computer connecting to unwanted sites and from sending personal data to other computers and sites without authorisation
- use of **robust passwords** (i.e. difficult passwords to guess) and **user IDs** to prevent illegal access to a computer or internet site.

Whilst **encryption** makes files unreadable if accessed illegally, it does not *prevent* illegal access (hacking) in the first place. It therefore would not prevent a hacker carrying out many of the harmful actions described in this section.

6.4 Effects of ICT on society

One moral issue that has emerged from the development of ICT is the **social divide** created by computer technology and ICT. This is often referred to as the **'haves and have-nots'** – those people who have the necessary ICT skills or money to purchase and use computer equipment will gain benefit from the new technology; those who are not able to access this new technology are left even further behind leading to this social divide.

ICT has affected many aspects of society. This section is going to look at just a few of these:

- the impact on employment
- the development of online shopping and banking
- policing of the internet
- the use of microprocessors in household appliances.

Impact on employment

The introduction of ICT has led to unemployment in many areas such as:

- manufacturing, where robots have taken over many tasks (e.g. paint spraying in a car factory)
- computer-controlled warehouses, which are automatic and require no personnel to be present
- labour-intensive work (e.g. in the printing industry, checking football pools, filing, etc.).

However, it is also true that some new jobs have been created with the introduction of ICT. These include writing software, maintenance of robots and other ICT equipment and work connected with internet sites (setting sites up, maintaining them, etc.).

The overall work- related effects on people can be summarised as follows:

- the need to be re-trained because of the introduction of new technology, e.g. how to operate or maintain the new machinery which is being introduced to do the work previously done by a person
- a cleaner working environment where robots have taken over many of the 'dirty' manual tasks

- de-skilling of the workforce, as jobs where high skills were needed in the past are now done by computer systems (e.g. the use of DTP software in the printing industry, CAD software in producing engineering drawings, etc.)
- a safer working environment (e.g. fewer people working in noisy factories)
- fewer manual tasks, since tasks such as heavy lifting are now done by robots.

Companies have also gained from the introduction of ICT systems. For example:
- there is no need to employ as many people to do the tasks, thus reducing labour costs
- robots do not take holidays, get sick or take coffee breaks, resulting in higher productivity
- whilst the quality is not necessarily better, there is greater consistency in the products made (e.g. every car coming off a production line will be identical).

Impact of using ICT for online shopping and banking

The development of online shopping and banking has led to changes in the type of employment in shops and banks. Fewer staff are now needed in traditional shops and banks, but new staff are needed to provide the online services (e.g. packing and sending out orders, courier services, and so on). As the amount of **online shopping** and **banking** increases, the impact on society begins to gain in significance. (The applications are covered in more depth in Chapter 7; this section will deal primarily with the impact of ICT.)

Online shopping and banking means that more and more people are staying at home to buy goods and services, manage their bank accounts and book holidays, etc. This would all be done using a computer connected to the internet and some form of electronic payment (usually a credit or debit card). The following notes give a comprehensive list of the benefits and drawbacks of using the internet to carry out many of these tasks.

Advantages

- There is no longer a need to travel into the town centre thus reducing costs (money for fuel, bus fares, etc.) and time spent shopping. It also helps to reduce town centre congestion and pollution.
- Users now have access to a worldwide market and can thus look for products that are cheaper. This is less expensive and less time consuming than having to shop around by the more conventional methods. They also have access to a much wider choice of goods.
- Disabled and elderly people can now get access to shops and banks without the need to leave home. This helps to keep them part of society since they can now do all the things taken for granted by able-bodied people.
- Because it is online, shopping and banking can be done at any time on any day of the week – this is termed 24/7. This is particularly helpful to people who work, since shops/banks would normally be closed when they finished work.
- People can spend more time doing other things. For example, going shopping to the supermarket probably took up a lot of time; by doing this online people are now free to do more leisure activities, for example.

Disadvantages

- There is the possibility of isolation and lack of socialisation if people stay at home to do all their shopping and banking.
- There are possible health risks associated with online shopping and banking (discussed in Section 6.7).
- Security issues (e.g.) are a major concern. These include:
  - hacking, stealing credit card details, etc. (discussed in Section 6.3)
  - viruses and other malware (e.g. phishing, pharming, etc., discussed in Section 6.5)
  - fraudulent websites (discussed in Section 6.5).
- It is necessary to have a computer and to pay for line rental to take part in online shopping and banking. Also the telephone line will be tied up if the user does not have a broadband connection.
- Unlike high street shopping, it is not possible to see (or try on) the goods first before buying them. The goods also take several days to arrive.
- There is a risk of lack of exercise if people do all their shopping and banking at the computer.
- High street shops and banks are closing because of the increase in online shopping and banking and this is leading to 'ghost towns' forming.

Effects on companies due to the spread of online shopping and banking

The discussion above focused on the effects of ICT on people. However, companies and other organisations have also been affected by the growth of ICT and online shopping and banking.

- Companies can save costs since fewer staff are required and they do not need as many shops and banks in high streets to deal with potential customers.
- Because the internet is global, the potential customer base is increased.
- There will be some new costs, however, because of the need to re-train staff and the need to employ more staff in despatch departments.
- There are also costs due to the setting up and maintaining of websites to enable online shopping and banking.
- Since there is very little or no customer-employee interaction, this could lead to a drop in customer loyalty, which could result in loss of customers. This could also be brought about by the lack of personal service associated with online shopping and banking.

Should the internet be policed?

This is a question which has raged for many years. Currently, the internet has no controlling body to ensure that it conforms to certain standards. There are many arguments in favour of control and as many arguments against.

Arguments in favour of some form of control

- It would prevent illegal material being posted on websites (e.g. racist/prejudiced material, pornographic matter, material promoting terrorist activities, etc.).
- People find it much easier to discover information which can have serious consequences (e.g. how to be a hacker, how to make bombs, etc.). Although most of this can be found in books, it is much easier to find the information using a **search engine**.

- It would prevent children and other vulnerable groups being subjected to undesirable websites.
- Since anyone can produce a website, there is no guarantee of the accuracy of information. Some form of control could reduce the amount of incorrect information being published.

Arguments against some form of control

- Material published on the websites is already available from other sources.
- It would be very expensive to 'police' all websites and users would have to pick up the bill.
- It would be difficult to enforce rules and regulations on a global scale.
- It can be argued that policing would go against freedom of information.
- Many topics and comments posted on websites are already illegal and laws currently exist to deal with the perpetrators.

Microprocessor-controlled devices in the home

Many common household devices are now fitted with microprocessors to control a large number of their functions. The devices fall into two categories:
- **labour-saving devices**, which include automatic washing machines, microwave ovens, ovens, and dishwashers
- other household devices, such as television sets, hifis, fridge/freezers and central heating systems – these are not labour saving, but they do have microprocessors to control many of their functions.

Tables 6.1 and 6.2 give the advantages and disadvantages of both types of devices.

Advantages	Disadvantages
<ul><li>They lead to more leisure time since the devices can be programmed to do the tasks.</li><li>People have more time to go out and socialise, and can go out when they want to.</li><li>They are becoming very sophisticated and can make use of embedded web technology.</li></ul>	<ul><li>They can lead to unhealthy diets (e.g. TV dinners).</li><li>People can tend to become lazy, since they rely on these devices.</li></ul>

Table 6.1 Advantages and disadvantages of microprocessor-controlled labour-saving devices

Advantages	Disadvantages
• They save energy, since they can switch off automatically. • It is easier to program the devices to do a task rather than having to set timings, dates, etc. manually.	• They lead to a more wasteful society: devices are thrown away if the electronics fail, since they are not economic to repair. • They can be more complex to operate for people who are not technology literate. • Leaving devices on standby (such as televisions) leads to a waste of resources.

Table 6.2 Advantages and disadvantages of other microprocessor-controlled devices

6.5 Information from the internet

The social and general impact of using the internet or devices which rely on microprocessors have been discussed in earlier sections. This section will now look at the *quality* of information found on the internet when using a **search engines**. There are four main aspects to consider:

- reliability of information
- undesirability of certain websites
- security issues
- other internet issues.

Reliability of information

- Information is more likely to be up to date than in books, since websites can be updated very quickly.
- It is much easier to get information from websites, as search engines quickly link key words together and find information that matches the criteria.
- There is a vast amount of information on the internet, which is easier to locate than using the indices in several books.
- However, information on the internet may be incorrect, inaccurate or even biased since it does not go through any checking process.
- There is a risk of information overload even if search engines are used properly. It is possible to get thousands of **hits**, which may make it difficult to find the information relevant to the user's search.

Undesirability of certain websites

- There is always the risk of finding undesirable websites (as discussed in Section 6.4).
- There is also a risk of doubtful websites which are not genuine and could lead to a number of problems such as undesirable web links, security risks, etc.
- Security risks are a very large problem and are discussed in the following section.

Security issues

The risk of viruses and hacking has already been discussed in Section 6.3. The use of passwords, user IDs, encryption, firewalls and other software protection was also discussed in Section 6.3. However, there are other security risks (not necessarily as a result of viruses or hacking) associated with connecting to the internet. These security risks are now discussed in some depth.

Phishing

Phishing is a fraudulent operation involving the use of emails. The creator sends out a legitimate-looking email, hoping to gather personal and financial information from the recipient of the email. To make it more realistic (and therefore even more dangerous!) the message will appear to have come from some legitimate source (such as a famous bank). As soon as an unsuspecting user clicks on the link they are sent to a spoof website where they will be asked for personal information including credit card details, PINs, etc. which could lead to **identity theft**.

Many ISPs now attempt to filter out phishing emails, but users should always be aware that a risk still exists and should be suspicious of any emails requesting unsolicited personal details.

Pharming

Pharming is a **scam** in which malicious code is installed on a computer hard disk or a server. This code has the ability to misdirect users to fraudulent websites, usually without their knowledge or consent.

Whereas phishing requires an email to be sent out to *every* person who has been targeted, pharming does not require emails to be sent out to everybody and can therefore target a much larger group of people much more easily. Also, no conscious action needs to necessarily be made by the user (such as opening an email), which means the user will probably have no idea at all that have been targeted. Basically, pharming works like this:

A hacker/pharmer will first infect the user's computer with a virus, either by sending an email or by installing software on their computer when they first visit their website. It could also be installed as part of something the user chooses to install from a website (so the user doesn't necessarily have to open an email to become infected). Once infected, the virus would send the user to a fake website that looks almost identical to the one they really wanted to visit. Consequently, personal information from the user's computer can picked up by the pharmer/hacker.

Certain **anti-spyware**, anti-virus software or anti-pharming software can be used to identify this code and correct the corruption.

Spam

Spam is electronic **junk mail** and is a type of advertising from a company sent out to a target **mailing list**. It is usually harmless but it can clog up the networks, slowing them down, or fill up a user's mail box. It is therefore more of a nuisance than a security risk.

Many ISPs are good at filtering out spam. In fact, some are so efficient that it is often necessary to put legitimate email addresses into a contacts list/address book to ensure that *wanted* emails are not filtered out by mistake.

Spyware

Spyware is software that gathers user information through their network connections without them being aware that this is happening. Once spyware is installed, it monitors all key presses and transmits the information back to the person who sent out the spyware. This software also has the ability to install other spyware software, read **cookies** and even change the default home page or web browser. Anti-spyware can be used to search out this software and correct the corruption.

Other internet issues

Although the following item is not regarded as a security threat, it can be a considerable nuisance to an internet user and is included here for completeness.

Cookies

Cookies are small files sent to a user's computer via their web browser when they visit certain websites. They store information about the users and this data is accessed each time they visit the website. For example:
- they remember who the user is and send messages such as 'Welcome Daniel' each time they log onto the website
- they recognise a user's buying preferences; e.g. if a user buys CDs, **pop ups** (adverts) related to their buying habits will appear on the user's screen each time they visit the website.

Without cookies, the web server would have no way of knowing that the user had visited the website before.

6.6 Internet developments

The internet has changed out of all recognition since it first started, and continues to develop. This section considers some of the most recent developments in the way the internet is used.

Web 2.0 refers to a second generation of internet development and design. This has led to a development of new web-based communication, applications and **hosted servers**. For example, the following will be considered in more detail in this section:
- blogs
- wikis
- digital media sharing websites
- social networking sites
- folksonomies.

Blogs

Blogs (which is an abbreviation for we**b logs**) are personal internet journals where the writer (or **blogger**) will type in their observations on some topic (e.g. a political view) or even provide links to certain relevant websites. No training is needed to do this.

Blogs tend to range from minor projects where people just gossip about some topic (such as the performance of an actor in a recent film) through to important subjects such as politics, advertising products or raising awareness of a certain key event taking place. However, comments made are *not* immune from the law and bloggers can still be prosecuted for making offensive statements about people!

Wikis

The word 'wiki' comes from a Hawaiian word meaning 'fast'. **Wikis** are software allowing users to easily create and edit web pages using any web browser. A wiki will support hyperlinks and has very simple **syntax** (language rules) for creating pages. They have often been described as 'web pages with an edit button'. Anyone can use wikis, which means that the content should always be treated with some caution. One of the most common examples of a wiki is the online encyclopedia Wikipedia.

Digital media sharing websites

Digital media sharing websites allow users to upload video clips and other media to an internet website. The video host, for example, will then store the video on a server and show the user the different types of code which can be used to enable them to view the video clip.

This development is becoming increasingly popular since most users don't have unlimited web space. One of the most common examples of this is YouTube.

Social networking sites

Social networking sites focus on building online communities of users who share the same interests and activities. They enable young people, in particular, to share photos of themselves, show people their favourite videos and music, what they like to do in their spare time, what they like to eat, etc.

Common examples include Facebook and Myspace, where users can join free of charge and interact with other people. It is possible to add friends and post messages on a bulletin/message board and update personal profiles to notify friends about themselves.

These are rapidly becoming the modern way of interacting socially and they allow young people, in particular, to communicate across the world and share their interests and views with many people.

Folksonomies

Folksonomies are closely related to **tagging** and literally mean 'management of people'. Tagging is a type of social **bookmarking** where a user can tag any web page with words that describe its contents. Anyone can view web pages corresponding to a specific tag. In folksonomies, the visual representation is a tag cloud – this is a sequence of words of different sizes that represent popular tags by showing them in a larger font size. One of the most common examples is Flickr.

6.7 Health and safety issues

There are many health and safety problems associated with regular use of computer systems.

Health and safety regulations advise that all computer systems have a minimum of tiltable and anti-glare screens, adjustable chairs and foot supports, suitable lighting, uncluttered work stations, and recommend frequent breaks and eye tests.

Although health and safety are closely related, they are very different subjects. Health issues are related to how to stop people becoming ill or affected by daily contact with computers. Safety is more concerned with the dangers which could lead to serious injury or even loss of life. They are discussed in separate sections below to help clarify the main differences.

Health aspects

Table 6.3 highlights a number of health issues, together with possible solutions to either minimise the risk or eliminate it altogether.

Health risk	Solution
Back and neck problems/strain	• use fully adjustable chairs to give the correct posture • use foot rests to reduce posture problems • use screens that can be tilted to ensure the neck is at the correct angle
Repetitive strain injury (RSI) – damage to fingers and wrists	• ensure correct posture is maintained (i.e. correct angle of arms to the keyboard and mouse, for example) • make proper use of a wrist rest when using a mouse or a keyboard • take regular breaks and do some exercise • use ergonomic keyboards • use voice-activated software if the user is prone to problems when using mouse and keyboard
Eyestrain (caused by staring at a computer screen too long or bad lighting in the room)	• ensure that there is no screen flicker, since this can lead to eye problems • change to LCD screens where flicker is less of a problem than with CRT screens • take regular breaks and try focusing on a point which is some distance away • make use of anti-glare screens if lighting in the room is a problem or use window blinds to reduce strong sunlight • have eyes tested regularly – middle-vision glasses should be prescribed if the user has a persistent problem such as eye strain, dry eyes, headaches, etc.)
Headaches	• use an anti-glare screen or use window blinds to cut out light reflections – bad lighting can cause squinting and lead to headaches, etc. • take regular breaks and do some exercise • have eyes tested regularly and use middle-vision glasses if necessary
Ozone irritation (dry skin, respiratory problems, etc.) – this is caused by laser printers in an office area	• ensure proper ventilation to remove the ozone gas as quickly as possible • house laser printers in a designated printer room • change to other types of printer if necessary (e.g. inkjet printers)

Table 6.3 Health risks and proposed solutions

Safety aspects

Table 6.4 gives a number of safety issues, together with possible solutions to eliminate or minimise the risk.

Safety hazard	Ways of eliminating or minimising hazard
Electrocution	• use of a residual circuit breaker (RCB) • check insulation on wires regularly • do not allow drinks near computers • check equipment regularly
Trailing wires (trip hazard)	• use cable ducts to make the wires safe • cover wires and/or have them neatly tucked away (under desks, etc.) • try and use wireless connections wherever possible, thus eliminating cables altogether
Heavy equipment falling	• use strong desk and tables to support heavy hardware • use large desks and tables so that hardware isn't too close to the edge where it can fall off
Fire risk	• have a fully tested CO2/dry fire extinguisher nearby (*not* water extinguishers!) • don't cover equipment vents, which can cause equipment to overheat • make sure hardware is fully maintained • ensure good ventilation in the room, again to stop overheating of hardware • do not overload sockets with too many items • change to low voltage hardware wherever possible (e.g. replace CRT monitors with LCD monitors)

Table 6.4 Safety hazards and proposed solutions

The ways in which ICT is used

In this chapter you will learn about:
- communication systems
- satellite and mobile phone network communications
- data handling applications
- modelling applications
- batch processing and online systems
- control and monitoring applications
- robotics
- batch processing applications
- automatic stock control systems (use of barcodes)
- online booking systems
- banking applications
- library systems
- expert systems.

7.1 Introduction

This chapter looks at how ICT is used in everyday life and discusses the many advantages and drawbacks of using computer systems to replace or enhance applications which were previously paper or manually based.

7.2 Communications applications

There are several communication applications that make use of ICT technology. These fall into two categories: methods of communication and ways of communicating information.

Methods of communication include:
- video conferencing
- voice over internet protocol (VOIP) systems
- emails.

These were discussed in Section 4.7, and so are not considered any further here.

There are a large number of ways of communicating information. The five considered here are:
- multimedia presentations
- printing flyers and posters
- use of websites
- music production
- cartoon animations.

Multimedia presentations

Presentations using animation, video and sound/music are generally much more interesting than a presentation done on slides or paper.

The presentations are produced using one of the many software packages on the market and then used with a **multimedia projector** so that the whole audience is able to see the presentation. Some of the advantages of this type of presentation include:
- the use of sound and animation/video effects
- interactive/hyperlinks built into the presentation
- the fact that it is more likely to hold the audience's attention.

Some of the disadvantages include:
- the need to have special equipment, which can be expensive
- sometimes the requirement for internet access within the presentation, if the user wishes to access files (e.g. music or video) from websites or up-to-date information (e.g. weather reports) which needs a live connection.

Paper-based presentations

It is always possible to produce presentations in a hardcopy format rather than the system described above. This has the following advantages:
- Disabled people do not have to go to the venue to see the presentation.
- It is possible to print it out in Braille for the benefit of blind people.
- The recipient can read the presentation at any time they want.
- The recipients have a permanent copy, which they can refer to at any time they want.

There are, however, disadvantages:
- The presentation needs to be distributed in some way.
- There are no special effects (sound, video, animation).
- There are printing costs (paper, ink, etc.).

Flyers and posters

Flyers and posters can be produced very easily using one of the many software packages available, most commonly **word processors** and **desktop publishers (DTP)**. Usually, the flyer or poster will have photos which have been taken specially or have been downloaded from the internet. The following sequence is fairly typical of how such a document would be produced on a computer system:
- A word processor or DTP application is opened.
- The user creates frames, boxes and text boxes.
- If necessary, photos are taken, using a camera.
- The images are uploaded from the camera, loaded from a CD/DVD, scanned from hard-copy photos or downloaded from the internet.
- The photos are saved to a file.
- The photos are imported or copied and pasted into the document.
- The photos are edited and text typed in or imported from a file and then put into the required style.

Websites

Rather than producing flyers and posters by printing them out, it is possible to use websites for advertising and communication. There are a number of advantages and disadvantages of using this technique.

Advantages include:
- the ability to add sound/video/animation
- links to other websites/**hyperlinks**
- the use of **hot spots**
- buttons to navigate/move around the website
- hit counters to see who has visited the websites.

Disadvantages include:
- the fact that websites can be hacked into and modified or viruses introduced
- the need for a computer and internet connection
- its lack of portability compared with a paper-based system
- the need to maintain the website once it is set up.

Music production

The generation of music and the production of music scores can now be done by computer systems with the appropriate software, for example:
- music samplers and mixers allow the original tracks that were recorded in the studio to be modified in any way that the producer wants
- electronic instruments (like guitars and organs) can play back through electronic effects machines
- synthesisers combine simple wave forms to produce complex music creations
- electronic organs can mimic any other instrument
- music scores can be generated from the music itself using software
- software can automatically correct music notes in a score
- there is no need to understand music notation to write a music score
- music notes are automatically printed out in the correct format.

Cartoon animations

Animation can be produced using computer hardware and software. With **3D animation**, objects are designed on a computer and a 3D skeleton produced. The parts of the skeleton are moved by the animator using key frames (these frames define the start point and end point to give a smooth animation effect). The difference in the appearance of the skeleton in these key frames is automatically calculated by the software and is known as **tweening** or **morphing**. The final stage is to make a realistic image by a technique known as **rendering**.

7.3 Satellite and mobile network communications

This section considers three applications which make use of satellite technology and/or mobile phone network technology:
- mobile phone networks
- embedded web technology (EWT)
- global positioning satellite systems (GPS).

Mobile phone networks

Mobile phones communicate by using towers inside many cells networked together to cover large areas, illustrated in Figure 7.1. The towers allow the transmission of data throughout the mobile phone network.

Each tower transmits within its own cell. If you are driving a car and get to the edge of a cell the mobile phone signal starts to weaken. This is recognised by the network and the mobile phone then picks up the signal in

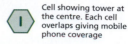

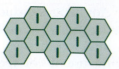

Cell showing tower at the centre. Each cell overlaps giving mobile phone coverage

Figure 7.1 A network of mobile phone cells

one of the adjacent cells. If a person is making a call or sending a text to somebody in a different country then satellite technology is used to enable the communication to take place.

Mobile phone technology can now be used by computers. A plug-in device (using one of the available USB ports) allows the computer to connect to the mobile phone network, which then allows access to the internet. This service is usually provided through a monthly contract which gives a download limit.

Embedded web technology

Embedded web technology (EWT) is a relatively new development that uses the internet in real time to control or interact with a device in the home or a device which is part of an industrial application. The device must contain an **embedded microprocessor** for this system to work.

The device can be controlled by an authorised user from a computer anywhere on a network or from a **web-enabled mobile phone**.

Consider the scenario of an oven equipped with an embedded processor. An authorised person can use their web-enabled mobile phone, for example, to send instructions to control the oven remotely (e.g. switch it on at a given time, set the timings and set the temperature) from their office before setting off for home. Any device with an embedded microprocessor can be controlled in this way; examples include a DVD recorder, a washing machine, a central heating system or even a scientific experiment in some remote location (e.g. in outer space or under the sea).

Global positioning satellite (GPS) systems

Global positioning satellite (GPS) systems are used to determine the exact location of a number of modes of transport (e.g. airplanes, cars, ships, etc.). Cars usually refer to GPS as **satellite navigation systems** (sat navs).

Satellites surrounding the Earth transmit signals to the surface. Computers installed in the mode of transport receive and interpret these signals. Knowing their position on the Earth depends on very accurate timing – atomic clocks are used in the satellites which are accurate to within a fraction of a second per day. Each satellite transmits data indicating its position and time. The computer on board the mode of transport calculates its exact position based on the

Figure 7.2 Calculation of position using satellites

information from at least three satellites, illustrated in Figure 7.2.

In cars, the on-board computer contains pre-stored road maps. With these sat nav systems the car's exact location, based on satellite positioning, can be shown on the map and the driver can also be given verbal instructions such as: 'After 100 metres, take the next left turn onto the A1234'. A screen on the sat nav device will also show the car's position in relation to the road network (see Figure 7.3).

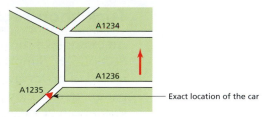

Figure 7.3 Car position shown on a sat nav screen

Advantages

- The driver does not have to consult paper maps while driving, so it is far safer.
- It removes errors, as it can warn drivers about one way streets, street closures, etc.
- The system can warn the driver about the location of speed cameras, again aiding safety.
- The system can estimate the time of arrival.
- It is also possible to program in the fastest route, a route to avoid towns, etc.
- The system can give useful information such as the location of petrol stations.

Disadvantages

- If the maps are not kept up to date, they can give incorrect instructions.
- Unless the system is sophisticated, road closures, due to accidents or road works, can cause problems.
- Loss of satellite signals can cause problems.
- If an incorrect start point or end point is keyed in, the system will give incorrect information.

7.4 Data handling applications

A number of applications make use of simple data handling techniques, such as:
- surveys
- tuck shop (i.e. school sweet shop) records
- clubs and society records
- record keeping (e.g. a book shop).

Surveys

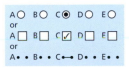

Figure 7.4 Methods of filling in questionnaires

Suppose a small business is interested in finding out information about the buying habits of a number of customers. Questionnaires or surveys will be either handed out to people or posted on a website to allow them to be filled in online. Paper questionnaires will be filled in either by shading in circles, ticking in boxes or connecting two points to select the correct response (see Figure 7.4).

Online questionnaires would tend to use the first option (using **radio buttons**) since this is a quick and easy method for gathering data.

Paper surveys are then scanned in using **optical mark recognition (OMR)** or **optical character recognition (OCR)** methods and the information is transferred to a database. The advantages of doing this rather than checking each one by hand are that:
- it is faster to get results
- there are fewer errors
- it is easier to do a statistical analysis
- it is less expensive to carry out, since it needs fewer people.

Online questionnaires have the added advantage that no data preparation is needed, as the results are sent directly to a database for analysis.

Tuck shop records

An example of the use of **spreadsheets** to keep school tuck shop accounts is given in Section 7.5. Simple financial applications such as these use spreadsheets to keep a record of prices and takings. The advantage is that it is much easier to vary different parameters to show how to optimise profits or to see why a loss is being made. The system can be programmed (using macros) to automatically warn of any problems.

Club and society records

Clubs and societies need to keep records of their membership. The information held typically includes payment details, contact details (phone number, address), interests, etc. A simple database is often used to hold all this information, making it unnecessary to keep paper records. Consequently, if a particular item of interest (e.g. a talk on F1 motor racing) comes up then the computer system can quickly scan all the records on file and find out who would be interested in this topic. The organisation can then automatically contact the member by email or, using **mail merging**, send out a letter and flyer.

It is also easy to check on membership subscriptions and send out reminders. This all saves having manual records on paper, which take time to search, can be easily lost, can have some details missing. It is also less expensive (cost of paper, filing, etc.) and saves on space in the office area.

It is worth noting that data stored by the club/society may be of a personal nature and must therefore obey the rules of a data protection act.

A typical data protection act

The purpose of a data protection act is to protect the rights of the individual about whom data is obtained, stored and processed (i.e. collection, use, disclosure, destruction and holding of data). Any such act applies to both computerised and paper records.

Any data protection act is based on eight simple principles:

1   Data must be fairly and lawfully processed.

2   Data can only be processed for the stated purpose.

3   Data must be adequate, relevant and not excessive.

4   Data must be accurate.

5   Data must not be kept longer than necessary.

6   Data must be processed in accordance with the data subject's rights.

7   Data must be kept secure.

8   Data must not be transferred to another country unless they too have adequate protection.

Failure to abide by these simple rules can lead to a fine and/or imprisonment to anyone who holds data about individuals.

There are general guidelines about how to stop data being obtained unlawfully:

● Don't leave personal information lying around on a desk when not being used.
● Lock all filing cabinets at the end of the day or when an office is unmanned for any length of time.
● Do not leave data on a monitor if unattended or log off from a computer system if it is to be unattended for a time.

- Protect passwords and don't give them out to anybody else.
- Change passwords regularly and select passwords which are difficult to 'crack'.
- Make sure anything in a fax/email is not of a sensitive nature (ask yourself the question: 'Would I write that on a post card?')

All of the above are in addition to the number of safeguards discussed throughout this book (such as ways to prevent hacking, phishing, pharming, etc.).

Record keeping

To evaluate the advantages of using a computer system for record keeping, we will consider the case of a small bookshop. This shop keeps files on the books in stock and on their customer base. Using a simple database it would be easy to keep this information in electronic form. This would make it easy to contact customers if a particular book was just published or to check on their buying habits. If a customer came into the shop it would also be far easier to search for a particular book (based on title, author or ISBN). No paper records would need to be kept which would lead to the following advantages to the shop:

- Less room would used up in the shop since no paper record would need to be kept.
- It would be quicker and easier to find details of a particular book or find out whether or not it was in stock.
- The system would be less expensive, since it wouldn't be necessary to employ somebody to do all the filing and searching.
- There would be fewer errors since no manual checking of paper files would be done.

There are some disadvantages of the system:

- The shop would need to buy a computer and software to run the system.
- It would take a lot of time and effort to transfer all the paper files to the database.

7.5 Modelling applications

A **simulation** is the creation of a **model** of a real system in order to study the behaviour of the system. The model is computer generated and is based on mathematical representations.

The idea is to try and find out what mechanisms control how a system behaves and consequently predict the behaviour of the system in the future and also see if it is possible to influence this future behaviour.

Computer models have the advantage that they save money, can help find a solution more quickly and can be considerably safer (discussed further below). There are many examples of simulations, ranging from simple spreadsheet representations through to complex flight simulators. This section gives two examples: a model for showing a shop's profit/loss and a traffic light simulation.

Tuck shop model

This example uses a spreadsheet to do the modelling. It models the school tuck shop mentioned in Section 7.4. The numbers in the spreadsheet model are shown in Figure 7.5, with Figure 7.6 showing the formulae that produce these numbers.

	A	B	C	D	E	F	G
1	Item	Price	Selling	Profit per	Weekly	Number sold	Total profit
2	name	each ($)	price ($)	item	shop cost ($)		per item ($)
3							
4	chew	1.00	1.50	0.50	200.00	35	17.50
5	chox	2.00	2.50	0.50	200.00	45	22.50
6	gum	3.00	3.50	0.50	200.00	30	15.00
7	crisps	1.00	1.50	0.50	200.00	45	22.50
8	cake	2.00	2.50	0.50	200.00	40	20.00
9							
10					200.00	Profit/Loss ($)	-102.50

Figure 7.5 Results in the spreadsheet model for a tuck shop

	A	B	C	D	E	F	G
1	Item	Price each	Selling	Profit per	Weekly	Number sold	Total profit per
2	name	($)	price ($)	item	shop cost		item ($)
3							
4	chew	1	1.5	=(C4-B4)	200	35	=(D4*F4)
5	chox	2	2.5	=(C5-B5)	200	45	=(D5*F5)
6	gum	3	3.5	=(C6-B6)	200	30	=(D6*F6)
7	crisps	1	1.5	=(C7-B7)	200	45	=(D7*F7)
8	cake	2	2.5	=(C8-B8)	200	40	=(D8*F8)
9							
10					200	Profit/Loss ($)	=SUM(G4:G8)-E10

Figure 7.6 Expressions in the spreadsheet model for a tuck shop

Thus, by varying the values in column C or in column F it would be possible to model the shop's profit or loss. This is a very simple model but it shows the principal of using spreadsheets to carry out any type of modelling that can be represented in a mathematical form.

Traffic light simulation

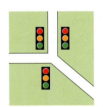

Figure 7.7 A junction controlled by traffic lights

To demonstrate a more complex simulation, the following scenario has been chosen: a set of traffic lights are to be modelled at a Y-junction, as shown in Figure 7.7.

In this simulation it is necessary to consider:
- how and what data needs to be collected
- how the simulation is carried out
- how the system would work in real life.

Data collection

Since the success (or failure) of a simulation model depends on how realistic it is, data needs to be collected by watching traffic for a long period of time at the Y-junction. This is best done by using induction loop sensors which count the number of vehicles at each junction. Manual data collection is possible but is prone to errors and is difficult to do over an 18-hour period per day, for example. The following data is an indication of what would need to be collected:
- the number of vehicles passing the junction in all directions
- the time of day for the vehicle count
- how many vehicles build up at the junction at different times of the day
- how vehicle movements change at weekends, bank holidays, etc.
- how long it takes a vehicle to clear the junction
- how long it takes the slowest vehicle to pass through the junction
- the movements made by vehicles (e.g. left turns, right turns, filtering, etc.)
- additional environmental factors, such as whether there are pedestrian crossings nearby.

Carrying out the simulation

Data from the above list is entered into the computer and the simulation run. The results of the simulation are compared with actual traffic flow from a number of data sets. Once the designers are satisfied that it simulates the real situation accurately, then different scenarios can be tried out. For example:

- vary the timing of the lights and see how the traffic flow is affected
- build up the number of vehicles stopped at part of the junction and then change the timing of the lights to see how the traffic flow is affected
- increase or decrease traffic flow in all directions
- how emergency vehicles affect traffic flow at different times of the day.

Using the simulation

This simulation can then be used to optimise the flow of traffic through the junction on an ongoing basis.

- Sensors in the road gather data and count the number of vehicles at the junction.
- This data is sent to a control box or to a computer. It may need to be converted first into a form understood by the computer.
- The gathered data is compared to data stored in the system. The stored data is based on model/simulation predictions which were used to optimise the traffic flow.
- The control box or computer 'decides' what action needs to be taken.
- Signals are sent out to the traffic lights to change their timing if necessary.

Why simulations are used

- They are less expensive than having to build the real thing (e.g. a bridge).
- On many occasions it is safer to run a simulation – some real situations are hazardous (e.g. chemical processes).
- With simulations, various scenarios can be tried out in advance.
- It is nearly impossible to try out some tasks in real life because of the high risk involved or the remoteness (e.g. in outer space, under the sea, in nuclear reactors, crash testing cars, etc.).
- It is often faster to do a simulation than the real thing. Some applications could take years before a result was known (e.g. climate change calculations, population growth, etc.).

There are some limitations to using simulations:

- They are only as good as the data used and the mathematical algorithms representing the real-life situations. They therefore have a limited use in some very complex applications (e.g. simulating a nuclear process).
- They can be very expensive to set up and often require specialist software to be written.
- They frequently require very fast processors/computer systems (which can be expensive) to do the necessary 'number crunching'; many simulations are made up of complex mathematical functions and use several thousand data sets.

7.6 Types of processing

There are three basic types of processing:

- batch processing
- real-time (transaction) or online processing
- real-time process control.

Batch processing

With **batch processing**, a number of tasks (**jobs**) are all collected together over a set period of time. The jobs are then loaded into a computer system (known as a **job queue**) and processed all at once (in a **batch**). Once the batch processing starts, no user interaction is needed. This type of processing can only be done where there are no timing constraints, i.e. files don't need to be updated immediately or a response from the computer is not needed straight away.

A big advantage of batch processing is that the jobs can be processed when the computer system is less busy (e.g. overnight), so the use of resources is being optimised. Areas where batch processing is used include billing systems (e.g. electricity, gas, water and telephone), payroll systems and processing of bank cheques. Section 7.9 considers batch processing applications in more detail.

Real-time (transaction) processing

Real-time (transaction) processing is an example of **online processing**. When booking seats on a flight or at the theatre, for example, this type of online processing is required. The response to a query needs to be very fast in order to prevent 'double booking' and seats need to be marked as 'unavailable' immediately the booking is confirmed. (Booking applications are covered in more detail in Section 7.11.)

Examples of the use of this type of processing include flight bookings, cinema and theatre bookings and use of an **automatic teller machine (ATM)** when getting money.

Real-time process control

Although this is still an example of **online processing**, it is very different to real-time (transaction) processing. This system usually involves sensors and feedback loops (e.g. monitoring and control applications – these are covered in more detail in Section 7.7).

In real-time (transaction) processing, files are updated in real time (e.g. booking flights) but in real-time process control, physical quantities (such as a temperature) are continually monitored and the input is processed sufficiently quickly to influence the input source.

7.7 Control applications

This section is split into two parts: turtle graphics and the use of sensors to control or monitor applications.

Turtle graphics

This is based on the computer language called LOGO and is now usually known as **turtle graphics**. It is essentially the control of the movement of a 'turtle' on a computer screen by a number of key instructions which can be typed in. The most common commands are given in Table 7.1. Thus, to draw the shape shown in bold in Figure 7.8, the instructions listed in Table 7.2 need to be carried out. Note that there are two possible sequences of instructions, which will both draw the same shape – the second option makes use of 'Repeat' instructions and so is more efficient in its coding.

Command	Meaning
FORWARD x	Move x cm forward
BACKWARD x	Move x cm backward
LEFT d	Turn left through d degrees
RIGHT d	Turn right through d degrees
REPEAT n	Repeat next set of instructions n times
ENDREPEAT	Finish the repeat loop
PENUP	Lift the pen up
PENDOWN	Lower the pen

Table 7.1 Common turtle graphics commands

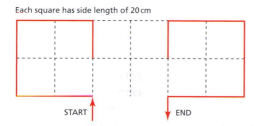

Each square has side length of 20 cm

START   END

Figure 7.8 Shape to be drawn by the turtle

Option 1 instructions		Option 2 instructions	
Pendown	Forward 40	Pendown	Pendown
Left 90	Left 90	Left 90	Forward 20
Forward 40	Pendown	Repeat 3	Repeat 3
Right 90	Forward 20	Forward 40	Right 90
Forward 40	Right 90	Right 90	Forward 40
Right 90	Forward 40	Endrepeat	Endrepeat
Forward 40	Right 90	Forward 20	
Right 90	Forward 40	Penup	
Forward 20	Right 90	Left 90	
Penup	Forward 40	Forward 40	
Left 90		Left 90	

Table 7.2 Instructions to draw the shape in Figure 7.8

Applications using sensors

There is a difference between *monitoring* and *controlling* an application using a computer and sensors. In both cases, sensors are used to send data to a computer where the data is processed – it is what happens next where the differences occur: In **monitoring**, the computer simply reviews the data from the sensors (by comparing it to data stored in memory) and updates its files and/or gives a warning signal if the values are outside given parameters. *No changes to the process are made* during monitoring.

In **control applications**, the computer again reviews the data from the sensors (by comparing it to data stored in memory). But if the values are outside the given parameters it *takes action to try and get the values within acceptable ranges*. It does this by sending signals to devices controlling the process (such as motors, valves, etc.). For example, if the temperature in a greenhouse is too high, it might send a signal to a motor to open a window until the temperature is within acceptable parameters; once the temperature dropped to acceptable values, the computer would instruct the motor to close the window again.

There are many examples of monitoring and control applications.

Monitoring:
- monitoring a patient's vital signs in a hospital
- monitoring a scientific experiment in a laboratory
- a burglar alarm system
- environmental monitoring (e.g. oxygen levels in a river).

Control:
- controlling a chemical process
- controlling a nuclear reactor
- controlling a greenhouse environment
- controlling a central heating system
- controlling a set of traffic lights.

Remember also that it was stressed in Section 5.5 that the **analogue** data from the sensors needs to be converted into **digital data** using an **analogue to digital converter (ADC)** so that the computer can understand and process the data from the sensors. If the computer sends signals to motors, valves, etc. then this data also needs to be converted to analogue using a **digital to analogue converter (DAC)** so that the computer can effectively control these devices.

We will now consider a number of monitoring and control applications. There are so many examples to choose from that it is important that you understand the principle behind each process so that this can be adapted to suit other examples.

Monitoring example: monitoring a patient's vital signs in a hospital
- Sensors read key vital signs (such as pulse/heart rate, temperature, blood pressure, respiration, etc.).
- The data from the sensors is converted into digital using an ADC.
- The data is stored in the computer's memory.
- The computer compares the data from the sensors with the values stored in its memory.
- The results are output on a screen in the form of graphs and/or digital read-outs.
- An alarm is activated if any of the data is outside acceptable parameters.
- The system continues to monitor the patient until the computer is turned off.

Monitoring example: measuring oxygen levels in a river (environmental monitoring)

The monitoring system and the positions of the sensors are shown in Figure 7.9.

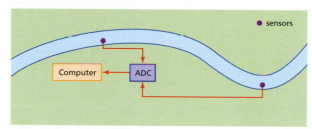

Figure 7.9 A monitoring system for measuring oxygen levels in a river

- Sensors read data from the river (oxygen levels and acidity levels using a pH sensor).
- The data from the sensors is converted into digital using an ADC.
- The computer stores the received data.
- The oxygen levels and acidity levels are compared to the historical data stored in memory and they are also compared to alarm levels stored in memory.
- One of two things will now happen: *either* the data is transferred to a CD/DVD or to a memory stick and taken away for analysis later *or* the computer is connected into a mobile phone network and transmits the data back automatically to the monitoring station.

Advantages of using computers and sensors for monitoring

- The computer will not forget to take readings.
- The computer's response time is much faster, which is particularly important in the patient monitoring example.
- Doctors, nurses, scientists, etc. can all get on with other tasks while the monitoring is done automatically.
- Computers give 24 hours cover every day (i.e. 24/7).
- The readings will tend to be more accurate.
- Readings can be taken more frequently if they are done by a computer and sensors.
- It could also be safer if whatever is being monitored may have potential hazards (e.g. children falling into the river whilst attempting to take readings).

Control example: a greenhouse environment

Five different sensors could be used to control a greenhouse environment: humidity, moisture, temperature, pH and light sensors. The system is shown in Figure 7.10.

Because of the number of sensors, this is clearly quite a complex problem. Let us consider the humidity sensor only. This sends a signal to an ADC which then sends a digital signal to the computer. This compares the input with stored values and decides what action needs to be taken (follow the orange lines in Figure 7.10). If humidity is too high, the computer sends a signal to a DAC to operate the motors to open windows thus reducing the humidity. If it is too low, the computer sends a signal to open valves to spray water into the air (follow the green lines in Figure 7.10 overleaf). This continues as long as the system is switched on. The process is similar for all five sensors.

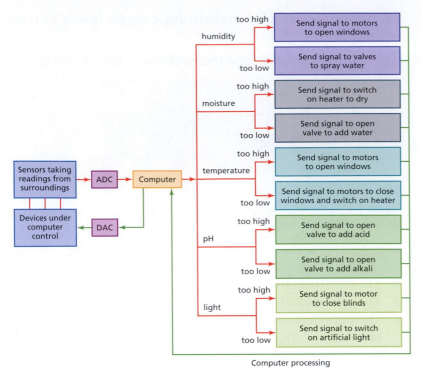

Figure 7.10 The control system for a greenhouse

Control example: chemical process

A certain chemical process only works if the temperature is above 70 °C and the pH (acidity) level is less than 3.5. Sensors are used as part of the control system. A heater is used to warm the reactor and valves are used to add acid when necessary to maintain the acidity. The following description shows how the sensors and computer are used to control this process.

- Temperature and pH sensors read data from the chemical process.
- This data is converted to digital using an ADC.
- The computer compares the incoming data with 'ideal' data stored in memory:
  - If the temperature is too low, a signal is sent to switch on the heaters.
  - If the temperature is too high, a signal is sent to switch off the heaters.
  - If the temperature is within an acceptable range, no action is taken.
  - If the pH is too high, a signal is sent to open a valve and acid is added.
  - If the pH is too low, a signal is sent to close this valve.
  - If the pH is within an acceptable range, no action is taken.
  - The computer signals will be changed into analogue signals using a DAC so that it can control the heaters and valves.
  - This continues as long as the computer system is activated.

Advantages of using sensors and computer systems to control processes

The advantages given earlier for monitoring systems also apply to control systems. However, there are a number of additional advantages:

- The response time if some parameter is out of range is much faster.
- This is safer, as some processes are potentially dangerous if they go wrong – the computer can control the process in a more accurate way, ensuring that the conditions are always correct.
- If a process is dangerous, it is better to control it from a distance.

7.8 Robotics

Robots are used in many areas of manufacturing, from heavy work right through to delicate operations. Examples include paint spraying of car bodies, welding bodywork on cars, manufacturing of microchips, manufacturing electrical goods and automatic warehouses.

Control of robots is either through embedded microprocessors (see Section 7.3) or linked to a computer system. Programming of the robot to do a task is generally done in one of two ways:

- The robot is programmed with a sequence of instructions which allow it to carry out a series of tasks (e.g. spraying a car body with paint).
- Alternatively, a human operator manually carries out a series of tasks and how each task is done is relayed back to the robot (embedded processor) or controlling computer. The sequence of instructions is remembered so that the robot can automatically carry out each task identically each time (e.g. assembling parts in a television).

Robots are often equipped with sensors so they can gather important information about their surroundings. Sensors also prevent them from doing 'stupid things', such as stopping a robot spraying a car if no car is present, or stopping the spraying operation if the supply of paint has run out, etc.

Robots are very good at repetitive tasks. However, if there are many different tasks (e.g. making specialist glassware for some scientific work) then it is often better to still use human operators.

Advantages

- Robots can work in environments harmful to human operators.
- They can work non-stop (24/7).
- They are less expensive in the long term. Although they are expensive to buy initially, they don't need wages.
- Productivity is higher, since they do not need holidays, are not ill, etc.
- There is greater consistency – every car coming off a production line is identical.
- They can do boring, repetitive tasks, leaving humans free to do other more skilled work.

Disadvantages

- Robots find it difficult to do 'unusual' tasks (e.g. one-off glassware for a chemical company).
- They replace skilled labour, leading to unemployment.
- Since robots do many of the tasks once done by humans, there is a risk of de-skilling.
- Because robots are independent of the skills base, factories can be moved anywhere in the world, again causing unemployment.

7.9 Batch processing applications

There are several applications that make use of batch processing, the most common ones being payroll, billing (electricity, gas, water and telephone) and cheque processing.

Payroll

At the end of each pay period (usually weekly or monthly) a company needs to pay its employees. Payroll systems are used to calculate wages and print out pay slips.

- The **inputs** are: employee details from file (e.g. rate of pay, tax code, bank details), number of hours worked (often obtained from a timesheet), any overtime working, holidays, etc.
- The **processing** done is calculation of: gross pay, any deductions (tax, national insurance), net pay, etc.
- The **outputs** are: printed pay slips, updating of the employee file, transfer to Bankers Automated Clearing Service (BACS) if wages paid into a bank account, etc.

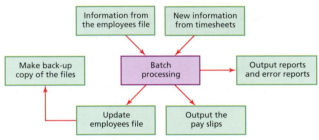

This is run as a batch system, where all the timesheets, etc. are gathered together before the payroll calculations are done in one go (often over night). Since there is no need for any further input, nor is it urgent to get the output (unlike in, for example, a booking system), batch processing works efficiently. The process is shown in Figure 7.11.

Figure 7.11 The stages in batch processing

Billing systems

Because companies send out their bill/invoices on a pre-determined date, all the information is gathered together and then processed in one go (batch). Consider an electricity billing system:

- The **inputs** are: customer details (address), charge per kW (unit) of power, previous readings, new readings taken from the electricity meter, bank account details (if using direct debit), etc.
- The **processing** done is calculation of: number of units of electricity used (i.e. new reading minus old reading), customer's cost (i.e. units used times charge per unit), monthly payments made (if using direct debit), outstanding amount owed or carried over to next bill, etc.
- The **outputs** are: bill showing all the details, updating of customer file, production of request for payment if not done through direct debit, etc.

The diagram of this process is very similar to that shown in Figure 7.11 for the payroll system.

7.10 Automatic stock control system

Automatic stock control systems rely on the use of **barcodes**.

Barcodes now appear on most products sold in shops. They allow quick identification of product details once the barcode has been scanned by a **barcode reader**. Supermarkets, in particular, use **electronic point of sale (EPOS) terminals**, which incorporate a barcode reader that scans the barcode, retrieve the price of the article and relay information back to the computer system allowing it to update its files.

Figure 7.12 An example of a barcode

Barcodes are made up of alternating dark and light lines of varying thickness, as shown in Figure 7.12. A number underneath the barcode usually consists of four parts: country code, manufacturer's code, product code and a **check digit**. The check digit is a form of **validation** which is used to make sure no errors occurred during the reading of the barcode.

The check digit can be calculated in a number of ways. The method discussed here works for codes which contain 11 digits.

Consider the following code:

```
1   3   5   7   9   11        odd digit positions
 5  1  0  4  3  1  1  2  0  1  7
   2   4   6   8   10         even digit positions
```

1   Add together the digits in the *odd* positions and multiply the sum by 3:
$5 + 0 + 3 + 1 + 0 + 7 = 16$
$16 \times 3 = 48$

2   Add together the digits in the *even* positions:
$1 + 4 + 1 + 2 + 1 = 9$

3   Add the two results together: $48 + 9 = 57$

4   To find the check digit, calculate what needs to be added to 57 to make the next multiple of 10 i.e. 60. Thus, the check digit is **3**.

Hence the final code is **5 1 0 4 3 1 1 2 0 1 7 3**.

Every time the barcode is read, this calculation is performed to ensure that it has been scanned correctly.

Barcodes are used in the following applications:
- library book systems (see Section 7.13)
- administration systems (e.g. in hospitals)
- passport and ID card systems
- some burglar alarm systems
- equipment checking systems (safety records on maintenance of equipment)
- automatic stock control systems (described in this section).

The following description is a detailed account of how barcodes are used to control stock levels automatically in a supermarket. Other retailers use similar systems with only minor differences.
- Barcodes are attached to all the items sold by the supermarket.
- Each barcode is associated with a stock file, which contains details such as prices, stock levels, product descriptions. The barcode acts as the primary key in the file.
- A customer takes their trolley/basket to the EPOS terminal once they have completed their shopping.
- The barcode on each item is scanned at the EPOS.
- If the barcode cannot be read, then the EPOS operator has to key in the number manually.
- The barcode is searched for on the stock file record by record until a match is found.
- The appropriate record is accessed.
- The price of the item is sent back to the EPOS, together with a product description.
- The stock level for the item is found in the record and is reduced by 1.
- The new stock level is written back to the file.

- If the stock level of the item is less than or equal to the re-order/minimum stock level then the computer *automatically* orders a batch of items from the suppliers. (Supplier information would be found on another file called the order file or supplier file – the barcode would be the link between the two files.)
- Once goods have been ordered, a **flag** is assigned to this item in the file to indicate an order has been placed; this now prevents re-order action being triggered *every time* this item is scanned before the new stock arrives.
- The above procedure is repeated until all the items in the customer's basket/trolley have been scanned.
- When all the items have been scanned, the customer is given an **itemised bill** showing a list (with prices) of everything they have bought.
- The computer updates the files containing the daily takings.
- If the customer has a loyalty card, the system will also automatically update their points total.
- When new goods arrive, the barcodes on the cartons will be used to update the stock files. Also, any flags associated with these goods will be removed so that the stock checks can start to be made again.

Some newer supermarkets now allow customers to scan their own items at special checkouts. These basically work in the same way as the normal EPOS terminals.

7.11 Online booking systems

Online booking systems rely on the ability to update files immediately, thus preventing double booking, which could happen if the system response time was slow. Booking systems are used for transport (flights, trains and buses), cinemas and theatres.

We will consider the theatre booking system to describe how this system works. With this example, we have assumed that the customer has already logged on to the theatre booking website.

- The customer clicks on the performance they wish to see.
- They enter the date and time of the performance and the required number of seats.
- A seating display at the theatre is then shown on the screen and the user clicks on where they would like to sit.
- The database is then searched to check the availability of the selected seats. If the seating plan is shown on screen, this step is not required.
- If the seats are available, the seat numbers are shown together with the total price.
- If the customer is happy with this, they select 'confirm' on the screen.
- The seats are now temporarily set at 'no longer available'.
- The customer then enters their personal details or indicates that they are a returning customer (in which case the website being used will already have their details).
- They select a payment method and make the payment.
- The theatre seats are then booked in the customer's name.
- The final details are shown on the screen, together with a reference number (in case there are any customer queries later on).
- An email is sent to the customer which they print out as their proof of purchase. In some cases, this also acts as their printed ticket when they go to the theatre – an **e-ticket**.
- The database is updated with the transaction.

Booking seats at the cinema is very similar. However, booking flights is slightly more complex since it involves choosing airports, etc. Figure 7.13 shows an example of an online webpage for choosing flights.

7.12 Banking applications

The use of computer technology has revolutionised how we do our banking transactions, for example:

- internet banking (discussed in Chapter 6)
- the use of automated teller machines (ATMs)
- chip and PIN technology.

Figure 7.13 An online flight booking system

Automated teller machines (ATMs)

Automated teller machines (ATMs) are places where customers can get cash (or carry out certain other banking activities such as order a statement) using their credit or debit card. Table 7.3 summarises the process.

Sequence at ATM	What goes on behind the scenes
Customer puts card into ATM.	• Contact is made with bank's computer.
PIN is entered using the keypad.	• PIN is checked to see if it is correct. • Card is checked to see if it is valid.
A number of options are given: • change PIN • top up mobile • see balance • get money.	
The customer selects the cash option. A number of cash amounts are shown.	
The customer accepts one of the options or types in a different amount.	• The customer's account is accessed to see if they have sufficient funds. • It is checked to see if they are withdrawing more than their daily limit.
The customer is asked if they want a receipt.	
The card is returned.	• Transaction is OK.
Money is dispensed.	• Customer's account is updated.

Table 7.3 Process for withdrawing cash from an ATM

Although ATMS are very convenient for customers, they do have a few disadvantages:
- They are often in places where theft can take place unnoticed.
- 'Fake' ATMs can be set up to gather information about the card and retain the card.
- Some banks charge customers for the use of ATMs.
- Someone else could see the PIN being entered and could use this to commit fraud at a later date (also known as 'shoulder surfing').

Chip

Figure 7.14 A chip and PIN card

Chip and PIN

Many credit cards are equipped with a chip as well as a magnetic stripe (see Figure 7.14) – this contains key information such as the PIN.

This system is designed to enhance security since it is better than relying only on a signature. When paying for items using a chip and PIN card, a form of **electronic funds transfer (EFT)** takes place. In this example, a customer pays for a meal in a restaurant using a chip and PIN card:

- The waiter inserts the card into the chip and PIN reader.
- The restaurant's bank contacts the customer's bank.
- The card is checked to see if it is valid (expiry date, whether stolen card, etc.).
- If the card is stolen or expired then the transaction is terminated.
- The customer enters the PIN using a keypad.
- The PIN is read from the chip on the card and is compared to the one just keyed in.
- If they are the same, then the transaction can proceed.
- If they are different, the transaction is terminated.
- A check is then made on whether they have enough funds.
- If there are not enough funds available, then the transaction is terminated. Otherwise, the transaction is authorised.
- An authorisation code is sent to the restaurant.
- The price of the meal is deducted from the customer's account.
- The same amount of money is credited to the restaurant's bank account.
- A receipt is produced as proof of purchase.

Exercise 7b

Indicate which of the following tasks is batch processing or online (both types).

Description	Batch	Online
Producing a monthly payroll		
Processing bank cheques at the end of the month		
Using an ATM to obtain cash		
Booking seats for a train journey		
Monitoring a patient in an intensive care unit		
Manual stock taking system done at the end of each day		
Welding of a car body using a robot		
A satellite navigation system		
Producing and updating a dictionary or encyclopedia		
Printing out mobile phone bills at the end of the month		
Getting prices of items at an EPOS terminal in a supermarket		

7.13 Library systems

Many library systems are computer controlled. They usually involve the use of barcodes on the books being borrowed and on the borrower's library card (see Figure 7.15).

ISBN 85-263-0548-4

a) 9 788526 305489

213 213 004 55

This card must be produced when items are borrowed

| NAME | Mr A. N. Other |
| LIBRARY | H & S Library |

This card should only be used by the person named.

b)

Figure 7.15 Barcodes on a) a library book and b) a library card

- The following describes a computerised library system based on barcodes.
- There are two files:
  - **Book file** (this contains a number of records made up of the following fields):

Barcode	Book title	Name of author	Date published	Number of books	Date due back

  - **Borrower's file** (this contains a number of records made up of the following fields):

Borrower's number	Borrower's name	Borrower's details	Barcode of book borrowed

- When a borrower takes out a book, the book's barcode is scanned. The book details are then found on the **book file**.
- The borrower's library card barcode is then scanned for the borrower's unique number. The **book file** is linked to the **borrower's file** and both files are updated to indicate which book has been borrowed and when it is due back.
- On a daily basis, the **borrower's file** is interrogated by the computer to see which books are overdue for return:
  - The computer reads a record from the book file.
  - It compares the date due back with the current date.
  - If the date due back is **less than (or equal to)** the current date (i.e. earlier date) …
  - … using the barcode number of the book …
  - … the book file is linked to the borrower's file …
  - … and the corresponding record is read from the borrower's file.
  - The customer details are then found and a letter or email is automatically sent out.
  - The next record in the book file is then read …
  - … until the whole file has been checked.

7.14 Expert systems

These systems have been developed to mimic the expertise and knowledge of an expert in a particular field. Examples include:

- diagnosing a person's illness
- diagnostics (finding faults in a car engine, finding faults on a circuit board, etc.)
- prospecting for oil and minerals
- tax and financial calculations
- chess games
- identification of plants, animals and chemical compounds
- road scheduling for delivery vehicles.

A basic expert system is made up of a number of elements, illustrated in Figure 7.16.

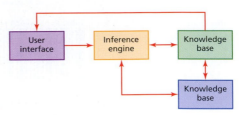

Figure 7.16 Elements of an expert system

How to set up an expert system

- Experts in the field are interviewed to find out what is needed in the expert system.
- Data is then collected from these experts.
- A **knowledge base** (defined below) is designed and then created.
- The **rules base** (defined below) is designed and created.
- An **inference engine** (defined below) is designed and created.
- The **input screen** and output format are also designed and created – this is known as the **user interface**.
- The **expert system** is tested against known conditions and scenarios.
- It is also checked to see if it meets the original specification.
- Experts are interviewed about how effective it is before the expert system goes out on general release.

Advantages

- Expert systems provide consistent answers.
- They never 'forget' to answer a question when determining the logic.
- Using expert systems reduces the time taken to solve a problem.
- A less skilled work force is needed, which gives the potential of saving money, but also allows areas of the world access to expertise which they could not normally afford.

Disadvantages

- They tend to lack common sense in some of the decision-making processes.
- Errors in the knowledge base can lead to incorrect decisions being made.
- It can be expensive to set up in the first place.
- Considerable training is necessary to ensure the system is used correctly by the operators.

Example of an expert system: oil prospecting

- An interactive user screen appears.
- Questions are asked about geological profiles.
- Answers to the questions and information about the geological profiles are typed in.
- The inference engine searches the knowledge base using the rules base.
- The system:
  - suggests the probability of finding oil as an output
  - indicates the probable depth of deposits
  - makes predictions about geological deposits above the soil
  - produces contour maps showing concentration of minerals, rocks, oil, etc.

Definitions of knowledge base, inference engine and rules base

Knowledge base

This is a database designed to allow the complex storage and retrieval requirements of a computerised knowledge-based management system (in support of an expert system).

Inference engine

This is software that attempts to derive answers from the knowledge base using a form of reasoning. It is how expert systems appear to use human-like reasoning when accessing information from the knowledge base in an effort to find a conclusion to a given problem. The inference engine is a type of reasoning engine.

Rules base

This is made up of a series of 'inference rules' (e.g. IF the country is in South America AND the language used is Portuguese THEN the country must be Brazil). These inference rules are used by the inference engine to draw conclusions. They closely follow human-like reasoning.

CHAPTER 8

Systems analysis and design

In this chapter you will learn about systems analysis and design, specifically:
- the analysis stage
- the design stage:
  - validation
  - verification
- the development stage
- the testing stage
- the implementation stage, particularly changeover methods
- documentation
  - user documentation
  - technical documentation
- evaluation.

8.1 Introduction

A **systems analysis** team is often brought in to review an existing system and suggest a number of improvements. The existing method used may be either a manual paper-based system or a computer-based operation that is no longer regarded as adequate for the task.

There are many stages in systems analysis, as shown in Figure 8.1. These are covered in Sections 8.2 to 8.7.

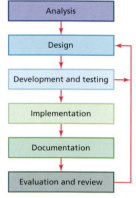

Figure 8.1 The stages in systems analysis

8.2 Analysis stage

The basic steps in the **analysis** stage can be summarised as follows:

1 fact finding/collecting data from the current system

2 description of the current system – establishing the inputs, outputs and processing being done

3 identification of the problems with the current system

4 agreeing the objectives with the customer

5 identifying and agreeing the customer's requirements

6 interpreting the customer's requirements

7 producing a cost-benefit analysis

8 producing a data flow diagram.

Stages 2 to 7 are sometimes referred to as the **feasibility study** and this can be further broken down as shown in Figure 8.2.

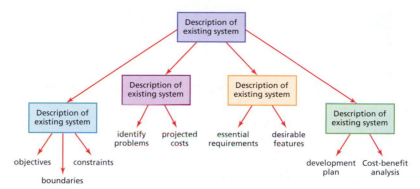

Figure 8.2 Stages in a feasibility study

Let us now consider the first item in the analysis stage – **fact finding**. There are four common methods used in fact finding, which have been summarised in Table 8.1 overleaf. The methods are: **observation, questionnaires, interviews** and **looking at existing paperwork**.

8.3 Design stage

Once the analysis has taken place and the systems analyst has some idea of the scale of the problem and what needs to be done, the next stage is to **design** the key parts of the recommended system. A list of tasks is summarised here, but is by no means exhaustive:

- designing data capture forms/input forms
- designing screen layouts
- designing output forms and reports
- producing systems flowcharts and/or **pseudo code**
- selecting and designing validation rules that need to be used
- selecting the most appropriate data verification methods
- designing and agreeing the file structures and tables
- selecting and designing the hardware requirements
- selecting and designing the software requirements
- producing algorithms or program flowcharts
- designing a testing strategy/plan.

We will now consider in more depth two of these tasks: **verification** and **validation**.

Verification

Verification is a way of preventing errors when data is copied from one medium to another (e.g. from paper to disk/CD). There are two common ways that verification checks are carried out:

- **Double entry**: in this method, data is entered *twice*, using two different people. The computer compares the two entries, either after data entry or during the data entry process, and identifies any differences.
- **Visual check**: this is the checking for errors by comparing entered data on the screen with the data in the original document (this is *not* the same as proof reading).

Validation

Validation is a process where data is checked to see if it satisfies certain criteria when input into a computer, for example to see if the data falls within accepted boundaries. A number of validation techniques exist and Table 8.2 highlights some of the more common ones used when writing computer software.

Name of method	Description	Advantages	Disadvantages
Observation	Involves watching personnel using the existing system to find out exactly how it works.	• The analyst obtains reliable data. • It is possible to see exactly what is being done. • It is a relatively inexpensive method.	• People are generally uncomfortable being watched and may work in a different way. • If workers perform tasks that violate standard procedures, they may not do this while being watched!
Questionnaires	Involves sending out questionnaires to the work force and/or to customers to find out their views of the existing system and find out how some of the key tasks are carried out.	• The questions can be answered quite quickly. • It is a relatively inexpensive method. • Individuals can remain anonymous if they want. • It allows quick analysis of the data.	• Often the number of returned questionnaires is low. • The questions are rather inflexible since they have to be generic. • There is no immediate way to clarify a vague or incomplete answer to a question.
Interviewing	Involves a one-to-one question-and-answer session between the analyst and the employee/customer.	• It gives the opportunity to motivate the interviewee into giving open and honest answers to the analyst's questions. • It allows the analyst to probe for more feedback from the interviewee, as it is easier to extend a question. • It is possible to modify questions as the interview proceeds and ask questions specific to the interviewee. • It is a good method if the analyst wants to probe deeply into one specific aspect of the existing system.	• It can be rather time consuming. • It is relatively expensive, due to the use of the analyst's time. • The interviewee cannot remain anonymous.
Looking at existing paperwork	Allows the analyst to see how the paper files are kept, look at operating instructions and training manuals, check the accounts, etc.	• It allows information to be obtained which was not possible by any of the other methods. • The analyst can see for themselves how the paper system operates. • It allows the analyst to get some idea of the scale of the problem, memory size requirements, type of input/output devices needed, etc.	• It can be very time consuming. • Because of the analyst's time, it is a relatively expensive method.

Table 8.1 Different fact finding methods

Validation check	Description	Example/s
Range check	Checks whether data is within given/acceptable values.	A person's age should be in the range > 0 but < 150.
Length check	Checks if the input data contains the required number of characters.	If a field needs six digits then inputting a five- or seven-digit number, for example, should cause an error message.
Character/type check	Checks that the input data does not contain invalid characters.	A person's name should not contain any numbers but a person's height should only contain digits.
Format/picture check	Checks that data is in a specific format.	Date should be in the form dd/mm/yyyy.
Limit check	Similar to range check except that only *one* of the limits (boundaries) is checked.	Input data must be > 10.
Presence check	Checks if data is actually present and has not been missed out.	In an electronic form, a person's telephone number may be a required field and if no data is present this should give rise to an error message.
Consistency check	Checks if fields correspond (tie up) with each other.	If 'Mr' has been typed into a field called **title** then the **gender** field must contain either 'M' or 'Male'.
Check digit	Looks at an extra digit which is calculated from the digits of a number and then put on the end of the number (see example in Section 7.10).	Check digits can identify three types of error: • if two digits have been inverted during input, e.g. 13597 instead of 13579 • an incorrect digit entered twice, e.g. 13559 typed in instead of 13579 • a digit missed out altogether, e.g. 1359 typed in instead of 13579.

Table 8.2 Common validation methods

8.4 Development and testing

Once the design stage is completed, it is then necessary to create the system and fully test it. This section considers some of the development stages and testing strategies which are often adopted by systems analysts.

Development stages

If the system contains files (e.g. a database) then the file structure needs to be finalised at this stage (e.g. what type of data is being stored in each field, length of each field, which field will be the key field, how the data files will be linked, etc.). Once the file structure has been determined, it is then created and fully tested to make sure it is robust when the system actually goes live.

Since it is important that the correct data is stored in files, there are certain techniques that need to be adopted to make sure the data populating the file/s and database/s is at least of the right type and that it conforms to certain rules. Validation routines and verification methods (discussed in Section 8.3) are used to ensure this happens. Again, these routines have to be fully tested to ensure they do trap unwanted data but also to make sure any data transferred from a paper-based system to an electronic system has been done accurately.

Any system being developed will have some form of user interface. The types of hardware were chosen in the design stage. How these are used to interface with the final system now needs to be identified, for example how the screens (and any other input devices) will be used to collect the data and the way the output will be presented. If specialist hardware is needed (e.g. for people with disabilities), then it will be necessary to finalise how these devices are used with the system when it is implemented. This will be followed by thorough testing to ensure the user screens are user friendly and that the correct output is associated with the inputs to the system.

Testing strategies

Testing of each module needs to be done to ensure each one functions correctly on its own. Once the development of each module is completed, the whole system needs to be tested (i.e. all modules functioning together). Even though each individual module may work satisfactorily, when they are all put together there may be data clashes, incompatibility and memory issues, etc.

All of this may lead to a need to improve the input and output methods, file and database structures, validation and verification methods, etc. Then the system will need to be fully tested again. It is a very time-consuming process but the system has to be as perfect as possible before it goes live.

Testing will use many different types of data, which will fall into one of three categories: normal, extreme or abnormal. Let us suppose one of the fields in a database is the date and this must be in the form dd/mm/yyyy, where each element of the date must be numeric:

- **Normal**: this is data which is acceptable/valid and has an expected (known) outcome, e.g. the month can be *any* whole number in the range 1 to 12.
- **Extreme**: this is data at the limits of acceptability/validity, e.g. the month can be either of the two end values i.e. 1 *or* 12.
- **Abnormal**: this is data outside the limits of acceptability/validity and should be rejected or cause an error message. For example, all the following values are not allowed as inputs for the month:
  - negative numbers (e.g. –1, –15)
  - any value greater than 12 (e.g. 32, 45)
  - letters or other non-numeric data (e.g. July)
  - non-integer values (e.g. 3.5, 10.75).

8.5 Implementation

Once the system is fully tested, the next stage is to fully implement it. Some of the stages in this process are shown in Figure 8.3.

We will now consider **changeover** to the new system in more depth. As indicated in Figure 8.3, there are four common methods used for changing over from the old system to the new system. Each one has advantages and disadvantages, shown in Table 8.3, which need to be weighed up before the most appropriate method is chosen for a particular application.

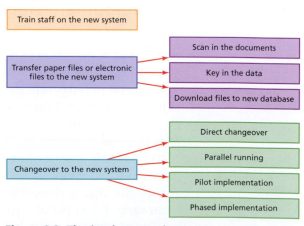

Figure 8.3 The implementation stage

Changeover method	Description	Advantages and disadvantages
Direct	The old system is stopped overnight and the new system introduced immediately.	• The benefits are immediate. • Costs are reduced – since only one system is used there is no need to pay for two sets of staff. • There is less likelihood of a malfunction since the new system will have been fully tested. • This method can be disastrous if the new system fails.
Parallel running	The old and new systems are run side by side for a time before the new system takes over altogether.	• If the new system fails, the old system is still available as a back-up. • It is possible to train staff gradually. • Staff have time to get used to the new system. • It is more expensive than direct changeover, since extra staff are needed to run both systems together.
Pilot implementation	The new system is introduced into one part of the company (e.g. into a warehouse of a supermarket) and its performance assessed.	• If the new system fails, only one part of the company is affected. • It is possible to train staff in one area only, which is much faster and less costly than parallel running. • The costs are also less than parallel running, since only one part of the system is being used in the pilot. • It is more expensive than direct changeover, since each pilot scheme needs to be evaluated before the next stage is introduced.
Phased implementation	Initially, only part of the new system is introduced. Only when it proves to work satisfactorily is the next part introduced, and so on, until the old system is fully replaced.	• If the latest part fails, it is only necessary to go back in the system to the point of failure, hence failure is not disastrous. • It is possible to ensure the system works properly before expanding. • This is more expensive than direct changeover, since it is necessary to evaluate each phase before moving to the next stage.

Table 8.3 Changeover methods

Table 8.4 compares the costs, input requirements and risk of failure for all four changeover methods.

Changeover method	Relative costs	Input needed by the user	Input needed by systems team	Impact of failure
Direct	Low	Medium	Low*	High
Parallel	High	High	Low	Low
Pilot	Medium	Low	Medium	Low
Phased	Medium	Medium	Medium	Medium

* Low if successful, otherwise *very high* amount of input needed

Table 8.4 Comparison of the four changeover methods

8.6 Documentation

Once the new system is fully developed, a considerable amount of documentation needs to be produced a) for the end user, and b) for people who may need to modify or develop the system further at some later stage. There is some overlap between the two types of documentation, but the basic requirements are shown below.

User documentation

User documentation is designed to help users to learn how to use the software or system. This can consist of any of the following:
- the purpose of the system/program/software package
- how to log in/log out
- how to load/run the software
- how to save files
- how to do a search
- how to sort data
- how to do printouts
- how to add, delete or amend records
- screen layouts (input)
- print layouts (output)
- hardware requirements
- software requirements
- sample runs (with test data and results)
- error handling/meaning of errors
- troubleshooting guide/help lines/FAQs
- tutorials.

Technical documentation

Technical documentation is designed to help programmers and analysts who need to make improvements to the system or repair/maintain the system. This can consist of any of the following:
- purpose of the system/program/software
- program listing/coding
- programming language used
- flowchart/algorithm

- input formats
- hardware requirements
- software requirements
- minimum memory requirements
- known bugs in the system
- list of variables used (and their meaning/description)
- file structures
- sample runs (with test data and results)
- output formats
- validation rules
- meaning of error messages.

8.7 Evaluation

Once a system is up and running it is necessary to do some **evaluation** and carry out any maintenance, if necessary. The following is a list of some of the things considered when evaluating how well the new system has worked. This can ultimately lead back to a re-design of part of the system if there is strong evidence to suggest that changes need be made. If you look back to Figure 8.1 in Section 8.1, you will see that the evaluation stage feeds back into the design stage. To evaluate the system, the analyst will:

- compare the final solution with the original requirement
- identify any limitations in the system
- identify any necessary improvements that need to be made
- evaluate the user's responses to using the new system
- compare test results from the new system with results from the old system
- compare the performance of the new system with the performance of the old system
- observe users performing set tasks, comparing old with new
- measure the time taken to complete tasks, comparing old with new
- interview users to gather responses about how well the new system works
- give out questionnaires to gather responses about the ease of use of the new system.

Some results from the evaluation may require changes to either hardware or software. Hardware may need to be updated because:

- of feedback from end users
- new hardware comes on the market, making change necessary
- there are changes within the company which require new devices to be added or updated.

Software may need to be updated because:

- of feedback from end users
- changes to the company structure or how the company works may need modifications to the software
- changes in legislation may need modifications to the software.

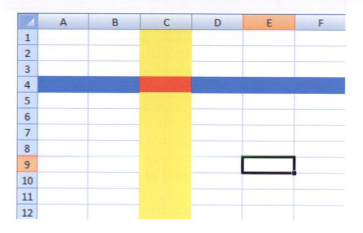

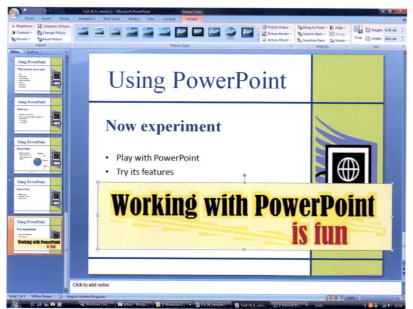

Part 2

Communication

In this chapter you will learn how to:

- open your mailbox
- organise your mail
- use email etiquette
- send an email
- send a file as an email attachment
- receive an email
- receive and save a file as an email attachment
- reply to an email
- forward an email
- copy an email to another mail recipient
- manage your email contact lists
- locate and download information from the internet
- use the internet to locate information on a specified website
- use the internet to search for information using a search engine.

For this chapter you will need this source file from the CD:
- STYLE1.CSS

9.1 Using email

Email is short for 'electronic mail' and is a method of sending text-based messages from one computer to another or using mobile phones. Email is usually received instantaneously by the recipient's mail provider and frequently waits there until the user accesses their mailbox. Some mail providers will allow users to have their messages forwarded to their mobile phones. All mailboxes have a storage limit and it can be very easy to fill your mailbox. If this happens, you will not be able to receive the messages sent to you.

To use email you must have a mailbox with an email address. These can be web based like *Windows Live Mail* or use an internally hosted mailbox, which is common in many schools. For this chapter, I have created a new email account with *Windows Live Mail*. Although I will use this for the exercises in this chapter, most of the skills are transferable to other email editors and the underlying structures are the same.

Hint

Your email system will be protected by a password. Make sure that you keep your password secure.

9.2 Opening your mailbox

To open your mailbox, go to the *Windows* taskbar, usually found along the bottom of the screen. Select the icon for *Windows Live Mail* (it looks like a white envelope) and click the left mouse button on this icon to open the email editor.

Hint

If this icon does not appear, select the **Start** button, followed by **All Programs** and **Windows Live Mail**.

Your email editor will open and look similar to this. You may need to enter your email address and password in some systems.

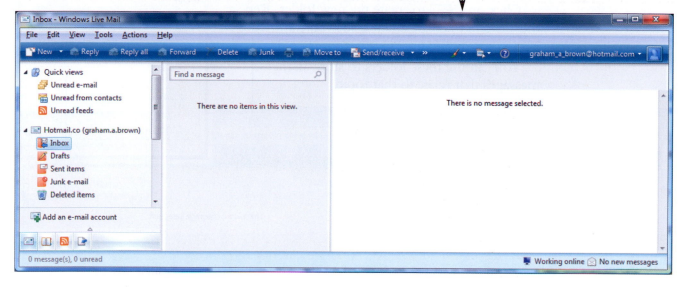

9.3 Organising your mail

At the moment the mailbox is empty, but it will soon fill with a flood of messages. These will need organising into logical groups. You need to decide on the groups you want and then create and name folders to match these groups.

Hint

If the menu bar is not visible, click on the **New** button, and select **Folder** from the pull-down list.

Task 9a

Create new folders in your email editor called 'IGCSE ICT' and 'Friends'.

Select your email account by clicking on your email address in the left column of the email editor.

Select the **File** menu, followed by **Folder**, then **Create new folder…** like this.

In the **Create Folder** window, enter the text 'IGCSE ICT' in the **Folder name:** box.

Click on [OK] to create the new folder. Repeat this process to create a new folder called 'Friends'. The editor should look similar to this.

You can use these folders to store all the messages that relate to that topic.

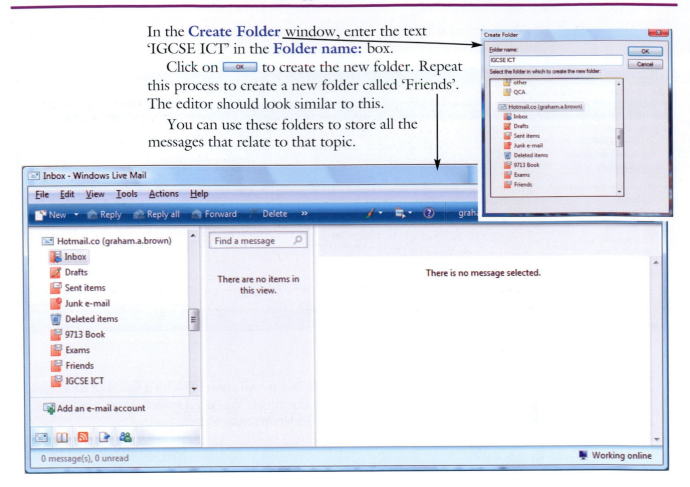

9.4   Email etiquette

When using email, use these basic rules to help you to gain respect of other online users:

- Do not type using all capital letters – this is read as shouting in an email.
- Do not leave the subject line blank.
- Do not use coloured text and backgrounds. These are more difficult to read and can take up a lot of space in an email inbox.
- When sending a number of people the same email use 'bcc' rather than 'cc' as it protects their email addresses from being passed on and reduces the chance of them getting junk mail.
- Do not forward chain letters and similar types of email as these can take up valuable space in an email inbox.
- Do not give out any personal details like phone numbers, passwords, bank account details, etc. in emails.
- Email communication is private. In most countries, you are likely to be breaking the law if you post the content of an email to you in a public place without the sender's permission.
- Compress or **zip** email attachments where possible before sending them. This will allow larger documents or other files to be sent quickly and take up less storage space in the inbox.

9.5 Sending an email

Task 9b

Send an email message to David Watson. Use the email address david.w.watson@hotmail.com and let him know that some of the source files for Chapter 15 of the book are almost complete. Copy this message to a user with the email address a.n.other@hoddereducation.co.uk and send a blind carbon copy to best.book@hoddereducation.co.uk.

Make the subject line for the email '0417 IGCSE text book'

Open your email editor and access your mailbox, using your email address and password. Click on **New** to create a new email message.

This opens the **New Message** window. Enter the email address of the person that you wish to send the email to in the **To:** box. In this case the message will be sent to David Watson.

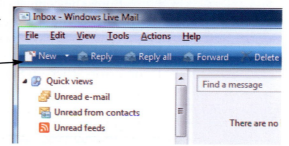

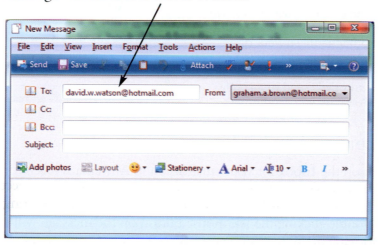

Make sure that you type the address accurately, carefully checking spelling and punctuation. One error in your typing will mean that the message will not be sent to the correct person. This person will not be aware that you have ever sent them a message. If you have contacts that you email often, add them to your contacts list (sometimes called an address book), and select them from there. This reduces the chance of errors when typing the email address. Clicking the left mouse button on the [ ] **To:** icon opens the contacts list.

If you wish to send a copy of the message to another person, add their name to the **Cc:** (carbon copy) box. Again, if the person's name is already in your contacts list, use the [ ] **Cc:** icon to find and add their email address. For this task, a copy of the message will be sent to a.n.other@hoddereducation.co.uk so include this address in the carbon copy box.

Hint

If the Cc: and Bcc: options cannot be seen, click on **Show Cc & Bcc** to get these boxes

You can also copy the message to another person using **Bcc** (blind carbon copy). None of the people receiving the message will be aware that a copy of it has been sent to anyone in the **Bcc:** box. It also prevents the email address that was used for the blind carbon copy being passed to other people. For this task a blind carbon copy is to be sent to best.book@hodder education.co.uk, so include this address in the **Bcc:** box.

The subject line of a message lets the person receiving the email know what the message is about. This will allow them to read the most urgent messages first. Add the subject line '0417 IGCSE text book' in the **Subject:** box.

Enter the content of the message in the main message box. Remember to use a greeting at the start of the message and a salutation at the end.

When you have checked your email to make sure that there are no errors, click on **Send**. The email will then be sent to the mailbox of each person in the **To:**, **Cc:** and **Bcc:** boxes.

Activity 9a

Send an email to your teacher with the subject line 'email'. Copy this to two other people in your class, informing them that you can now send them messages using email. Your tutor will send you a reply, which will set you another task.

9.6 Receiving an email

Click on the **Inbox** for your email account. Any emails received will appear in this window. In this example, the new email message has been received and can be seen here. New (unopened) messages appear in bold in this centre column of the window.

Double clicking the left mouse button on the message will open it in a new window and will look similar to this.

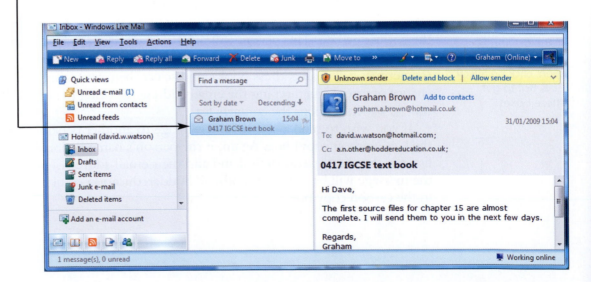

To reply to the message click on **Reply**, or to reply so that all the people placed in the **To:** box and **Cc:** box in the original message can see the reply click on **Reply all**.

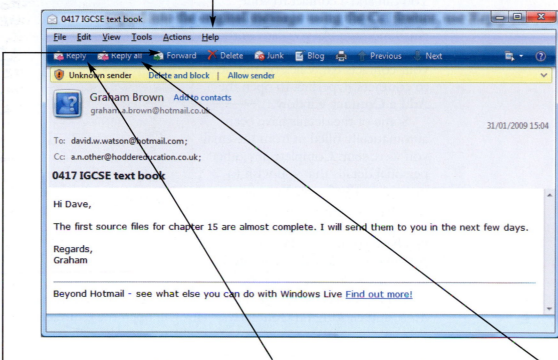

If you wish to send this message to another person without adding to the contents use **Forward**.

Using the **Reply** or **Reply all** options allows you to add your text to the message, but send the original message as well. You may notice that the email addresses of the people who were blind carbon copied into this message are not visible to the other people receiving the message, unlike those who were carbon copied.

9.7 Managing your contacts

You can add a contact to your address book when they send you an email message. As you can see there is an option to add this sender to your contacts list. Click on the **Add to contacts** hyperlink to open the **Add a Contact** window.

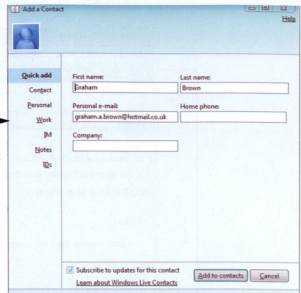

Some of the details have been automatically filled in from the email you were sent. Complete any other personal details that you wish to include on the forms. You can include more contact details using the tabs down the left side. When you have completed the form, this person can be added to your list of contacts by clicking on [Add to contacts].

Your contacts list can be managed by selecting the **Tools** menu in *Windows Live Mail*, and clicking on **Contacts…**. This will open the **Contacts** window.

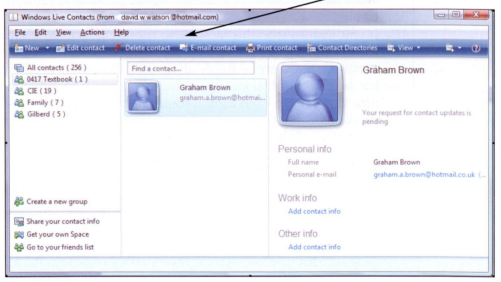

New contacts can be added, existing contact details edited and contacts deleted from this window. You can also organise your contacts into groups. You can use these groups to send a single email to all of the people in a group at the same time by selecting the group name rather than contact name. You can create multiple groups and contacts can belong to more than one group. Groups can be deleted by right mouse clicking on the group name then selecting **Delete Category** from the drop-down menu. Deleting a group does not delete the contacts in it and removing a contact from a group does not delete the contact from your address book. Your contact details can be shared with others using this system, but this is not recommended.

Activity 9b

Add the email addresses and other contact details of two of your friends to your contact list. Check that these contact details work by sending them a test email. Reply to messages sent by your friends letting them know that the details are correct.

9.8 Sending a file using email

Task 9c

Send an email message to David Watson and a copy to a.n.other@hoddereducation.co.uk with the file STYLE1.CSS (from the CD) attached to the message. Make the subject line for the email 'First stylesheet'.

Prepare the email for sending as you did in Task 9.2. Enter the email addresses, subject line and the body of the message. The completed message should look similar to this.

Click on **Attach** to start the process of attaching the file to the message. This opens the **Open** file window.

Select the file to be sent before clicking on Open.

This will add the file as an attachment to the message. This process can be repeated to attach multiple files to a message. When you have checked the message and it is ready to be sent, click on **Send**.

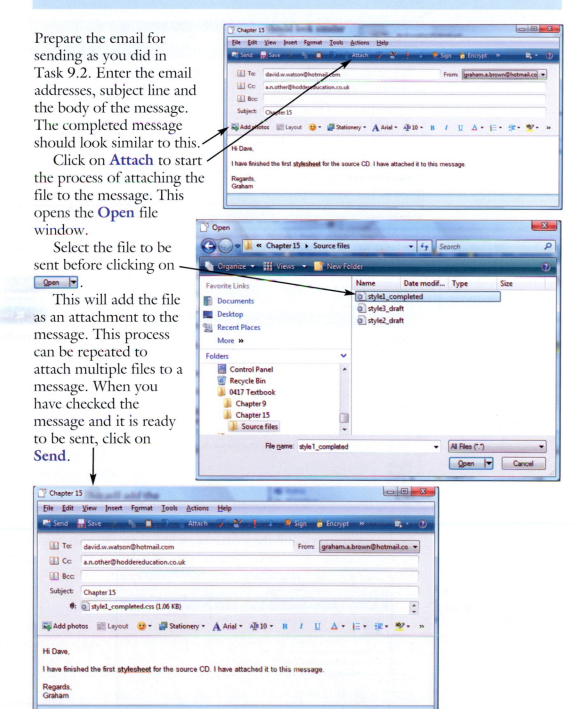

Activity 9c

Read the reply that your teacher sent you after Activity 9a. Reply to this email, sending them the document that they have asked for with your notes in it.

9.9 Receiving and saving a file using email

Click on the **Inbox** for your email account. All messages that you have received will appear in this window. In this example, a new email message has been received. The paperclip shows that the message has an attachment. Open this message by double clicking the left mouse button on the sender's name. The message will look similar to this.

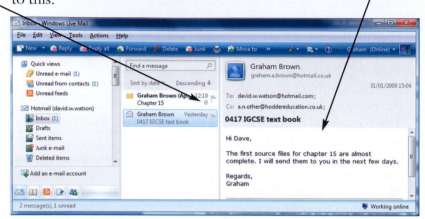

To open the attachment, double click the left mouse button on the attachment name. Then click on Open in the **Mail Attachment** window.

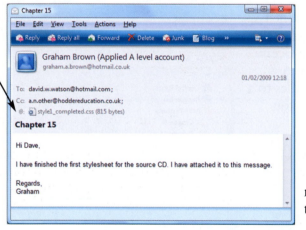

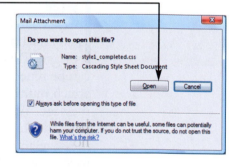

If you prefer to save the file, right mouse click on the attachment name to get a drop-down menu.

To save a single file use **Save as...**
(**Save all...** is useful for multiple files), which opens the **Save Attachment As** window. Choose the filename and the folder location for the file, then click on Save .

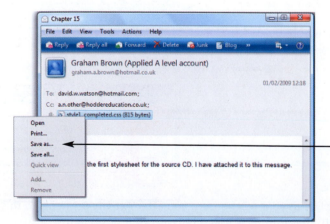

9.10 Using the internet

The internet is a **wide area network**, made from a number of individual computers and networks linked together to form one large network. It is worldwide and can be accessed by anyone with an internet connection. Anyone can add information to or have a server on the internet. This means that some information on the internet is incorrect, biased or unreliable, although other information is reliable and factual.

There are two ways of locating information from the internet. The first is by accessing sites that you know about using their URL. The second method is finding the information that you are looking for, but you do not know where to look. This method involves using a search engine.

9.11 Opening a website from a URL

URL is short for **uniform resource locator**, which is the unique address given to any document found on the internet. The URL contains two parts: the first is the type of protocol being used (e.g. http://) and the second is the name of the computer (e.g. www.cie.org.uk). There may be a third part which gives the pathway within this computer. Open your web browser and type the URL of the site that you require in the Address bar, followed by the <Enter> key. In this case the address added is for the homepage of the CIE website.

If you know the URL for a page within the website, you can type the full entry into the browser to get to a particular page. For example if you wanted the 0417 page within this site you would enter this URL: http://www.cie.org.uk/qualifications/academic/middlesec/igcse/subject?assdef_id=969 to obtain this page of the website.

To avoid having to retype long URLs like this, use the **Add to Favorites** icon to store this URL in your browser. To open your stored favourites, use the **Favorites** icon.

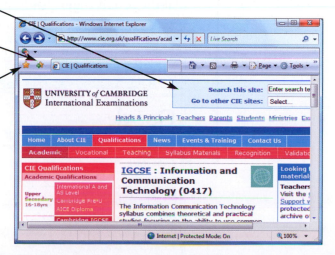

9.12 Using a search engine

A **search engine** is useful if you do not know the URL of a website or if you want information and do not know where to look. There are many search engines that appear to use different methods, but the underlying function of all search engines is the same. They take the words that you enter as a **search string** and look up in their database of **webpages** those that appear to match your search string. The more detail that you put into your search string the more likely the search engine is to find the results you require.

Task 9d

Search the Internet for information on 'learn to scuba dive' in your country in preparation for a scuba diving trip to the Red Sea.

Open a webpage with a search engine. In this case you are going to use the URL www.google.com. As this has been entered into the browser, this has been re-routed to a local version of the website hosted in the UK.

To search for a topic enter the search string in this box.

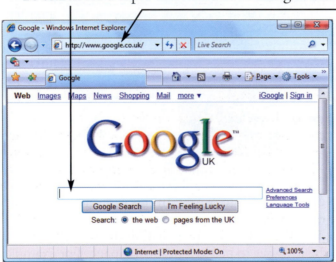

Your choice of search string is very important. If you type only the words 'scuba dive' then click on [Google Search], the search engine will find these results. You can see that the search engine has found eleven and a half million possible webpages.

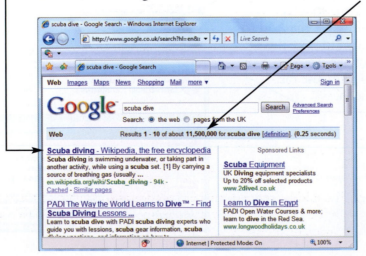

To improve the search you can select the **pages from the UK** radio button (this may vary depending upon your location). This would make sure that only local sites are included in the search results. Changing the search string to include 'learn to scuba dive' will also reduce the number of web pages found.

These two stages have reduced the number of possible webpages to just over thirty thousand.

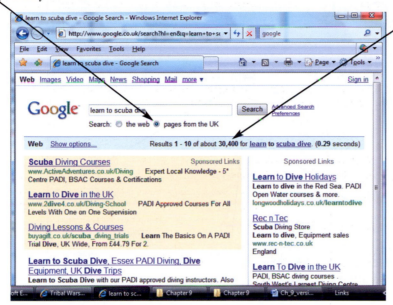

The results of this search appear on the page.

Most search engines will show sponsored links as the first few results of the search. These are websites that have paid money to have their webpages at the top of the results, in the hope that this will bring them more customers. These are not always the best links to use. Some search engines will tell you that this has happened like this.

This search could be refined further by adding the name of the local town or city in the search string. A better way to refine your searches is to use the advanced search option available in many search engines.

Selecting this will take you to the **Advanced Search** window.

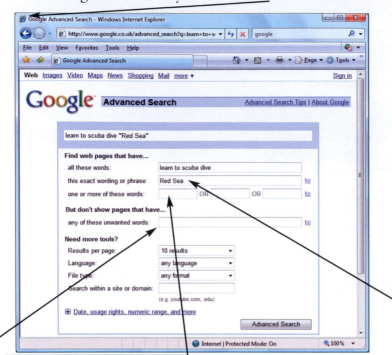

If an exact phrase needs including in the search, like 'Red Sea', place this text here.

This would find any websites relating to the phrase 'Red Sea' but not find either the word 'Red' or the word 'Sea' on their own.

If there are words that you need to have one OR another included in the search these can be placed here.

If there are other words that you want excluding from the search place these here.

All of these options could be used to find the site or sites that you require. Look carefully at the URLs and brief descriptions of each site to help you decide which site or sites might be more suitable for you.

Search engines can also be used in a website to search only within that site. These are sometimes used in the practical examinations. If you need to use one of these, take care to enter meaningful search strings, taken directly from the information in the question paper. Each search engine works in a different manner and instructions on saving and downloading are always given.

Hint

Spelling errors in search strings are the most common reason for search errors. To help solve these problems, enter the search string into your word processor, check the spelling, then cut and paste the search string into your web browser.

CHAPTER 10

Document production

In this chapter you will learn how to:
- enter data from an existing file
- key in and edit text
- import images from a variety of sources
- place and manipulate images
- set the page size and orientation
- set page margins
- use headers and footers
- set page, section and column breaks
- use columns
- set font styles and sizes
- emphasise text
- use lists
- use tables
- align text
- set line spacing
- correct errors.

For this chapter you will need these source files from the CD:

- ACTIVITY3.RTF
- SNOWBALL.JPG
- TABLE1.CSV
- TABLE2.CSV
- TEXT1.RTF
- TEXT2.RTF
- TEXT3.RTF
- TEXT4.RTF
- TEXT5.RTF
- TEXT6.RTF
- TEXT7.RTF
- TREES.JPG

You will also need this source image for scanning:
- SNOWANGEL

You will find this image at the end of the book, on page 300.

10.1 Generic file types

The practical examinations will ask you to open and edit data that is supplied to you in the examination. These files will be saved in a file format that can be opened in suitable software on all types of computer. For the examinations you must be able to open documents from generic file types and understand their features and limitations. Common generic files include:

- **comma separated values**: these files have a **.csv** file extension. This file type takes data in the form of tables (that could be used with a spreadsheet or database) and saves it in text format, separating data items with commas
- **text**: these files have a **.txt** file extension. A text file is not formatted and can be opened in any word processor
- **rich text format**: these files have a **.rtf** file extension. This is a text file type that saves some of the formatting within the text.

10.2 Entering data from existing files

Task 10a

Open the file TEXT1.RTF and insert the file TABLE1.CSV as a table within the document. Change the document heading to 'Winter weather forces schools to close'. Save the document as Ch_10_Task_10a in your word processor's normal format.

You can use a variety of text and document formats and include them as part of your finished document. These include .doc (*Microsoft Word* documents), .docx (also *Word* documents), .rtf and .txt formats. Open *Word*. To open a document, select the **Office** button in the top left corner of the window, then click on **Open** to obtain this window.

Change the file types that can be opened using the drop-down menu. If you are unsure of the file type and wish to see all the available files in a folder select **All Files**. You can now see a list of all the available files, including the file TEXT1. To open this file, click the left mouse button on the filename, followed by **Open**.

Use the **Office** button and **Save As...** to save this document with the filename Ch_10_Task_10a as a *Word* document, rather than in rich text format.

Now open the file TABLE1.CSV as a new *Word* document. An alternative to copying and pasting the table into the document would be to place the .csv file in the document as an **embedded object**. This is really useful if you wanted to update the table within another package like a spreadsheet, but is not as useful in the practical examinations where it is unlikely that you will have time to keep updating objects embedded into a document.

The file TABLE1.CSV looks like this when it has been opened in *Word*.

Now you need to edit it, to turn the comma separated values into a table and copy it into the file that you recently saved. Highlight all the text and then select the **Insert** tab.

Hint

If you have to combine more than one file (sometimes with different file types), open each file as a new document, then copy and paste from one document to another. This method can reduce any problems that could occur with embedded objects.

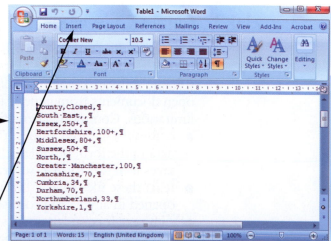

Select the **Table** icon, then **Convert Text to Table....** Because the text is highlighted it will be placed within the cells of a table.

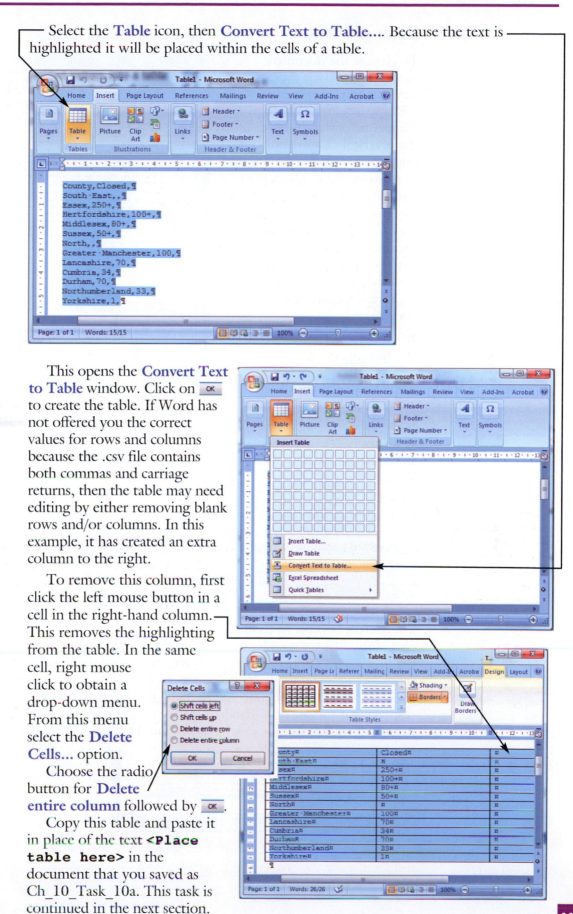

This opens the **Convert Text to Table** window. Click on OK to create the table. If Word has not offered you the correct values for rows and columns because the .csv file contains both commas and carriage returns, then the table may need editing by either removing blank rows and/or columns. In this example, it has created an extra column to the right.

To remove this column, first click the left mouse button in a cell in the right-hand column. This removes the highlighting from the table. In the same cell, right mouse click to obtain a drop-down menu. From this menu select the **Delete Cells...** option.

Choose the radio button for **Delete entire column** followed by OK.

Copy this table and paste it in place of the text **<Place table here>** in the document that you saved as Ch_10_Task_10a. This task is continued in the next section.

10.3 Keying in text

To change the document heading, highlight the existing heading and overtype this with the new heading. Although this seems one of the easiest tasks in the practical examinations, it is one where a significant number of students fail to check their data entry. You will need to be one hundred per cent accurate with all data entry, including the use of capital and lower case letters. The document should now look like this.

Save the changes to this document.

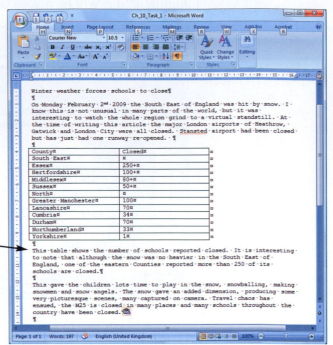

10.4 Editing text

Task 10b

Open the file Ch_10_Task_10a.
Move the last sentence in the document so that it becomes the last sentence in the first paragraph.
Add a new subtitle 'School closures' just above the table, and add this short paragraph: The dramatic change in the weather has meant that a number of areas are experiencing transport problems. This means that many schools across the country have been closed.' between the subtitle and the table.
In the third paragraph change the word 'was' to 'is', and add the word 'has' between 'Counties' and 'reported'.
Save the document as Ch_10_Task_10b in your word processor's normal format.

There are a number of techniques that could be used to move the last sentence to the end of the first paragraph. These include **cut** and **paste**, **copy** and paste then delete the original and drag and drop. It is recommended that you learn and practise all of these methods.

All three methods require you to highlight the correct section of text. A useful tip (especially if you are right-handed) is to highlight from the end of the text back to the beginning rather than the other way around. Highlight the text like this.

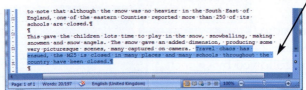

You can now choose your method from:

1. Cut and paste

Right mouse click within the highlighted area to get the drop-down menu, then select **Cut**. This removes the sentence and places it in the windows clipboard. Move the **cursor** to the end of the first paragraph and right mouse click to obtain the drop-down menu again. This time select **Paste**.

2 Copy, paste and delete

Right mouse click within the highlighted area to get the drop-down menu, then select **Copy**. This copies the sentence to the clipboard but does not remove it. Move the cursor to the end of the first paragraph and right mouse click to obtain the drop-down menu and select **Paste**. Move back to the original sentence, highlight it and press the <Delete> key on the keyboard. Although this method takes longer than method 1, it does not remove the original sentence until the end of the process, so if you accidentally lose the sentence from the clipboard the original is still present.

3 Drag and drop

Click the left mouse button in the highlighted area and hold this down, moving the cursor to the end of the first paragraph. Release the left mouse button at that point and you will drop all of the highlighted text there.

Whichever method you have used, make sure that the character spacing between the sentences and the line spacing between paragraphs matches the rest of the document. In the practical examinations you are likely to be penalised for any inconsistencies.

To add the subtitle, move the cursor to the end of the first paragraph and press the <Enter> key twice. (This will keep the same paragraph spacing as the rest of the document). Now type the text 'School closures' followed by the <Enter> key. Type the new paragraph. Go back and check for data entry errors and the consistency of spacing. Correct any errors.

To change the word 'was' to 'is', locate the word and highlight it. Type in the word 'is' and it will replace the original. To insert the word 'has', place the cursor between the words 'Counties' and 'reported'. Ensure that there is a single space on each side of the cursor before you type the word 'has'.

Save your document with a new filename. The finished document should look like this.

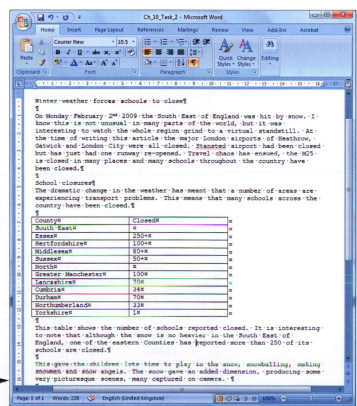

Hint

To import images from a scanner or digital camera, the hardware device must have been installed on the computer first or the device will not work.

Activity 10a

1 Open the file TEXT2.RTF and insert the file TABLE2.CSV as a table within the document after the paragraph that ends 'This table shows the number of schools closed in some of the local authorities:'.
2 Change the document heading to 'Snow brings disruption to Britain'.
3 Move the last paragraph in the document so that it becomes the first paragraph.
4 Add the text 'Heavy snowfalls were reported to the north of London. London was also affected but not to the same extent as the disruption that had been caused the week before.' as a new paragraph immediately before the paragraph that starts 'Flights were suspended ...'.
5 In the last paragraph change the word 'weird' to 'unusual' and add the word 'national' between 'many' and 'newspapers'.
6 Save and print this document.

10.5 Importing images

Images for the practical examination can be imported from clip art, a digital source like a scanner or digital camera, a file supplied to you, or an image from a website.

Task 10c

Open the file Ch_10_Task_10b.
Add a suitable image from clip art, from a scanner, from a digital camera and from the file SNOWBALL.JPG.

Importing an image from clip art

To import an image from clip art, select the **Insert** tab and click on the **Clip Art** icon.

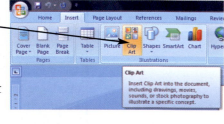

This will open the **Clip Art** pane to the right of the document. As there are thousands of clip-art images available in some packages it is sensible to search for images of a type to see what is available. In this case the article is about snow, so you can add this as your search string in the **Search for:** box. In the **Search in:** box, choose from the drop-down list where you wish to search for the images: it could be on the local machine or via a web search. This may also depend upon the network settings of your system. Local searches will result in fewer images being found (when I tried this search I only obtained one result), but searching **Everywhere** may take a long time depending upon your network connection speeds. You must also define the type of resource that you wish to include. This is found in the **Results should be:** box which opens a drop-down menu. In this case you want clip art, so ensure that only this tick box is selected. Click on Go.

The results of the search may look like this.

Move your cursor to the end of the document and double click the left mouse button on the image you want to place on the page. You will manipulate this image later in the chapter.

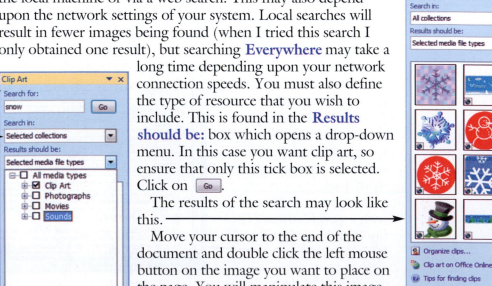

Importing an image using a scanner

Images can be scanned and added to your clip-art collection. Select the **Insert** tab and click on the **Clip Art** icon to open the **Clip Art** pane. Click on the **Organize clips...** icon.

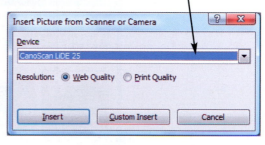

This opens the **Microsoft Clip Organizer** window. Select the **File** menu, followed by **Add Clips to Organizer**, then **From Scanner or Camera...**.

This will open the **Insert Picture from Scanner or Camera** window. Select the scanner in the **Device** box and click on `Insert`. Scan the image – the instructions for this will vary depending upon the scanner software.

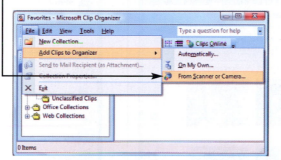

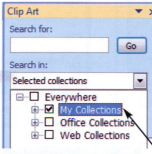

The image you have scanned will be added to the images stored on the local machine and can be obtained from the **Clip Art** pane. Remove the search string from the **Search for:** box. In the **Search in:** section, use the drop-down list and select only the option for **My Collections**.

In the **Results should be:** box, tick the boxes for **Clip Art** and **Photographs**. When these options have been selected click on `Insert`. The scanned image, plus any others stored locally, will appear like this.

Double click the left mouse button on the scanned image to place it on the page.

Importing an image using a digital camera

You can import an image from a digital camera in one of two ways. Both methods require you to attach the digital camera to the PC, turn on the camera and, if required, select the PC setting on the camera. All cameras are slightly different in this respect.

The first method is similar to using the scanner, and adds an image or images from the camera into the clip-art images stored on the local machine. As for the scanner, select the **Clip Art** pane, the **Organize clips...** icon, then **File**, **Add Clips to Organizer** and **From Scanner or Camera...**. Choose the camera from the available options like this.

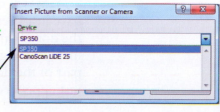

Click on the 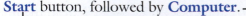 button to open the **Get Pictures from...** window. Depending upon your camera, you may need to find the correct folder. When you have found this you will see all the pictures available on the camera. Click the left mouse button to select an image or use the left mouse button and <Shift> or <Ctrl> keys to select multiple images. When you have chosen the images that you want, click on Get Pictures. This image will now be available as clip art, like the image scanned earlier in this section.

The second method is to attach the digital camera to the PC and click on the **Start** button, followed by **Computer**.

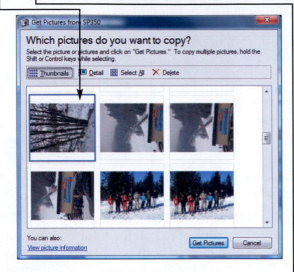

This opens the **Computer** window and allows you to browse the available storage devices. Select the **Removable Disk** option (it may have the camera name here). Copy the image file and paste it into the word-processed document.

Importing an image provided for the task

Select the **Insert** tab, followed by **Picture**. This opens the **Insert Picture** window. Browse through the folders and files until you locate the file SNOWBALL.JPG.

Click the left mouse button on this file followed by the Insert button. This will insert the image into the document. Save the document with a new filename.

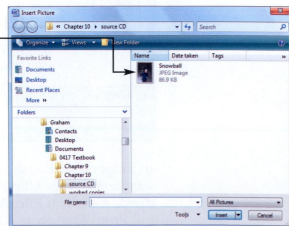

You will notice that the images have just been placed at the end of the document. These will now need manipulating so that they become a part of the document, rather than just appended to the end.

10.6 Resizing images

Task 10d

Open the file Ch_10_Task_10c.

Resize the image SNOWBALL.JPG to 8 centimetres high and maintain its aspect ratio. Place this at the top right of the first paragraph.

Resize the clip-art image to 2.8 centimetres high and 2 centimetres wide. Place this image at the top left of the second paragraph. Ensure that the text wraps around both of these images.

Place the scanned image to the right of the table, aligned to the right margin. Resize this image if needed.

Place the image from the digital camera to the bottom left of the page. Crop the image to remove the top 25 per cent of it. Ensure that all the text and images fit on a single page.

Find the image SNOWBALL.JPG in your document. To obtain a drop-down menu, right click with the mouse on this image. From this menu select the **Size...** option. This opens the **Size** window.

The task instructs you to resize the image maintaining its aspect ratio. This means to keep the height and width in the same proportions as the original image, usually to ensure that you do not distort it. To do this, ensure that the two tick boxes related to the aspect ratio are both selected.

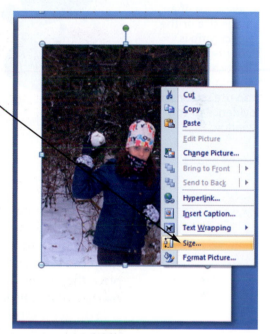

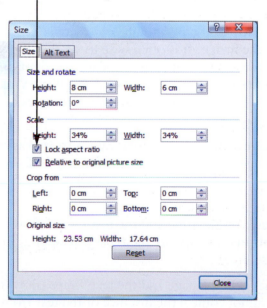

Change the **Height:** of the image to 8 centimetres and click on Close.

Use a similar method to resize the clip-art image to 2.8 centimetres high by 2 centimetres wide. Select the clip-art image and open the **Size** window for that image. In this case different lengths and widths have been specified, but you have not been instructed to crop the image.

This means that you will probably distort the image from its original proportions. To do this, ensure that both of the aspect ratio tick boxes have their ticks removed.

Use the **Height:** box to change this setting to 2.8 centimetres and the **Width:** box to 2 centimetres.

This will change the proportions of the image from this, to this.

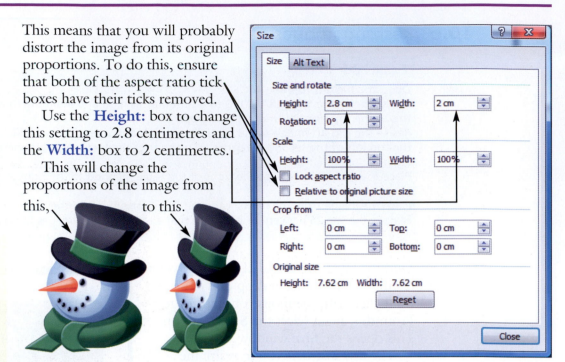

Notice how the second image is slightly thinner but the same height. This task is continued in the next section.

10.7 Wrapping text around images

Task 10d requires you to place the resized SNOWBALL.JPG image at the top right of the first paragraph. A question like this would expect you to align the image to the margins and to the top of the paragraph, and there is a further instruction to warp the text around the image. It is often wise to set the text wrapping first, then place the image. To set the text wrapping of the image, right click with the mouse on this image. From the drop-down menu, select the **Text Wrapping** option.

You get a sub-menu with the layout options. Useful ones include:

1. **In Line with Text**
   This places the image as an in-line graphic and is treated as a text character within a line of text. It will move with the text surrounding it if new text is inserted or deleted.

2. **Square**
   This places the image on the page and the text wraps (flows) around it. Use **More Layout Options...** to specify the type of wrapping that you require.

3. **Tight**
   This places the image on the page and the text wraps (flows) around it, like **Square**, but you cannot control the distance of the text from the image for the top and bottom settings, although you can to the left and right, using **More Layout Options....**

4. **Behind Text**
   This places the image behind the text. It can be used to set a background image in a document.

5 In Front of Text
This places an image over the top of the text.

6 Top and Bottom
This places the image with the text above and below the image, but not wrapped to the side.

7 More Layout Options
This can be used to give more options to the selected layout types above. For example: if a **Square** layout is selected you can specify where you wish to flow the text around the image and the distance of the text from the image on each side. This option also allows you to control the positioning of the image on the page.

For this task, set the **Text Wrapping** of the image to **Tight** using the sub-menu.

To move and place the image, click and hold the left mouse button on the image and drag it to the top right corner of the first paragraph. When you have roughly placed this image, right click on the image again. Select the **Text Wrapping** option, followed by **More Layout Options...**, to get the **Advanced Layout** window. Click on the **Picture Position** tab.

In the practical examinations you will be expected to place images precisely. To align the text to the right margin, in the **Horizontal** section, first select the **Alignment** radio button and then set the image **Right** aligned relative to the **Margin**.

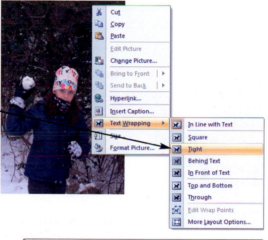

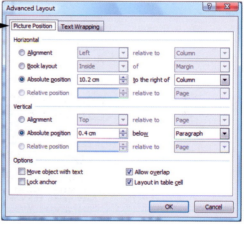

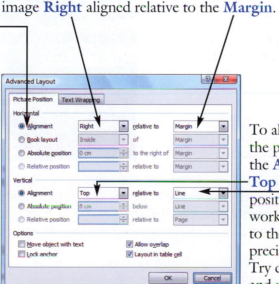

To align the image to the top line of the paragraph, in the **Vertical** section, select the **Alignment** radio button and then **Top** relative to the **Line**. To set the position, click on OK. Check that this has worked correctly. If not, this is usually due to the image being placed with too little precision when it was dragged and dropped. Try dragging and dropping the image again and repeat the process.

Repeat both procedures for the clip-art image, wrapping the text using **Tight**, and placing the image with a **Horizontal** alignment of **Left** relative to the **Margin** and a **Vertical** alignment of **Top** relative to the **Line**.

To place the scanned image to the right of the table, aligned to the right margin, follow the same procedures as above, set the wrapping and align the image with the right margin. The image is still too large for the space; no size has been specified, but it needs resizing without changing its aspect ratio. Use the drag handle in the corner to resize the image (do not use the drag handles in the middle, as they will affect the aspect ratio).

The resizing has been completed so that the paragraph below the scanned image does not have to wrap around it. This has been done to ensure that the final instruction within this task to 'Ensure that all the text and images fit on a single page' can be completed.

The image from the digital camera may need to be rotated before it can be placed on the page or resized. Click the left mouse button on the image to select it. You will notice a rotate handle as well as the drag handles used to resize the previous image. Hold down the Shift key, then click and hold the rotate handle and drag it in a clockwise direction (like the arrow). When the image has rotated through 90 degrees (so that it is upright) let go of the mouse button.

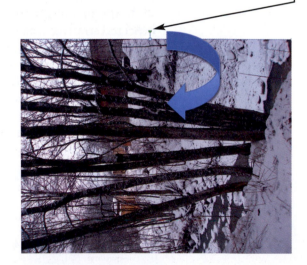

The rotated image will need resizing to fit the available space. It is recommended that you resize the image to a smaller size than required at this stage. This image should have the text wrapping set to **Tight**, and placed with a **Horizontal** alignment of **Left** relative to the **Margin** and a **Vertical** alignment of **Bottom** relative to the **Bottom Margin**. Then resize the image to fit the available space. The page should look like this. This task is continued in the next section.

10.8 Cropping images

To crop the image from the digital camera, click the left mouse button on the image, then on the **Format** tab (which should have the text **Picture Tools** displayed above it) at the top of the window. From the **Size** section of this toolbar click on the **Crop** icon.

This will change the drag handles used to resize the picture to crop handles, which are used to cut off a portion of the image. Drag the top handle down so that approximately the top 25 per cent (a quarter) of the picture has been removed. To resize the image again, you must click your left mouse button back on the text, then on the image, so that the crop tool has been removed and use the drag handles to resize the image.

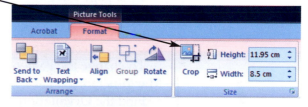

Activity 10b

1 Open the file saved in Activity 10a. Add the image TREES.JPG (from the CD) and rotate it through 180 degrees. Resize it to 7 centimetres wide, maintaining its aspect ratio. Place it at the top left of the first paragraph. Ensure that the text wraps around this image.

2 Scan the image SNOWANGEL. Place and resize this image at the start of the second paragraph, so that it left and right aligns with the text wrapped around the first image like this:

3 Crop the top and bottom of the SNOWANGEL image so that the child is within 5 millimetres of the edge of the image.

4 Add an image of a car or train from clip art and place this at the bottom of page 1 so that it moves the table onto page 2.

5 Add a suitable image from a digital camera of a car, train or snow and place this in an appropriate place on page 2.

6 Save and print this document.

10.9 Formatting pages

In the practical examinations, you may be presented with documents with different page layouts and given instructions to reformat them. Do not assume that a document is already set as specified. If it is in text (.txt) format, it will use the default settings of your word processor. If it is opened in rich text format (.rtf) or was saved as a *Word* document, it will keep the settings used to save the file.

Task 10e

Open the file saved in Task 10b.
Change the page size to A5 and the orientation to landscape. Set the top and bottom margins to 3 centimetres and the left and right margins to 3.5 centimetres.
Save the file with a new name and print the document.

Open the file saved in Task 10b and select the **Page Layout** tab. Double click the left mouse button on the icon at the bottom right corner of the box, to open the **Page Setup** window.

This window can be used to change the page size, orientation (to make the page tall or wide)

and the page margins. To change the paper size, select the **Paper** tab. The **Paper size:** can be selected from the drop-down list. For this task, select A5 from this list.

To change the page orientation, select the **Margins** tab.

Find the **Orientation** section of the window. Click the left mouse button on the **Landscape** icon to change from portrait to landscape.

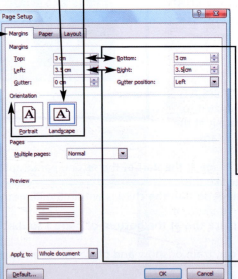

To set the top and bottom margins to 3 centimetres, select the **Margins** section, then either; highlight the text within the **Top:** and **Bottom:** boxes and type in the new values, or use the scroll handles to change the values in each of the boxes.

Change the left and right margins to 3.5 centimetres using a similar method in the **Left:** and **Right:** boxes. Click on OK.

If the document is to be part of a bound book, a **gutter** may be needed. This is an area outside the margins that is used to bind the book together. If you need to use a gutter, this can also be set in the same way using the **Margins** section of the window. The gutter can be placed to the left or top of the page, depending upon the type of binding to be used. Save the document.

10.10 Using headers and footers

A **header** is the area of a document between the top of the page and the top margin. A **footer** is the area of a document between the bottom of the page and the bottom margin. You can insert text or graphics into headers and footers. This might include the author's name, the document's filename, page numbering, or even a company logo. Headers and footers can be found in many printed documents, including those that have been word processed or desktop published, and in presentations, reports from spreadsheets and databases and in **webpages**.

> ### Task 10f
>
> Open the file saved in Task 10e.
> Place your name in the centre of the header. Place the date and time on the left, an automated page number in the centre and the filename on the right in the footer. Save the file with a new name.

To use the document header or footer select the **Insert** tab. In the **Header & Footer** section click on the **Header** icon. This offers a range of built in header styles; simple **Blank** settings are all that should be required for the practical examinations. If you select the **Blank (Three Columns)** option, this will allow you to put text on the left, in the centre and on the right within the header. This moves the cursor into the header and changes the toolbar to give you options for the header, like changing the position of the header relative to the edge of the page.

For Task 10f you are instructed to place your name in the centre of the header. Move the cursor over the centre placeholder that says **[Type Text]** and type in your name.

Your text will replace the placeholder. For this task you were not instructed to place anything in the left or right placeholders. These must be deleted or you may be penalised in the examination. Select each placeholder in turn and press the <Delete> key. The header should now look similar to this.

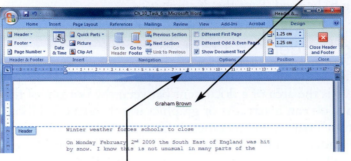

To set up the page footer, do *not* click on the **Go To Footer** icon. Although this takes you into the footer, it neither sets up the placeholders nor correctly positions the tab stops for the centre and right aligned text. Whilst this works fine for a standard document, if you have changed the margin settings of a document, as in Task 10e, the tab stops do not align with the margins as shown here. You can see in this example that the centre tab stop is not set to 7 centimetres which would be the centre of this page with these margin settings.

To set up the page footer, click on the **Footer** icon on the **Header & Footer** section of the toolbar and then the **Blank (Three Columns)** option. This will allow you to set all three areas of the footer.

In Task 10f you are instructed to place the date and time on the left in the footer. Click the left mouse button on the left placeholder to highlight it. Then click on the **Date & Time** icon on the toolbar.

This will open the **Date and Time** window. In this task, the format of the date and time has not been specified so you can select either of the options that shows both the date and the time. Click the left mouse button on the format that you choose. Make sure that if you wish the date and time to update automatically, this tick box is completed before clicking on OK.

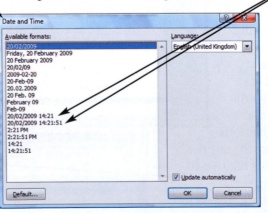

You were also instructed to place an automated page number in the centre of the footer. Click the left mouse button on the centre placeholder, then click on the **Page Number** icon from the toolbar. This gives you a drop-down menu, from which you need to select the option for **Current Position**. Select the format for the page numbering; again, in this task the format of the numbering has not been specified so you can select whichever option you choose. Check carefully that the automated page numbering has not placed an extra carriage return into the footer; if it has remove this using the <←Backspace> key.

Hint

If you are not sure whether a carriage return exists in the text, header or footer, select the **Home** tab on the toolbar, then the **Show/Hide ¶** icon.

Carriage returns will appear in the document as ¶.

You were also instructed to place the document's filename on the right in the footer. Click the left mouse button on the right placeholder, then click on the **Quick Parts** icon on the toolbar.

This will allow you to select a number of automated functions, most of which are beyond the scope of this book. Select **Field...** to open the **Field** window. In the **Field names:** box, scroll down through the list and select **FileName**. Select the **Format:** for the filename from the list of available options. If the full path of the filename is required select the **Add path to filename** tick box before clicking on OK. The completed footer should look similar to this.

To exit from the header or footer back into the document, either click on the **Close Header and Footer** icon, or double click the left mouse button on the body text of the document. Save the document.

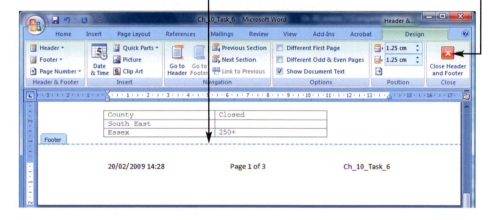

Activity 10c

Open the file ACTIVITY3.RTF. Change the page size to A4 and the orientation to portrait. Set all the margins to 4 centimetres and remove the gutter. Place the date on the left, the filename in the centre and the time on the right in the header. Place your name on the left and an automated page number on the right in the footer. Ensure that the header and footer are 2 centimetres from the top and bottom of the page respectively. Save and print the document.

10.11   Widows and orphans

If you start a paragraph of text on one page but there is not enough room on the page to get the last line typed in, the single line of text which appears at the top of the next page is called a **widow**. Similarly, sometimes you start a paragraph at the bottom of a page but you can only type in one line before the rest of the text goes onto the next page. The first line of the paragraph at the bottom of the page is called an **orphan**. These should be avoided when producing a document and you are likely to be penalised if you include these in any submission for the practical examinations. They can be manually avoided by inserting a **Page Break**, which does not show the reader that you have forced the page break at this point. For more information on breaks, refer to Section 10.12.

You can set up *Word* to automatically avoid widows and orphans. To do this select the **Page Layout** tab, then in the **Paragraph** section click on the expand icon to open the **Paragraph** window.

Now select the **Line and Page Breaks** tab so that the window looks like this. To get *Word* to automatically avoid widows and orphans, select the **Widow/Orphan control** tick box and click on OK.

10.12 Using page, section and column breaks

Breaks can be used within a document to force text onto a new page or into the next column (if columns are being used), or to define areas with different layout, for example where part of a document is formatted in landscape orientation and part is in portrait. For the practical examinations you will only need to use these effects:

1 Page break
This forces the text onto the start of a new page, leaving **white space** at the end of the previous page. It is particularly useful for removing widows and orphans from your document, although *Word* can be set up to do this for you (see Section 10.11).

2 Column break
This forces the text into the top of the next available column, which may be on the same page or may be on the next page.

3 Section break
A section break is used to split areas of a document with different layouts. There are two types of section break: one forces a page break as well as the change in layout and the other is a continuous break, that allows different layouts on the same page.

Task 10g

Open the file saved in Task 10f.
Add the text 'Winter wonderland or woe' as a new title at the start of the document. Keep the two titles on the first page of the document. Set the orientation of the first page to portrait and the rest of the document to landscape. Set all of the body text except the table into two columns, with a 2 centimetre spacing and vertical line between the columns.
Save the file with a new name.

Open the file saved in Task 10f and add the text 'Winter wonderland or woe' to the start of the document as a new title.

Move the cursor to the place where the first break needs to be inserted. This will be just before the text 'On Monday ...'. Because this break will be the separator between two different types of layout (page 1 being portrait and page 2 onwards being landscape), a section break for a new page needs inserting rather than just a page break. To do this, select the **Page Layout** tab and click on the **Breaks** icon.

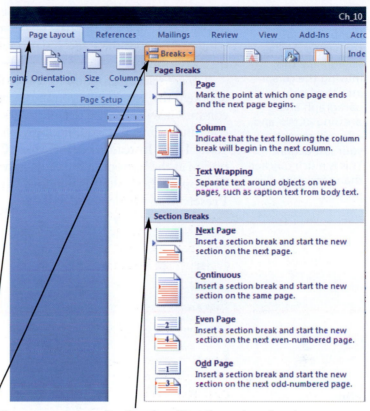

This drop-down list will appear. Select the **Section Break** option for the **Next Page**.

As the document is currently in landscape orientation, move the cursor to page 1, the section that needs to be changed to portrait orientation. Then select the **Page Layout** tab again, followed by the **Orientation** icon and click on **Portrait**. You will notice that the word processor has only changed the orientation of this page (because you inserted the section break) and that all of the header and footer settings have been automatically amended for the new layout of this page. This task is continued in the next section.

10.13 Using columns

Columns can be used to give a layout similar to that found in a newspaper and you may be required to format a document, or part of a document into a number of columns. If you are going to have different column settings for different parts of the document, you must decide where you are going to split the document into the different sections. This information is often given to you in the examination questions.

For Task 10g you need to add two more section breaks to the document, so that the body text and the table can have different layouts. These section breaks need to be at the start and end of the table. Because the text and table do not need to be on different pages you need to set these as continuous section breaks. Move the cursor to the place where you want each break inserted (i.e. before and after the table), then in the **Page Layout** tab click on the **Breaks** icon, followed by the **Section Breaks** option

Hint

If you have just
formatted the first
section like this,
moving the cursor
into the final
paragraph and
pressing <Ctrl> and
<Y> will repeat
your last action.
This is much quicker
than repeating this
process.

for **Continuous**. Click the left mouse button to place the cursor within the text of the first paragraph. From the **Page Layout** tab click on the **Columns** icon.

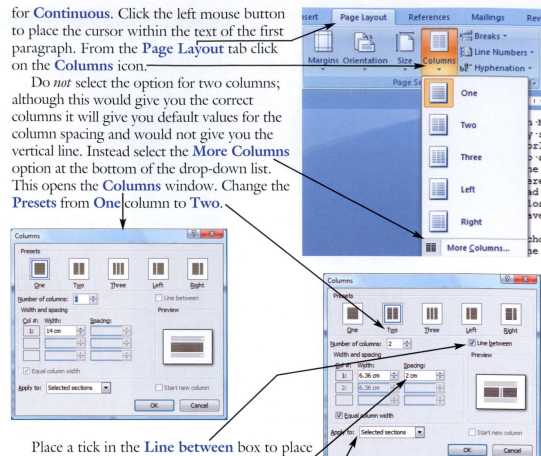

Do *not* select the option for two columns; although this would give you the correct columns it will give you default values for the column spacing and would not give you the vertical line. Instead select the **More Columns** option at the bottom of the drop-down list. This opens the **Columns** window. Change the **Presets** from **One** column to **Two**.

Hint

Column breaks can
be inserted to force
text into the next
column using the
Page Layout tab,
the **Breaks** icon in
the **Page Setup**
section, followed
by the **Column**
option.

Place a tick in the **Line between** box to place the vertical line. Change the **Spacing:** from its default value to 2 centimetres. Make sure that the **Apply to:** box contains a reference to the **Selected sections** before clicking on OK. Move the cursor into the paragraph after the table and repeat this process for the final section of the document. Save the completed document, which will look like this.

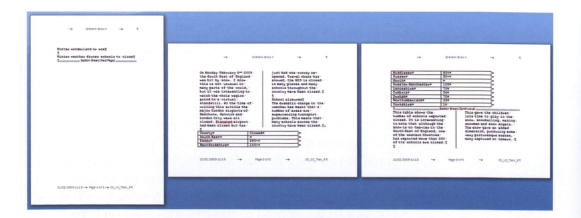

Activity 10d

Open the file saved in Activity 10c.
Change the body text of only the first page so that it is set in two columns with a
1 centimetre spacing and a vertical line between the columns.
Save the file with a new filename.

Activity 10e

Open the file saved in Activity 10d.
Change the page margins to 2 centimetres and the alignment of the header and footer to fit the margins. Ensure that the header and footer are 1 centimetre from the top and bottom of each page.
Add a new title 'Arctic blast grips the United Kingdom' at the start of the document. Place the two titles on a single portrait page with a single column. All other text should be on landscape pages, in three columns with 1.5 centimetre column spacing.
Save the file with a new filename.

10.14 Font styles and sizes

Text can be changed to have different font faces, colours and sizes and can have a number of enhancements added. These are useful for making text stand out. Font faces are grouped into two main categories: **serif** fonts and **sans serif** fonts. These are not the name of the font face, but are the generic categories that describe the properties of the font. A serif font looks like this: This is serif font and a sans serif font looks like this: This is a sans serif font. The word 'serif' describes the short strokes at the end of individual letters. Sans serif fonts do not have these short strokes. If you are asked to set text into a sans serif font, you must find any font in your word processor that does not have these serif strokes.

Serif fonts are often used in newspapers and books as they are easier to read than sans serif fonts. It would be appropriate to use sans serif fonts for emphasis of text or for titles or sub-titles. It is not sensible to use more than two different font faces on any page. You can use other enhancements to make text stand out, as can be seen later in this chapter.

Font sizes are measured in points. There are 72 points to an inch (which is just over 2.5 centimetres). If you are asked to produce text of an appropriate size, for most adults 10 points is appropriate as **body text**, but older readers may prefer 12 point. Anything above 14 point is generally unsuitable as body text for adults, but may be ideal for children. In stories for children learning to read (aged 4 to 6) it may be appropriate to use a 20 or 24 point font size to make it easier to make out the letter shapes. Different font sizes would also be appropriate as body text for the partially sighted.

Two fonts can be the same size but appear to be different heights. For example, all of these fonts are 11 points high: Goudy, Comic Sans, *Brush Script Std*, **Impact**, Tekton and **Arial**. The height of the font is measured using the measurement from the top of the letter with the tallest **ascender** (often the letter 'h'), to the bottom of the one with the longest **descender** (often the letter 'p').

Task 10h

Open the file saved in Task 10g.
Set all of the text on the first page to an 18 point sans serif font. Make the sub-heading a 13 point sans serif font and the body text a 13 point serif font.
Save the file with a new filename.

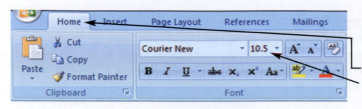

Open the file saved in Task 10g and highlight all of the text on the first page. Select the **Home** tab, then the **Font** section. Use the drop-down list to show a list of available fonts.

Hint

A document may contain a table (like this one) or a database extract. Make sure that these are formatted with the same font face and size as the body text of the document.

The list of available fonts will look similar to this, showing the currently selected font in the box, the most recently used fonts below and a full list of all the fonts below; many more are available using the scroll bar.

For this task you need an 18 point sans serif font to use as the title for a document, so choose an appropriate font such as **Arial Black**. Use the drop-down list box for the point size. Select 18 if it is available, or type this size into the box.

To set all the body text to a 13 point serif font, highlight all of the body text (including the table) and the sub-heading, then, using the method shown above, change the font size to 13. Setting the font size for both the body text and the sub-heading, and then changing the font face of the sub-heading, will be quicker than doing each section individually. Select an appropriate serif font such as **Times New Roman**; as this is body text do not choose one that is complex and difficult to read.

To set the sub-heading into a sans serif font (it is already 13 point), highlight the text 'School closures' and select the same font face that you used on page 1, in this case **Arial Black**. Save the completed document, which will look like this.

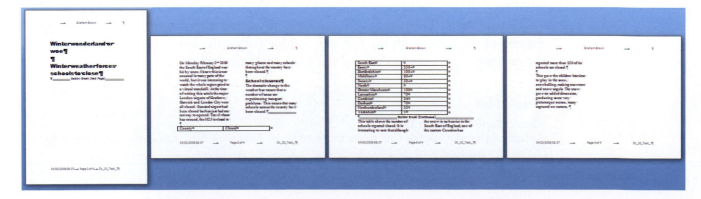

Activity 10f

Open the file saved in Activity 10e. Set all of the text on the first page to a 24 point sans serif font. Make the body text, headers and footers an appropriate 11 point serif font.

10.15 Emphasising text

Text can be emphasised in many ways. These include using colour, emboldening (making the text bold), underlining or italicising the text. As you have seen from this book, different colours can be used to symbolise different things: any red text in this book is a reference to the glossary, blue text in this chapter tells you what to select in your work, etc. Background colours can also be used to give different meaning. In this book, for example, activities are always shown with a pale red background and tasks always shown on a blue background.

Task 10i

Open the file saved in Task 10h.
Make the text 'Winter wonderland or woe' red. Make the name of each airport in the text stand out by highlighting it in cyan.
Make all of the text in the top row of the table an italic font. Make the words 'snowmen' and 'snow angels' bold. Underline the sub-heading.
Set all of the text on the first page to an 18 point sans serif font. Make the sub-heading a 13 point sans serif font and the body text a 13 point serif font.
Save the file with a new name.

Open the file saved in Task 10h and highlight the text 'Winter wonderland or woe'. Select the **Home** tab, the **Font** section and then the drop-down arrow for the **Font Colour** icon.

This opens the initial colour palette. Select the colour you need from the choices given; for this task the red colour is specified. If the colour that you need is not shown, click on the **More Colors...** option.

To highlight each airport in the text, move the cursor to the highlight tool in the **Font** section and select the drop-down arrow. From the drop-down colour palette for the highlighter pen, use the left mouse button to select cyan.

As you move the mouse pointer over the page you will notice that it has changed to a small highlighter pen. Use this to highlight the names of the airports. When you have finished, go back to the drop-down colour palette for the highlighter and select **Stop Highlighting**.

To italicise the top row of the table, highlight the top row of the table. Select the **Home** tab, the **Font** section and click on the **Italic** icon.

To embolden (make bold) the words 'snowmen' and 'snow angels', highlight the three words (if you hold down the <Ctrl> key whilst highlighting, you can select these words at the same time).

Select the **Home** tab, the **Font** section and then the **Bold** icon.

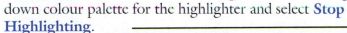

Hint

The countries you will need are England, Ireland, Scotland and Wales. Select the **Home** tab, **Editing** and then the **Find** icon to help you find all of these words in the document.

Hint

Use the Format Painter with care, it copies paragraph formatting as well as font formatting. For example, if the area copied from is part of a bulleted list, when the format is applied, the new text also becomes a bulleted list in the same style.

To underscore (underline) the sub-heading, highlight the text 'School closures'. Select the **Home** tab, the **Font** section and click on the **Underline** icon. Save the file.

Activity 10g

Open the file saved in Activity 10f.
Make all the text on page 1 green. Make the words United Kingdom on page 1 bold, italic and underlined. Make the name of each country in the text stand out by highlighting it in green. Save the file with a new name.

Using format painter

If you need to copy the formatting from one part of a document and apply it to another, for example if you have just set some text red and emboldened and want to copy that formatting onto another area of text you can use the **format painter**. Place the cursor within the text you wish to copy the formatting from and click the left mouse button. Select the **Home** tab, the **Clipboard** section and click on the **Format Painter** icon. Move the cursor to the text that you wish to format, if it is a single word then click the left mouse button anywhere within that word. If the area is more than one word, highlight the new text and the formatting from the original text will be applied to this text.

10.16 Using lists

There are two types of list that could be used in the practical examinations: bulleted lists and numbered (or sometimes lettered) lists. Bulleted lists contain a bullet point (character) at the start of each line to show that it is a new item in a list of other similar items.

Task 10j

Open the file TEXT3.RTF and place your name on the right in the header in a 14 point serif font. Place the filename in the centre of the footer.
Change the twelve items listed into a bulleted list. Use a bullet of your choice. Make sure that this bulleted list is indented by at least 3 centimetres.
Save the file with a new name.

Open the file and create the header and footer as described earlier. To add bullet points to a list, highlight all of the text to be added, in this case all twelve items. Select the **Home** tab, the **Paragraph** section and click on the **Bullets** icon. This will place bullet points next to each of the list items. To choose the type of bullets used, select the drop-down handle instead of the icon.

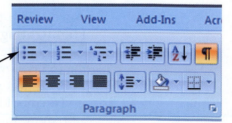

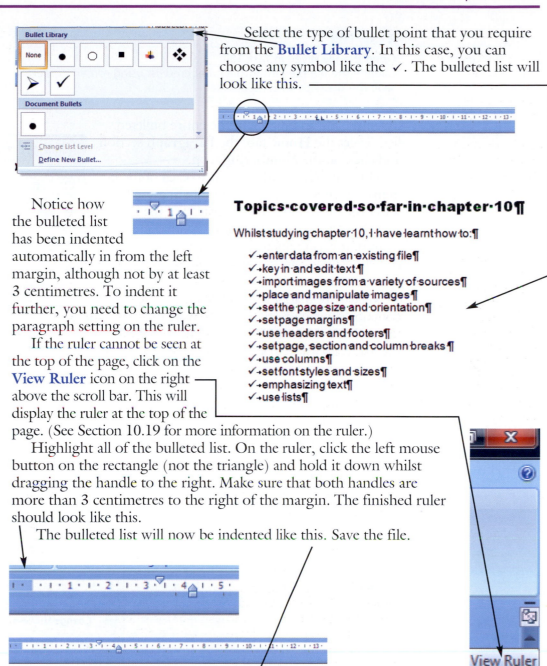

Select the type of bullet point that you require from the **Bullet Library**. In this case, you can choose any symbol like the ✓. The bulleted list will look like this.

Notice how the bulleted list has been indented automatically in from the left margin, although not by at least 3 centimetres. To indent it further, you need to change the paragraph setting on the ruler.

If the ruler cannot be seen at the top of the page, click on the **View Ruler** icon on the right above the scroll bar. This will display the ruler at the top of the page. (See Section 10.19 for more information on the ruler.)

Highlight all of the bulleted list. On the ruler, click the left mouse button on the rectangle (not the triangle) and hold it down whilst dragging the handle to the right. Make sure that both handles are more than 3 centimetres to the right of the margin. The finished ruler should look like this.

The bulleted list will now be indented like this. Save the file.

Topics·covered·so·far·in·chapter·10¶

Whilst·studying·chapter·10,·I·have·learnt·how·to:¶

    ✓→enter·data·from·an·existing·file¶
    ✓→key·in·and·edit·text·¶
    ✓→import·images·from·a·variety·of·sources¶
    ✓→place·and·manipulate·images·¶
    ✓→set·the·page·size·and·orientation¶
    ✓→set·page·margins¶
    ✓→use·headers·and·footers¶
    ✓→set·page,·section·and·column·breaks·¶
    ✓→use·columns¶
    ✓→set·font·styles·and·sizes¶
    ✓→emphasizing·text¶
    ✓→use·lists¶

View Ruler

Topics·covered·so·far·in·chapter·10¶

Whilst·studying·chapter·10,·I·have·learnt·how·to:¶

    ✓→ enter·data·from·an·existing·file¶
    ✓→ key·in·and·edit·text·¶
    ✓→ import·images·from·a·variety·of·sources¶
    ✓→ place·and·manipulate·images·¶
    ✓→ set·the·page·size·and·orientation¶
    ✓→ set·page·margins¶
    ✓→ use·headers·and·footers¶
    ✓→ set·page,·section·and·column·breaks·¶
    ✓→ use·columns¶
    ✓→ set·font·styles·and·sizes¶
    ✓→ emphasizing·text¶
    ✓→ use·lists¶

Task 10k

Open the file saved in Task 10j.
Change the bulleted list into a numbered list using roman numerals.
Save the file with a new filename.

Open the file and highlight the entire bulleted list. Select the **Home** tab, the **Paragraph** section and click on the **Numbering** icon.

This will place numbers next to each of the list items. To choose the type of numbering used, select the drop-down handle instead of the icon.

Select the type of numbering that you require from numbering library. In this case you can choose the roman numerals as that was specified in the task. Save the file.

Make sure that, if the bulleted list contains short items that would make up the end of a sentence, it has a colon before the list, each list item starts with a lower case character and only the last item in the list has a full stop.

Word will try to place capitals on each list item, but this is not correct as each one is not a new sentence. You must adjust these to get a list looking like this.

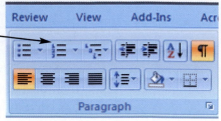

For breakfast I had:

- cereal
- toast
- a cup of tea.

When it was lunchtime

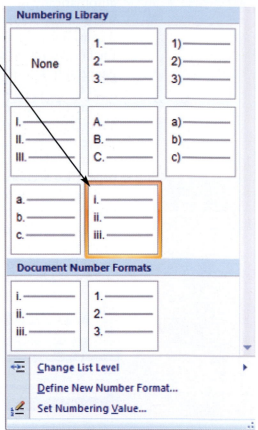

Activity 10h

Open the file TEXT4.RTF and place your name on the left, today's date in the centre and the filename on the right in the header. Make the blue text into a bulleted list, using a bullet of your choice. Make sure that this bulleted list is indented by at least 2 centimetres. Make the green text into a numbered list, using numbers followed by a bracket. Make the red text into a bulleted sub-list, indented from the numbered list using different bullet points. Change the colour of all the text to black.
Save the file with a new name.

10.17   Using tables

Task 10l

Open the file that you saved in Task 10i. Add to the end of the document the following text as a new paragraph:

'Temperatures recorded at one weather station in Ross-on-Wye during the week read:'.

Below this add the table shown opposite: Save the file with a new filename.

	Maximum	Minimum
2nd Feb	3	−1
3rd Feb	5	−3
4th Feb	5	−3
5th Feb	2	−1
6th Feb	2	−1
7th Feb	5	−3
8th Feb	4	−2

Tables of data may need inserting into your word-processed documents. You have already inserted a table from a .csv file in Task 10a.

Open the file that you saved in Task 10i and add the text as a new paragraph to the end of the document.

To create a new table you must first work out how many rows and columns the table contains. By counting them, you can work out that this table contains 3 columns and 8 rows. Move the cursor to the correct place in the document, then select the **Insert** tab, the **Pages** section and click on the **Table** icon in the **Tables** section.

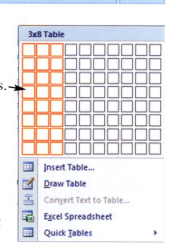

This will open the **Insert Table** drop-down menu. Move the cursor over the grid until it highlights the three columns and eight rows that you need, like this.

Click the left mouse button in the last highlighted cell of the grid and this will insert a 3 by 8 table into your document. Add the text from the task into this table. You can move the cursor into the next cell by pressing the <Tab> key. If you need more rows than the eight available, move the cursor into the last cell of the table and press the <Tab> key to create a new row. If you need lots of new rows, hold down the <Tab> key.

Activity 10i

Create a new document with the title 'Skills to practise using tables'. Create this table, below the title.

Function	How	Feature		
Insert	Insert tab	Table		
	Right click	Rows		
	Right click	Columns		
Delete		Rows		
Format		Cells	Alignment	Left, right, centre, fully justified
				Top, centre, bottom
			Colour, shading	
		Rows	Breaks across page	
		Gridlines	Show	
			Hide	
Text wrapping		Cells		

Task 10m

Open the file TEXT5.RTF and place your name on the right in the header.
Delete the second column and the 'Martial arts' row. Insert a new third column
with this data.
Insert a new row between the 'Dance workshop' and 'Discover Scuba' with
this data.

Craftworkshop	0	3	2	3

Merge cells 2 and 3 in the top row and cells 4 and 5 in the top row.
Save the file.

Second choice
1
2
21
18
2
3
10
5

Open the file TEXT5.RTF and place your name on the right
in the header. To delete the second column, move the cursor
to any cell in this column and click the right mouse button, to
get the drop-down menu like this.

Select **Delete Cells...**, which will open the **Delete Cells**
window. Select the radio button for **Delete entire column**
and click on OK.

Repeat this method to delete the
'Martial arts' row. Right mouse click
in any cell in this row and select
Delete Cells.... This time select the
radio button for **Delete entire row**
before clicking on OK.

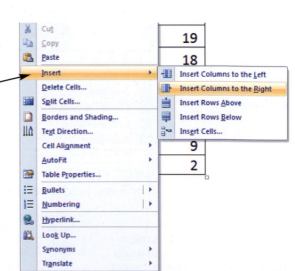

To insert a new third column,
right click the mouse in any cell in the
second column to obtain the drop-
down menu. Select **Insert**, then
Insert Columns to the Right. This
will insert the column. Enter the text
shown in the task into the cells.

Use a similar method to insert the
new row. Click the right mouse
button in any cell in the 'Dance
workshop' row. Select **Insert**, then
Insert Rows Below. This will insert
the new row. Enter the text shown in
the task into the cells.

	X population		Y population	
Activity	First choice	Second Choice	First choice	Second Choice
Jewellery making	0	1	1	2
Paintballing	39	2	37	19
Boulogne trip	52	21	56	18
Rock workshop	3	18	2	3
Dance workshop	0	2	2	10
Craft workshop	0	3	2	3
Discover scuba	4	3	8	8
Beauty	4	10	1	9
Ceramic painting	0	5	1	2

To merge cells 2 and 3 in the top row, highlight both these cells and then click the right mouse button on one of the highlighted cells to get the drop-down menu. Select **Merge Cells**. Repeat this for the two cells placed to the right of the cells that you have just merged. The completed table should look like this. Save the file.

Cut
Copy
Paste
Insert
Delete Cells...
Merge Cells
Borders and Shading...
Text Direction...
Cell Alignment
AutoFit
Table Properties...

Activity 10j

Open the file that you saved in Activity 10i. Delete the top row and second column of the table.

Insert a new row above the row containing the word 'Format'. Insert the text 'Columns' in cell 2 of this new row. Insert a new fourth column with this data.

In column 1, merge the cells containing 'Insert', Delete' and 'Format' with the blank cells below them. In column 2, merge the cells containing 'Cells' and 'Gridlines' with the blank cells below them. In column 3, merge the cell containing 'Alignment' with the blank cell below it.

Save the file with a new name.

Horizontal
Vertical

Tables can be formatted so that they can be aligned left, right or centrally between the margins. Text can be wrapped around the table or not as required. These features are found in the table properties: click the right mouse button in the cell of the table, then select **Table Properties...** and the **Table** tab within the **Table Properties** window. The table alignment can be selected in the **Alignment** section and text wrapping around the table can be switched on or off in the **Text wrapping** section.

Cells can be formatted so that the contents can be aligned both horizontally and vertically within the cell. Horizontal alignment can be set and changed by highlighting the relevant cells, selecting the **Home** tab and the **Paragraph** section and using the alignment icons within that section. See Section 10.18 for more details.

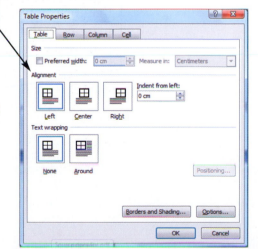

Task 10n

Open the file that you saved in Task 10m.
Right align all of the cells containing numbers in the second column. Centre align all of the cells in the top two rows.
Set the background colour of all cells in the top two rows to yellow. Ensure that there is no text wrapped within the cells of the table. Vertically align all data to the top of each cell.
Remove the gridlines from any unused cells.
Save the file with a new name.

To right align the numbers in the second column, highlight these cells, then select the **Align Text Right** ≡ icon in the **Paragraph** section under the **Home** tab. Repeat this method to centre align the cells in the top two rows: highlight these cells and click on the **Center** ≡ icon in the **Paragraph** section. While these cells in the top two rows are highlighted, select the **Home** tab, in the **Paragraph** section and click on the drop-down list for the **Shading** tool. Select the yellow colour from the palette, which will set the background colour for these cells.

To ensure that there is no text wrapped within the cells of the table, the column widths of the table need adjusting to fit the text within them. Make sure no cell within the table is selected before placing the cursor over the gridline between the cells. This cursor will change to appear like this. Without moving the mouse, double click the left mouse button. Repeat this for each column that needs resizing. Make sure that the completed table does not fit outside the margins of the page. This will be penalised in the practical examinations.

		X population		Y population	
		First choice	Second Choice	First choice	Second Choice
Activity					
Jewellery making	0		1	1	2
Paintballing	39		2	37	19
Boulogne trip	52		21	56	18
Rock workshop	3		18	2	3
Dance workshop	0		2	2	10
Craft workshop	0		3	2	3
Discover scuba	4		3	8	8
Beauty	4		10	1	9
Ceramic painting	0		5	1	2

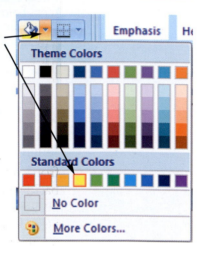

	X population		Y population	
	First choice	Second Choice	First choice	Second Choice
Activity				
Jewellery making	0	1	1	2
Paintballing	39	2	37	19
Boulogne trip	52	21	56	18
Rock workshop	3	18	2	3
Dance workshop	0	2	2	10
Craft workshop	0	3	2	3
Discover scuba	4	3	8	8
Beauty	4	10	1	9
Ceramic painting	0	5	1	2

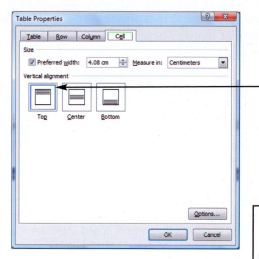

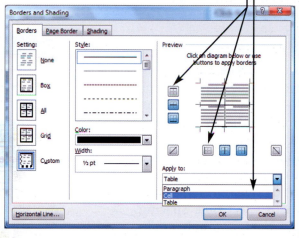

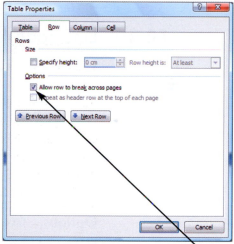

To vertically align all data to the top of each cell, highlight all the cells that require this. Right mouse click in the table, select **Table Properties...**, and select the **Cell** tab. Select the option for **Top** and click on OK.

To remove the gridlines from the unused cell in the top left corner, right mouse click in that cell of the table and choose **Borders and Shading...** from the drop-down menu to open the **Borders and Shading** window. Select the **Borders** tab.

Click the left mouse button on each of the lines that you wish to remove and in the **Apply to:** section select the option for **Cell**

from the drop-down list, before clicking on OK. Remember to remove the yellow background from this cell, using the method shown earlier in this section.

Sometimes, when text wrapping is present, a table row and its contents will be split between two different pages (or columns). To make sure that this does not happen, highlight the entire table, right mouse click and select **Table Properties...**, then the **Row** tab. Remove the tick from the **Allow rows to break across pages** tick box and click on OK.

Activity 10k

Open the file that you saved in Activity 10j. Right align all the cells in the first column. Left align all other cells in the table. Set the background colour of all cells in the first column to light grey. Ensure that there is no text wrapped within the cells of the table. Vertically align all data to the middle of each cell. Remove the gridlines from any unused cells. Save the file with a new name.

10.18 Text alignment

Text can be aligned in four basic ways. It can be aligned:
● to the left margin with a ragged right margin which is called left aligned
● to the centre of the page, which is called centre aligned
● to the right margin, which is called right aligned
● to both margins which is called fully justified.

As you saw in Section 10.17 the text is aligned by selecting the text and then using the using the alignment icons. These icons are found in in the **Paragraph** section under the **Home** tab.

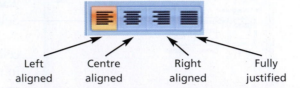

Left aligned   Centre aligned   Right aligned   Fully justified

Activity 101

Open the file TEXT6.RTF and place your name in the centre of the header. Make only the title a 36 point sans serif font that is centre aligned and fits in a single, full width column. Move the third paragraph so that it becomes the last paragraph. Fully justify the body text. Centre align the second paragraph. Left align the third paragraph. Right align the fourth paragraph. Make the first word 'grew' in the story 16 points high, the second 'grew' 20 points and the third 'grew' 24 points. Save the file with a new name.

10.19   Line spacing

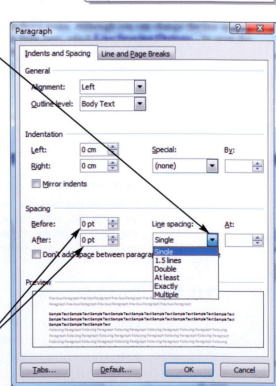

Different line spacing can be used to present different page layouts. The most commonly used layouts are single line spacing, 1.5 line spacing and double line spacing. To change the line spacing in a paragraph, select the **Home** tab, and look in the **Paragraph** section to find the **Line spacing** icon. Select this icon to open this drop-down menu. Although you can change the line spacing of a paragraph from here, select **Line Spacing Options...** to open the **Paragraph** window, which gives you more options.

To change the line spacing, select the **Line spacing:** drop-down menu. This will allow you to define an exact number of lines, which is very useful for title pages, where lines may be spaced out, perhaps needing to be five or six lines apart.

Ensuring that line spacing on a page is consistent is just as important as setting the line spacing. It is often wise to select all text and adjust the line spacing together. If you move, copy, insert or delete text from your document, always check that the line spacing is correct after you have made any change. Each paragraph and heading can have the spacing before and after it set using the same **Paragraph** window. This is set in the **Spacing** section, where the space before and after any paragraph (a title is counted as a paragraph) can be edited.

Activity 10m

Open the file that you saved in Activity 10l.
Make the first paragraph single line spacing, the second paragraph 1.5 line spacing and the third paragraph double line spacing. Do not change the line spacing in the rest of the document.
Set the heading spacing to 12 spaces before and 24 spaces after the paragraph.
Save the file with a new name.

Paragraphs can be formatted with different settings for the first line of a paragraph and the other lines in a paragraph. These settings are all changed on the ruler, which looks like this.

On the left side of the ruler are two settings for the left margin. The top triangle adjusts the first line of the paragraph, the bottom triangle aligns the rest of the paragraph, and the rectangle below moves the whole paragraph.

Task 10o

Open the file TEXT7.RTF and place your name on the left in the header.
Set the first line of the first paragraph as indented text, indented by 2.5 centimetres. Indent the whole of the second paragraph by 2.5 centimetres. Set the fourth and fifth paragraphs as hanging paragraphs with a 2.5 centimetre tab. In the fifth paragraph make the text 'Good Use' a sub-heading.
Save the file with a new filename.

Open the file and place your name in the header. Click the left mouse button in the first paragraph. Drag the top triangle to the right by 2.5 centimetres, like this.

To indent the whole of the second paragraph, click in that paragraph and then drag the small rectangle across to the right by 2.5 centimetres, like this.

Highlight both the fourth and fifth paragraphs and drag the bottom triangle to the right by 2.5 centimetres, like this.

To make the text 'Good Use' a sub-heading, remove the full stop and space at the end of it and replace it with the <Tab> key.

Activity 10n
Open the file that you saved in Activity 10g. Add the text 'History item 1' as a new line to the start of the document. Format this text in the same style as the rest of the page. Change the title 'Weather update' to 'February 2009'. Set all of the text on the first page to be spaced 5 lines apart and all other text in the document to be single line spacing with no spacing before each paragraph and 24 point spacing after each paragraph. Indent first line of each paragraph on the second page by 5 millimetres. Save the file with a new name.

10.20 Correcting errors

You will need to spell check all word-processed documents before submitting them for assessment. Select the **Review** tab and in the **Proofing** section click on the **Spelling and Grammar** icon. The spelling and grammar check starts automatically. Any words or phrases found in a document that are not in the dictionary will be flagged as an error. Do

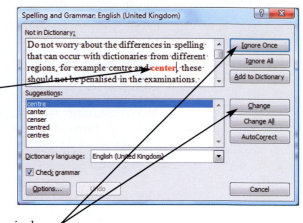

not worry about the differences in spelling that can occur with dictionaries from different regions, for example 'centre' and 'center'; these should not be penalised in the examinations. For example, this has been flagged as an error, but was put into the text intentionally. Be careful not to change the spelling of names, especially for, companies, people or places. Each time an error is flagged, read it carefully and decide whether to change or ignore the spelling, using the buttons in the window.

It is important that you also read through all of the work and make sure that the text or data that you have typed is 100 per cent correct. A large number of marks can be lost in practical examinations through careless checking of your data entry. Check that your documents have consistency in all areas, not only fonts and styles, but also in line spacing and paragraph spacing. It is very easy to follow the instructions on a question paper, for example to remove a page break, only to find that you have an extra carriage return later, which will lose the consistency marks awarded for the document. If you have inserted section breaks or page breaks, make sure that there are no blank pages.

Part of the proofreading and error correction will be to check for widows and orphans. Even though you may have applied automatic widow and orphan control, it is always good practice to check that these have been removed. It is possible that you did not apply it to every paragraph. Make sure that other objects, like bulleted or numbered lists, tables, graphs and database or spreadsheet extracts are not split over two pages. Again, inserting appropriate breaks should avoid these problems.

Data manipulation

For this chapter you will need these source files from the CD:
- CARS.CSV
- STATIONERY.CSV

11.1 Understanding database structures

Traditional **flat-file databases** store data using a system of files, records and fields:
- A **field** is a single item of data like a forename or date of birth. Each field has a fieldname, which is used to identify it within the database. Each field contains one type of data, for example numbers, text, or a date.
- A **record** is a collection of fields, for example all the information about one person or one item. These may contain different data types.
- A **file** (in database terms) is an organised collection of records, usually where all the records are organised so that they can be stored together.

You will be using *Microsoft Access*, which is part of the *Microsoft Office* suite. *Access* stores its data in the form of **tables**, which are organised by rows and columns. Two or more of these tables can be joined together because *Access* is a relational database, rather than a flat file database, but this is beyond the scope of the practical section of this book. Each row in a table contains a record. Each column in the table represents a field and each cell in that column has the same, pre-defined field type.

Field types

When you create a new database you will set each field a field type. The field type will tell *Access* how to store and manipulate the data for each field. You will usually decide what field type should be used for each field. There are a number of field types that you can use and different packages may have different names for these. The list below shows the generic names for these field types (these will probably be used in the examination questions), but depending upon the package used, you may have different names. For example, in *Access* an **alphanumeric** field is called a text field. The three main types of field are **alphanumeric**, **numeric** and **Boolean**:
- **Alphanumeric** data can store alpha characters (text) or numeric data (numbers) that will not be used for calculations. In *Access* this is called a text field.
- A **numeric** field type (as the name suggests) is used to store numeric values that may be used for calculations. This does not include numeric data like telephone

numbers which should be stored in an alphanumeric field type. In *Access* this is called a number field. There are different types of numeric field including:

- **integer** fields, which store whole numbers. In *Access* you can select an integer field or a long integer field. It is wise to use a long integer field if it is going to contain three or more digits
- **decimal** formats, which will allow a large number of decimal places, or a specified restricted number, if this is set in the creation of the field properties when the database is set up
- **currency** values, which allow currency formatting to be added to the display. These include currency symbols and regional symbols. The database does not store these as this would use up valuable storage space
- **date and time** formats, which store a date and/or time as a number.

- A **Boolean** (or logical) field type is used to store data in a Yes/No (or True/False, 0/1) format.

There are other field types as well, like a memo type but these are not available in all packages, so will not be in the practical examinations. As stated above, you will be using *Access*. *Microsoft Excel* is not suitable for database tasks as you can **not** define field types.

Task 11a

You work for a small garage called 'Dodgy Dave's Motors'. This garage sells used cars. Using a suitable database package, import the file CARS.CSV. Assign the following data types to the fields.

Who manufactured the car?	Text
Model	Text
Colour	Text
Price that we bought the car for	Numeric/Currency/2 decimal places
Price that we will sell the car for	Numeric/Currency/2 decimal places
Year	Numeric/Integer
Extras	Text
Does the car need cleaning?	Boolean/Logical

Some fieldnames are inappropriate. Create appropriate and meaningful fieldnames for those fields. You may add another field as a primary key field if your software requires this. Save your database.

It is important to make sure that you use the fieldnames exactly as given in the question paper, unless you are asked to provide appropriate and meaningful fieldnames. In this task you are asked for appropriate and meaningful fieldnames, so start by looking at the detailed descriptions given instead of the fieldnames, or even examine the data to work out what information the fields contains.

For this task, the descriptions help you to work out meaningful fieldnames. These should always be short enough to allow printouts to fit easily onto as few pages as possible. The first example is **Who manufactured the car?**; this could be shortened to **Manufacturer** or even **Make**. **Make** is short, meaningful and appropriate, so use that. The **Price that we bought the car for** could be changed to **Purchase Price**, **Purchase**, **P Price**, **P_Price** or just **PPrice**. Although *Access* will allow any of these, do not use fieldnames with spaces in, as they may cause problems if you try to do more complex operations with the database. You could use any of the other three options, as all would be acceptable. For this task, use **PPrice**. Similarly, the next field can be called **SPrice**. For the final field, **Does the car need cleaning?**, simply using the fieldname **Clean** could give the wrong idea, as it could mean 'Does the car need cleaning?' or 'Is the car clean?'. In this case you can use **Valet** as the fieldname to avoid confusion. It is sensible to plan this and make the changes in the.csv file, before importing the data into *Access*.

Open the.csv file in *Excel*. Move into the relevant cells and type in the new fieldnames. Check the spelling carefully before re-saving the data file. Save it with the filename cars1.csv so you do not lose the original data file. Task 11a is continued in the next section.

11.2 Creating a database from an existing file

Open *Access* and use the **Office** button followed by **New** to open the **Blank Database** pane on the right-hand side in the window. Enter a **File Name:** for the database, for example 'cars' or a similar meaningful filename, and click on `Create`. This should open a new database similar to this.

Hint

Check that the data files are in the correct format for your regional settings before attempting this section. (See Introduction, page xi.)

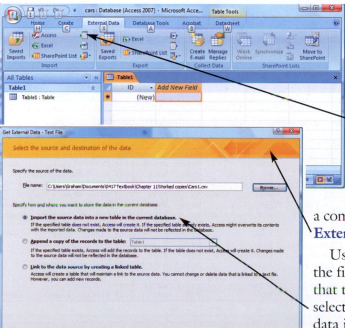

To import the file CARS1.CSV (remember we saved it with a new filename in an earlier section) for the task, select the **External Data** tab. Click on the **Import text file** icon, as files saved in.csv format are text files, with each data item separated from the next by a comma. This icon opens the **Get External Data** window like this.

Use the `Browse...` button to find the file CARS1.CSV and ensure that the top radio button is selected. This will ensure that the data is saved in a new data table. Click on `OK`.

The **Import Text Wizard** window will open. As comma separated value (.csv) files are delimited files (the comma is the delimiter), select the **Delimited** radio button and click on Next > .

For the next part of the wizard, make sure that the **Comma** is selected using the radio buttons (unless you have changed the.csv file so that it uses semi-colons as delimiters). Examine the first row of the data and decide whether this row contains the fieldnames that you need or if it contains the first row of data. If the first row contains the fieldnames click on the **First Row Contains Field Names** tick box. As you tick this box the first row changes from this, to this.

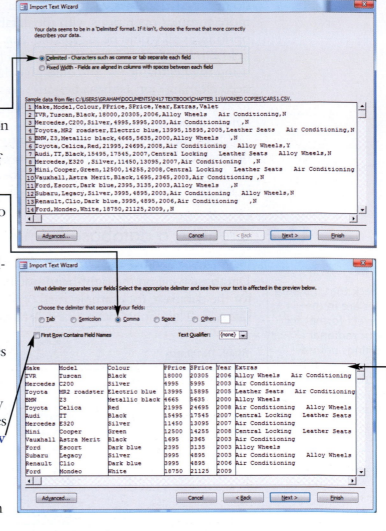

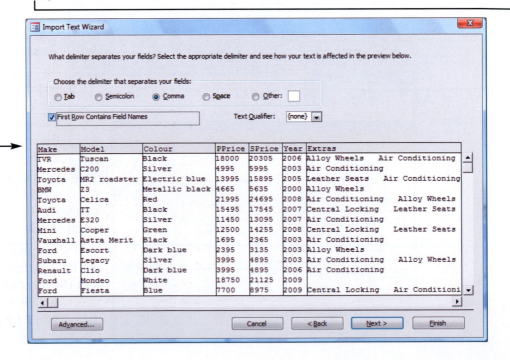

Click on **Advanced...** to open the **Import Specification** window.

Check that all the fieldnames and data types match those specified in the task. In this case the **PPrice**, **SPrice** and **Valet** fields are not correct. The **PPrice** and **SPrice** fields need changing to numeric (currency) fields and the **Valet** field needs changing to a Boolean (Yes/No) field.

To change the **PPrice** field into a numeric field with a currency sub-type, click on the **Data Type** cell for this field and use the drop-down list to select the **Currency** field type. Repeat this process for the **SPrice** field.

For the **Valet** field, use the drop-down list to change the **Text** field type into a **Yes/No** field type. When all of these changes have been made, click on **OK**. Select **Next >** twice. In the next screen, ensure that the radio button for **Let Access add primary key** is selected – this adds a new field called ID to the table and Access will use this as the **primary key** field. Click on **Next >** and in the **Import to Table:** box, enter **tblCars**. This is a meaningful table name, as 'tbl' shows you that it is a table and the 'Cars' gives relevance to the data. Click on **Finish** to import the data and on **Close** to close the wizard. Double click on tblCars to display the table like this.

Hint

The icon in the **Views** tab will let you change between **Datasheet** and **Design View**.

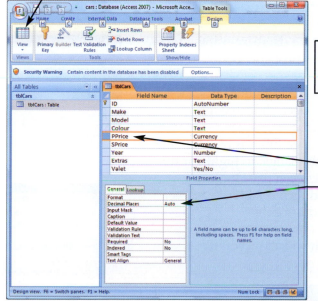

Changes to the field types or other properties, can be changed from the **Home** tab. In the **Views** section, click on the **Design View** icon.

The task instructed you to set the **PPrice** field to 2 decimal places. You can check this by clicking the left mouse button in the **PPrice** field and viewing the number of **Decimal Places** in the **General** tab at the bottom of the window.

As you can see this is not set to 2 decimal places but is set to automatic. Click on the cell containing Auto and use the drop-down list to set this to 2 decimal places. Repeat this process for the **SPrice** field.

Hint

If you need percentage values, set an integer or long integer field type and select Percentage from the Format drop-down menu for this field.

To change the Boolean field so that it displays Yes or No (it does not store the data like this), click in the **Valet** field and in the **General** tab select the **Format** cell. Use the drop-down list to select the **Yes/No** option. Save the database for later use.

Extras	Text
Valet	Yes/No

Field Prop

General | Lookup

Format	Yes/No	
Caption	True/False	True
Default Value	Yes/No	Yes
Validation Rule	On/Off	On
Validation Text		
Indexed	No	
Text Align	General	

Activity 11a

You work for a shop selling office supplies called 'Easy as ABC'. Using a suitable database package, import the file STATIONERY.CSV. Assign the following data types to the fields.

Code	Numeric/Integer
Type of product to be sold	Text
Description of the product to be sold	Text
Quantity of items in each pack	Numeric/Integer
Colour	Text
Sales Price	Numeric/Currency/2 decimal places
Purchase Price	Numeric/Currency/2 decimal places
Discount	Boolean/Logical

Some fieldnames are inappropriate. Create appropriate and meaningful fieldnames for those fields. Use the Code field as your primary key field. Save your database.

11.3 Entering data

Task 11b

Open the file that you saved at the end of Task 11a.
Add this new car to the database.

Make	Model	Colour	PPrice	SPrice	Year	Extras	Valet
Ford	Escort	Silver	4350	5285	2002	Alarm Central Locking Alloy Wheels	Y

Data would normally be entered into a database using a form, but in the practical examinations it is probably better to use the table to enter new data.

Open the database saved in Task 11a. Double click the left mouse button on the table name to open the table in **Datasheet View**.

To make sure that all the columns are fully visible, click the left mouse button on the small white triangle to highlight the entire datasheet. Move the cursor between two fieldnames until it looks like this and then double click. This will adjust the display widths of the columns. Scroll down the list of cars until you reach the entry with a star next to it which will allow you to add a **New** car at the bottom.

ID	Make	Model	Colour	PPrice	SPrice	Year	Extras	Valet	Add New Field
66	VW	Passat	Black	£6,495.00	£7,645.00	2005		No	
67	Ford	Escort	Silver	£3,450.00	£4,295.00	2004	Air Conditioning Central Locking	No	
(New)									

Click the cursor in the **Make** cell for the new car and add 'Ford'. The new ID number will automatically appear in the **ID** field, as you set this field as an AutoNumber type. Move the cursor and enter the **Model**, **Colour**, **Year** and **Extras** in the same way. You can always use copy and paste for some data. For example, if you need to make sure the spelling of Escort is correct, copy and paste it from record 67 above. For the **PPrice** and **SPrice** fields, enter only the numbers (and decimal point if this is required). Do not attempt to enter any other characters like the currency symbol. As you press the <Enter> key after adding the prices *Access* will set the data into currency format. The **Valet** field will automatically default to No. Move into this field and enter Yes in this cell. As you enter each item of data *Access* will automatically save it.

Check your data entry carefully using **visual verification**. This is when you compare the original data on paper (in this case, in Task 11b) with the data that you have entered into the computer. Any data entry error in a database may cause you errors when you try to use the database to search or sort. Save the database.

Task 11c

Open the file that you saved at the end of Task 11b.
Add a new field to the database called PDate. Add the purchase date of 30 September 2009 for the next record.

Open the database and open the table tblCars in **Design View**. Move to the empty row below the **Valet** field and enter the **Fieldname PDate**.

In the **Data Type** box use the drop-down list to select the **Date/Time** type. Choose the most appropriate **Format** for the question. In this case, the task asks for a **Long Date** format.

Save the database and select the **Datasheet View**. Move the cursor into the PDate field for the new record (the Silver Ford Escort) and use the **Calendar** icon to select the correct date.

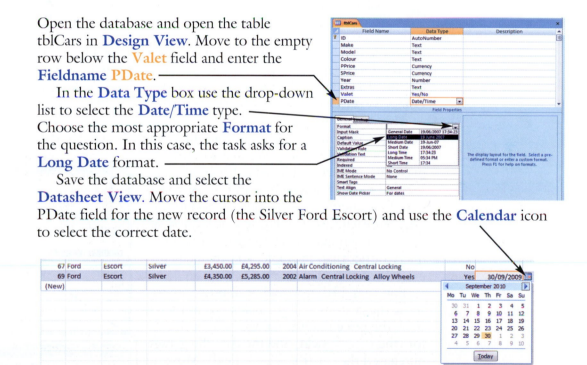

Code	Type	Description	Quantity	Colour	SPrice	PPrice	Discount
44282	Lever Arch File	Laminated Lever Arch Files	1	Red	57.22	28.96	N
44283	Lever Arch File	Laminated Lever Arch Files	1	Yellow	57.22	28.96	N
47478	Spine Label	Eastlight Spine Lables	100		30	13.86	Y

11.4 Performing searches

In Access you can search for data using a Query. This will allow you to select a subset of the data stored in your table. Each query is created and saved and can be used again later. Even if new data is added to the table, when you open a query again it will select the subset from all the data, including the new data.

Task 11d

Open the file that you saved at the end of Task 11c.
A customer would like a car made by Ford. Find the customer a list of all the cars in the garage made by Ford.

Open the database that you saved at the end of Task 11c. You do not need to open the table that you created earlier. Select the **Create** tab and find the **Other** section on the right. Click on the **Query Wizard** icon.

This is the easiest way of performing a search and opens the **New Query** window. Select the **Simple Query Wizard** and click on OK .

In the **Simple Query Wizard** window, make sure that the table name has been selected in the **Tables/Queries** box. As this is your first query this is the only option in this box, but each time you create a new query it will be shown here. If you select a previous query rather than the table, you are likely to get incorrect results.

For Task 11d, it would be appropriate to show the customer all the fields except the **ID** field, the price that the garage bought the car for (the **PPrice** field) and the date the garage purchased the car (the **PDate** field). Move all of the fields into the query using the double arrow key.

Select the **ID** field, the **PPrice** field and the **PDate** field in turn and click on the single arrow to remove them from the selection. When you have got only the required fields, click Next > . Select Next > again.

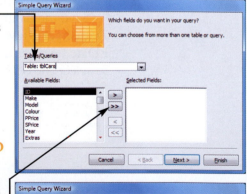

Enter a name for the query. This query may be turned into a report at some point and the name you give the query may become the title for the report. You may therefore wish to add your name to the query name.

Select the radio button for **Modify the query design** before clicking on Finish.

This opens the query in **Design View**. **Datasheet View** can be seen by selecting the drop-down list under the **View** icon. However, at the moment the query will still contain all of the records as we have not yet performed the search.

To perform the query, move the cursor into the **Criteria:** row of the **Make** field and type **Ford**. You do not need to use speech marks, as *Access* will put these in for you. This will extract only the cars made by Ford.

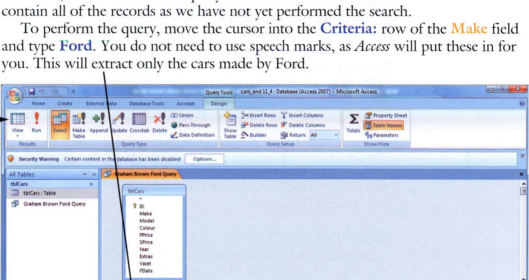

Now select the **Datasheet View** to see the results of the query. The number of records can be seen at the bottom of the window in this view. There should be 25 Ford cars in the query. Save the query.

Task 11e

Open the file that you saved at the end of Task 11d.
The manager would like to see all the details of all the Fords that need valeting.

Create the query in a similar way to the one for Task11d. Select all the fields and when you **Modify the query design**, enter **Ford** in the **Criteria:** row of the **Make** column and **Yes** in the same **Criteria:** row for the **Valet** column. The selection will look like this and only two cars will be found using this search.

Task 11f

Open the file that you saved at the end of Task 11e.
The manager would like to see all the details of all the cars made by Ford or Vauxhall.

Create the query in a similar way to the one for Task11e. In the **Simple Query Wizard** window, make sure that the table name has been selected in the **Tables/Queries** box. If you select one of the previous queries rather than the table, you are likely to get incorrect results.

Select all the fields and when you **Modify the query design**, enter **Ford or Vauxhall** in the **Criteria:** row of the **Make** column. The selection will look like this and 37 cars will be found using this search.

Task 11g

Open the file that you saved at the end of Task 11f.
The Sales Manager would like to see all the details of all the cars in stock not made by Ford.

Create the query in a similar way to the one for Task11f. Select all the fields and when you **Modify the query design**, enter **Not Ford** in the **Criteria:** row of the **Make** column. The selection will look like this and 43 cars will be found using this search.

Task 11h

Open the file that you saved at the end of Task 11g.
The manager would like to see all the details of all the cars that have alloy wheels.

By examining the data in the database you can see that the text 'Alloy Wheels' could appear in the Extras field. It may not be the only extra that a car has, there could be other extras listed before it or after it within the field.

To find all the cars with this extra you must create the query in a similar way as for Task11g. Select all the fields and when you **Modify the query design**, enter ***Alloy Wheels*** in the **Criteria:** row of the **Extras** column. The stars tell *Access* that

Hint

To search for something that is at the start of the data, use Text*, for example Bl* in the Colour field will find all the cars with the first Colour Blue or Black, but would not find colours like Light Blue. Placing the star at the start of a search string will only find those things ending with the search string.

you are performing a **wildcard search**. The selection will look like this and 35 cars will be found using this search.

Task 11i

Open the file that you saved at the end of Task 11h.
The Sales Manager would like to see details of all the cars in stock for sale for less than or equal to £4125.

Create the query in a similar way as for Task11g. Be careful not to use any symbols like < or £ in the query name. Select all the fields and when you **Modify the query design**, enter **<=4125** in the **Criteria:** row of the **SPrice** column. The selection will look like this and 18 cars will be found using this search.

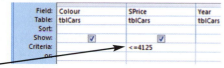

Similar mathematical formulae can be used, with < for less than, > for greater than, >= for greater than or equal to and = for equals. These mathematical formulae cannot be used for queries involving text fields, but can be used for any numeric, date or time fields.

Activity 11c

Open the file saved in Activity 11c.

Search the database to find the following information for your manager. For each search show all the fields in the table.

 1 Find all the blue stationery items.
 2 Find all the blue or black stationery items.
 3 Find all the items where the colour is not blue.
 4 Find all the red items where the discount is yes.
 5 Find all the items where the type contains the word 'file'.
 6 Find all the items where the description contains the word 'file'.
 7 Find all items with a quantity of less than or equal to 10.
 8 Find all items where the quantity is 10.
 9 Find all items with a quantity of greater than 1.
10 Find all items with a quantity of greater than or equal to 10.
11 Find all items where the sales price is less than £10.

11.5 Producing reports

The word 'report' can be quite confusing. A dictionary definition is 'a document that gives information about an investigation or a piece of research'. For the practical examinations a report has this generic meaning: 'a document that gives information'. This is often confused with a report created in *Access*. The report created in *Access* will often be the most suitable report for a task, but sometimes it may be better to produce a report in a word processor, copying and pasting information into a document. For each task, you will need to decide which method is the most suitable.

Task 11j

Open the database that you saved at the end of Task 11i.
Produce a report which:

- shows all the cars made by Ford
- displays only the Make, Model, Colour, SPrice, Extras and Valet fields within the width of a landscape page
- has your name on the left in the header of each page
- has a title 'All Ford cars in stock' centre aligned at the top of the first page
- has a subtitle 'request for Mr David Watson' right aligned at the top of the first page.

Hint

You *must* create the query first and then base the report upon the query.

Open the database saved in Task 11i. Select the **Create** tab and find the **Reports** section. Click on the **Report Wizard** icon to open the **Report Wizard** window.

In the **Tables/Queries** box you need to select the correct query. For this task, the report will be based upon the query to select only the Fords (you created this query in Task11d). Use the arrow buttons to move the correct fields from the **Available Fields:** into the **Selected Fields:** box like this, then click on Next > . Grouping is not needed at IGCSE level, so click on Next > again. For this task, you are not asked to sort the report (which will be covered later in the chapter), so click on Next > again to get this.

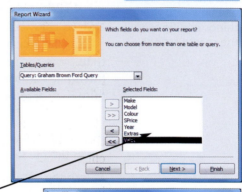

The task told you to select a single landscape page. The page orientation is chosen using the **Orientation** radio buttons. Select **Landscape**. Use the **Layout** section to choose how the page will be laid out; in this case a tabular format has been selected. Click on Next > .

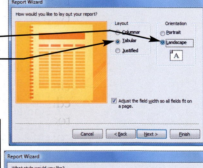

Choose the style for your report and click on Next > . Change the report name, so that it is 'All Ford cars in stock' (which is the title from the task). As you still need to add the subtitle and ensure that the layout is correct, select the **Modify the report's design** radio button and click on Finish . The design view of the report will look similar to this.

Each section of the report is shown with a light blue bar. The top section is the **Report Header**. Anything that you place in this section appears only once at the start of the document. Anything that you place in the **Page Header** is shown at the top of each page, in this case the fieldnames. Similarly, information in the **Page Footer** is shown at the bottom of each page. The **Report Footer** appears at the very end of a report, although in this example the Report Footer is empty (it is not shown in white) and therefore will not be shown in this document. The **Detail** section is the most important, as this single row is where the data is shown for each car. This single row will appear as many rows (as many as there are Ford cars in the database) and display the details of each record.

The task tells you to place your name on the left in the header of each page. Move the cursor to the top of the light blue bar showing the **Detail** row; click on this so that the cursor changes into an arrow. Hold the left mouse button down and drag the top of the detail row down about 5 millimetres. Select all of the controls (objects) in the **Page Header** by dragging (and holding) the left mouse button.

Move all of these controls down the page about 5 millimetres, so that they look like this. ➔

The **Design** tab should already be selected. Find the **Controls** section and click on the **Label** icon.

Drag a new control into the **Page Header** and type your name into this control. In this example, when you move the cursor out of the control and click anywhere else on the report it does not show the text clearly. This label needs editing so that the text is visible and it is left aligned. Select the control and use the tools in the **Font** section of the **Design** tab to set the font colour to white and the alignment to left.

To see what the report will look like at any time, find the **Views** section of the **Design** tab and select the **Report View**. Use this section to change back to the **Design View** at any time.

The title 'All Ford cars in stock' needs to be centre aligned. Click on the control containing this label, and use the drag handle to stretch the control to 28.2 centimetres (almost the edge of the page). If you stretch the control further to the right it will add another page width to the final printout, wasting paper when it is printed

and no longer fitting to a single page wide. Once the control fits the page width, then centre align the label using the **Center** icon.

To add the subtitle, drag the light blue bar for the **Page Header** down about 5 millimetres. Add a new label, the full width of the page, in the **Report Header**, just below the title. Type the text 'request for Mr David Watson' into this control. Set the font colour to white as before and right align this subtitle using the **Align Text Right** icon. The design view of the report looks like this.

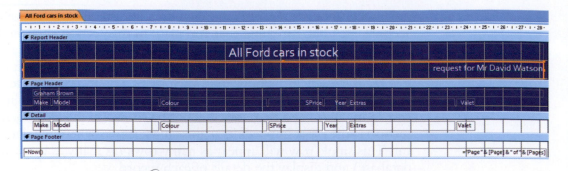

Activity 11d

Open the database that you saved at the end of Activity 11c. Produce a report which:

- displays all the data in the table within the width of a landscape page
- has your name on the right in the header of each page
- has a title 'All stationery in stock' centre aligned at the top of the first page
- has a subtitle 'request for the manager' right aligned at the top of the first page.

Task 11k

Open the database that you saved at the end of Task 11j.
Produce a report which:

- displays all the data for all the cars with alloy wheels within the width of a portrait page
- has your name in the report header followed by 'Cars with alloy wheels'.

Open the database saved in Task 11j. Select the **Create** tab and in the **Reports** section click on the **Report Wizard** icon. In the **Report Wizard** window, select the query for alloy wheels (that you created in Task11h) in the **Tables/Queries** box. As the task says 'display all the data', use the arrow buttons to move all the fields from **Available Fields:** to the **Selected Fields:** box. Go through the wizard as you did for the previous task, making sure that you set the page **Orientation** to **Portrait**. When the wizard has finished, the report is created and looks similar to this.

You can see that *Access* has attempted to make all the fields fit across the page, but this has not been successful as not all of the data is fully visible.

In the practical examinations you must show all of the required data in full. Select the **Create** tab, and in the **Views** section click on the **View** icon. Use the drop-down menu to select **Design View**.

Find the control for the **ID** field in the **Detail** section of the report. Use the left drag handle to make this control a little larger. It should change from this to this.

You can see that the control for the label in the **Page Header** has also been stretched. Use the **View** icon to change back to **Report View** to see the effect that this has made to the report. The left column now displays all of the figures (including the top row).

To make more space available for widening some fields, you will need to reduce the width of other fields. The **Make** field has taken more of the page width than it needs. Use the drag handle on the right of this field to shrink the field. Use the **Report View** to make sure that all of data is visible (you will need to scroll down through all the data), but space is not wasted. Repeat this for the **Model** and **Colour** fields. Stretch the **PPrice**, **SPrice** and **Year** fields so that all the data is visible. The **Design View** of the report should look like this.

At the moment, ignore the **Extras** field, as this is the longest field. Stretch the **Valet** and **PDate** fields so that all the data and labels fit within the width of the page. Make sure all the data and labels are fully visible. The data and labels may be different widths to those shown here, depending on the formats chosen for each field. Now stretch the **Extras** field until the **PDate** control just reaches the edge of the page but no further.

Change to **Report View** and the report appears like this. You can see that all of the **Extras** still do not fit within the space.

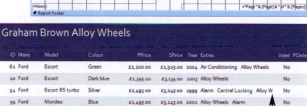

In **Design View**, move into the **Detail Row** and drag the bottom handle of the control for the **Extras** field down so that the control becomes exactly twice as high.

Change to **Report View** and check that all the data and labels fit within the width of a single page, like this.

Save this report.

Hint

The Discount field can appear as Yes/No, True/False or as a tick box. All of these would be correct for this question.

Activity 11e ✓

Open the database that you saved at the end of Activity 11d.

Produce a report which:

● displays all the data for all the items where the quantity is greater than or equal to 10 within the width of a portrait page
● has your name in the header of each page
● has a title 'Quantity >=10' centre aligned at the top of the first page.

Exporting data

Sometimes whole reports, queries or the data within them need exporting into other packages to be manipulated as part of a report for someone, or to create a graph or chart.

Task 11l ✓

Export the report saved in Task 11k into rich text format so it can be included in a word-processed document.

In the **Navigation** pane, find the report that you saved in Task 11k and right click the mouse button on the report name to get the drop-down menu.

Select the option to **Export**. This will open another drop-down menu. You need to export into .rtf format, so select **Word RTF File**. This opens the **Export - RTF File** window.

Click on the Browse... button to select a folder to save the document into. In the practical examinations you will need to use this file for another task, so select the tick box for **Open the destination file after the export operation is complete**, then click on OK . The exported file will appear. Close the **Export – RTF File** window.

Hint

If you need to export the report without any formatting, select the **Text File** option.

Task 11m ✓

Export all the details of all the cars with alloy wheels into a format that can be used to produce a graph.

The best package within the *Office* suite for creating graphs is *Excel*. You have just exported the report on all the details of the cars with alloy wheels into .rtf format. However, if you try to export the report into *Excel* you will not be able to do so, as the report holds its title and formatting as well as the data. Instead, you need to export the *query* for 'alloy wheels' rather than the *report*.

Right mouse click on the query name, then select **Export**, followed by **Excel** from the drop-down menus to open the **Export – Excel Spreadsheet window**. Rather than reformatting the data, select the tick box for **Export data with formatting and layout**, and the tick box for **Open the destination file after the export operation is complete**. Click on OK . Close the **Export – Excel Spreadsheet** window.

Hint

If you need to export the data into.csv format (comma separated values), Export it first into *Excel*, then save it in.csv format from *Excel*.

Activity 11f

Export the report saved in Activity 11g into:

● rich text format
● a format that can be used to produce a graph
● a comma separated value format.

Hiding data in a report

There are times when information in a report needs to be hidden in some way. In real applications a single report would be created for more than one task, and some data would be hidden. This process is often done automatically using a created report and a programming language. Although that is beyond the scope of this book, the ability to hide fields within a report is useful. An example of this is when an invoice would be produced for a customer, and the same document is used as a delivery note, so that it shows the details of the items ordered but the costs are hidden. In *Access* this can be done in one of two ways, the first is to make a control invisible; the second is to use a background colour that matches the text colour.

Task 11n

Open the report created in Task 11k.
Hide all the labels and data for the Valet and PDate fields from the report. Hide the PPrice data (but not the title) by setting a black background.

Before starting this task it is wise to back up the report that you created in Task 11k. In the **Navigation** pane, right mouse click on the report name and select **Copy**. Move the cursor onto the whitespace in the **Navigation** pane and right mouse click again.

Select **Paste** from the drop-down menu, renaming the report if required. Open the report in **Design View**. Right mouse click on any of the field controls and select **Properties** from the bottom of the drop-down menu to open the **Property Sheet** pane.

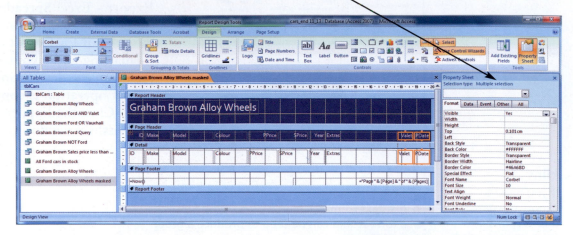

Select the four controls for the **Valet** and **PDate** fields (two for the labels and two for the data). These can be selected together by holding down the <Shift> key and clicking the left mouse button on each of the controls in turn. These should be highlighted like this.

In the **Property Sheet** pane, select the **Format** tab. Many of the options in the **Property Sheet** have small drop-down menus,

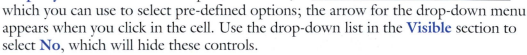

which you can use to select pre-defined options; the arrow for the drop-down menu appears when you click in the cell. Use the drop-down list in the **Visible** section to select **No**, which will hide these controls.

To set a black background for the **PPrice** data, in the **Detail** row of the report select the control for **PPrice**. Move the cursor into the **Property Sheet** pane, selecting the **Format** tab. Find the **Back Color** section and use the 🔲 icon to select the colour palette.

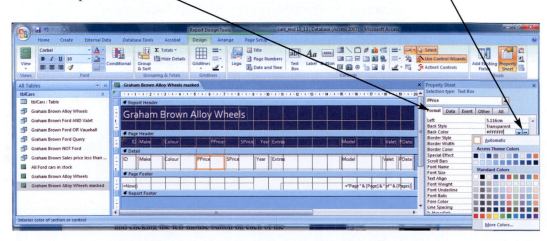

If you wish to change the display formats of any field, this can also be done in the **Property Sheet** pane using the **Format** tab. However it is better to set the formatting for the fields in the **Design View** of the table, as changing the display properties will not change the way that the data is stored and this could lead to errors if fields are used for calculations.

Select the black colour rather than the white background. You will notice that the colour code for this control has changed from #FFFFFF to #000000. You will learn more about this in Section 15.7. Change from **Design View** into **Report View** to see the changes. Save the changes to the report design. Close the report.

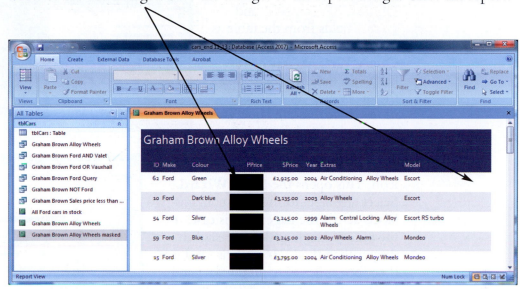

Activity 11g

Open the report created in Activity 11e.

Hide the label and data for the Discount field in the report and hide only the data in the PPrice field by setting a black background.

Producing labels

You may be required to produce other forms of output from your database, for example producing labels to advertise a product or address labels for mailing letters to customers.

Task 11o

Open the file that you saved at the end of Task 11n.
Find all the cars with a sale price of less than £4000 and for these cars produce labels which:

● have a page orientation of portrait
● fit two side by side on the page
● have a 16 point centre aligned heading 'Special Offer' at the top of each label
● show only the fields Make, Model, Colour, SPrice, Year and Extras, sorted into make and model order
● have your name at the bottom right of each label.

Design a new query to extract only the cars with a sale price of less than £4000, selecting only the **Make**, **Model**, **Colour**, **SPrice**, **Year** and **Extras** fields from the table as you step through the **Simple Query Wizard**. When you have selected these cars close the query and click the left mouse button on the query so that it is highlighted like this.

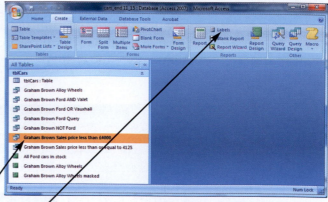

From the **Create** tab, find the **Reports** section and click on the **Labels** icon. This opens the **Label Wizard**. Select any label format that contains two labels across the page; in this case, use the C2244 labels as they are slightly deeper than the C2166 labels (and it is therefore easier to fit all the data and labels onto each label). Click on Next >.

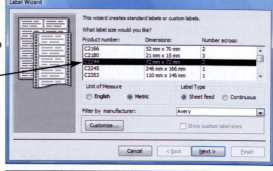

The next screen asks for the font size and colour of the text on the label. Leave this set to a small size (it is easier to enlarge this later if needed, than to reduce it), like 8 points high. Click on Next >.

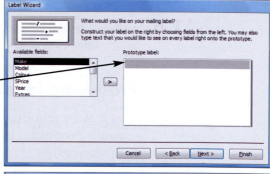

Type the text 'Special Offer' in the grey area as the top row of the label. Press <Enter> to move down to the second row. Each field needs moving onto the label – use the right arrow to move each field into the label, pressing <Enter> after each one to create a new row. You can type labels for each row if you wish to do so. When all of the fields have been moved across, add a final row with your name, then click on Next >.

Move the **Make**, then **Model** fields across into the right to sort the labels by make and model as specified in the task, then click on Next >.

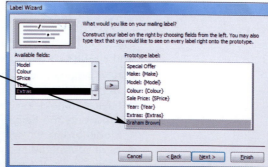

Give the labels an appropriate name and select the radio button for **Modify the label design**. Click on Finish.

Select the **Home** tab and use the text formatting tools to change this into this.

Notice how the heading has been set to 16 point and centre aligned and the other fields moved down. The **Extras** field has been given more space, so that all the data should be visible. This will need checking when the labels are produced, and edited again if necessary. Your name at the bottom of the label should also be right aligned.

Check the labels' layout using the **Office** button followed by **Print** and **Print Preview**. Save the labels.

Activity 11h

Open the database that you saved at the end of Activity 11g.

Find all the items where the discount is Yes and the sale price more than £30. For these cars produce labels which:

- have a page orientation of portrait and fit two side by side on the page
- have a 20 point right aligned heading 'Discount Offers' at the top of each label
- show only the fields Type, Description, Colour and SPrice, sorted into ascending order
- have your name centre aligned at the bottom of each label.

11.6 Using formulae in queries

You are sometimes asked to perform calculations at run time. This could be done in one of two ways. The first method is by creating a calculated field, so that each record has a calculation performed on it and the results are stored in a query. The other method is to calculate on all (or a selection of) the records, for example to add (sum) the data from a number of records.

Task 11p

Open the file saved in Task 11o.
Produce a new report from all the data which:

- contains a new field called Profit which is calculated at run time. This field will subtract the purchase price from the sale price
- has the Profit field formatted to currency with 2 decimal places
- contains a new field called Percent to calculate the percentage profit for each car at run time. This field will divide the profit by the sale price
- has the Percent field formatted as a percentage value with no decimal places.

To create a field that is calculated at run time, you must first open a query. For this task, the query will not be used to search for data, but be used to perform the calculation. Select the **Create** tab, then click on the **Query Wizard** icon and in the **New Query** window select the **Simple Query Wizard**. In the **Tables/Queries box** select the table **tblcars** as the source of the data. Select all fields using the double arrow key. Click on Next > twice, name the query **Profit calculation**, select the radio button for **Modify the query design**, then click on Finish .

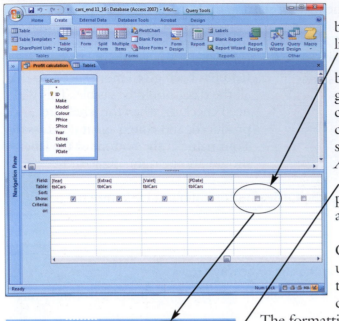

In the design view of the query, use the bottom scroll bar to scroll to the right and find the first blank field like this.

Move the cursor into the **Field** row for the first blank field. Enter the name (**Profit**) that you wish to give this calculated field followed by a colon. The colon tells *Access* that the next section is a calculation. Within the calculation, you must place square brackets [] around each fieldname so that *Access* looks up the data from the relevant field.

For this task, you need to subtract the purchase price from the sale price. The finished calculation will appear like this.

In the **Views** section select the **Datasheet View**. Calculate the profit for three or four cars by hand or using a calculator, and compare with the results in the query to check that you have entered the formula correctly.

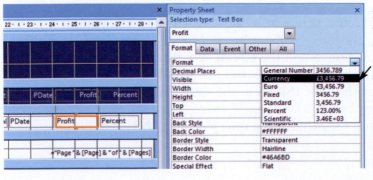

The formatting of the calculated field will be performed in the report. The task requires you to create a second calculated field so it would be sensible to include the new field now and complete the formatting later.

Hint

Use + for addition, – for subtraction, * for multiply and / for divide.

To create a new field called **Percent**, follow the same procedure, this time adding a formula to divide the profit by the sale price.

Again, check the calculations with a calculator to ensure that you have not made an error entering the formula. Save and close the query.

Create a new report using the **Report Wizard** as shown in Section 11.5. In the **Tables/Queries** box select the profit calculation query as the source of the data.

Select all fields using the double arrow key. Click on Next > three times before selecting a page **Orientation** of **Landscape**. Click on Next > twice more naming the report **Profit calculation**. Select the radio button for **Modify the report's design**, then click on Finish .

Move to the **Detail row** of the report and right mouse click on the control for the **Profit** data. Select **Properties** from the drop-down menu to display the **Property Sheet** pane.

Select the **Format** tab for this control, and use the drop-down menu for the **Format** option to select a **Currency** formatting style. Click on the **View** icon to go into **Report View** and check that the formatting for this field is correct and contains 2 decimal places. In this example it does.

Repeat this process for the **Percent** field, left mouse clicking on the control for **Percent** in the **Detail row** of the report. For this field select the **Percent** formatting style from the drop-down list. Again, go into **Report View** to check that the formatting for this field is correct and contains 0 decimal places. In this example, the data is displayed in with percentage formatting but has 2 decimal places.

Click on the **View** icon to return to **Design View**. Right click the mouse button

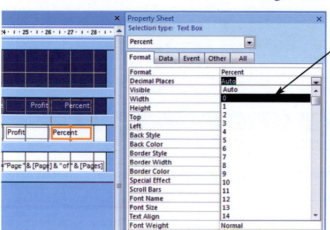

on the **Percent** control in the **Detail row**. Find the **Decimal Places** option and select 0 from the drop-down list.

Go into **Report View** to check that the formatting for this field is now correct and contains 0 decimal places. This is fine, but some field widths need adjusting so that all data and labels are fully visible. Adjust these before saving the completed report.

Activity 11i

Open the file saved in Activity 11h. Produce a new report from all the data which:

● contains a new field called **Profit** which is calculated at run time. This field will subtract the purchase price from the sale price
● contains a new field called **Percent** to calculate the percentage profit for each car at run time. This field will divide the profit by the sale price
● contains a new field called **UnitProfit**. This field will divide the profit by the quantity
● has the **Profit** and **UnitProfit** fields formatted to currency with 2 decimal places
● has the **Percent** field formatted as a percentage value with 1 decimal place.

11.7 Using formulae in reports

Other calculations may be needed on the data selected. These include calculating the sum (total), average, maximum or minimum values of selected data, or counting the number of items present in the selected data. All of these functions can be produced within a report in *Access*.

Task 11q

Open the file saved in Task 11p.
Produce a new report from all the data which:

● displays at the bottom of the report the total profit if all the cars were sold
● displays at the bottom of the report the maximum, minimum and average profit values
● displays the number of cars in this report.

You can use the report from Task 11p to help you with this task. Close this report (if it is open) and right mouse click on it once in the **Navigation** pane so that you get the drop-down menu. Select **Copy**, then **Paste** a new version into the pane with a name that relates to Task 11q. Open this report in **Design View**.

Click the left mouse button on the bottom edge of the **Report Footer** and drag this down about 2 centimetres, so that this footer is now visible. Select the **Design** tab and then click on the **Text Box** icon from **Controls** section. Move down into the

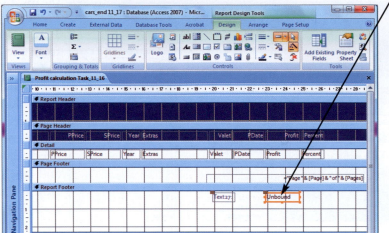

Report Footer and click the mouse button and drag to place a new control, in this case a text box directly below the **Profit** column. This positioning is important as this control will be used to calculate the total profit for the data in this report.

If the **Property Sheet** pane is not showing, right click the mouse button on the text box that you have just created, then select **Properties** from the drop-down menu. In the **Property Sheet**, select the **All** tab, find the **Control Source** row and type the formula **=SUM([Profit])** into this row. The **Property Sheet** will change to this.

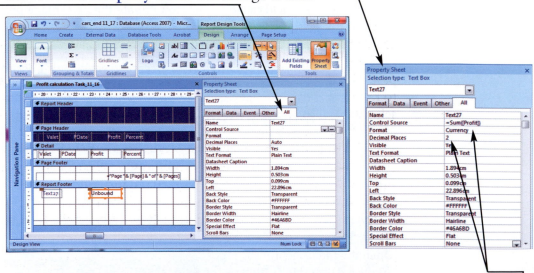

The round brackets are part of the SUM function, the square brackets tell *Access* that this is a field (in this case the **Profit** field calculated at run time). Format this control as **Currency** and set it to 2 decimal places.

Move the cursor into the label for this text box and type in the **Caption** 'Total profit'. This can be entered in the label or in the **Property Sheet** pane using the **Caption** row like this.

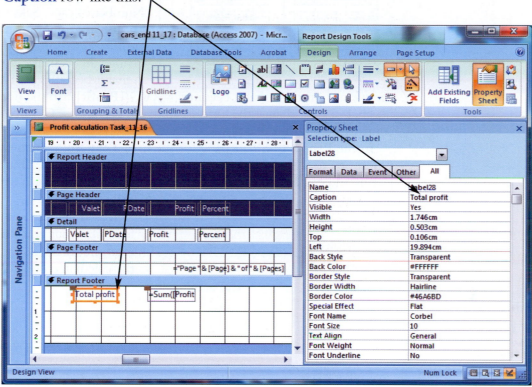

Change to the **Report View** and make sure that the control is in the correct place and appears to give the right answer (it is not too large or too small).

Rather than repeating this process four more times, it will be quicker to copy and paste these controls and edit each one to give the required results. Use the **lasso tool** to highlight both the **Text Box** and its **Label**. Click the right mouse button and select **Copy**, then click the right mouse button on the background in the **Report Footer** and use <Shift> and <Insert> to paste the copies of these controls. Using <Shift> and <Insert> pastes the new controls directly under the existing ones and you do not need to reorganise the controls. It also extends the bottom of the **Report Footer** as needed. If you right mouse click and use **Paste** from the drop-down menu, this pastes the controls in the top left-hand corner of the **Report Footer** and you then have to drag and position each set of controls. Repeat <Shift> and <Insert> until you have five sets of controls like this.

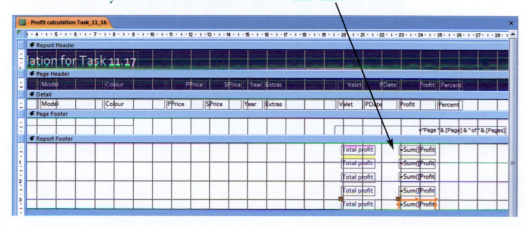

Total profit	=Sum([Profit])
Maximum profit	=Max([Profit])
Minimum profit	=Min([Profit])
Average profit	=Avg([Profit])
Number of cars	=Count([Profit])

In the last four controls containing labels, change the **Captions** to 'Maximum profit', 'Minimum profit', 'Average profit' and 'Number of cars'. Select the second **Text Box** (for the maximum profit) and change the formula so that it becomes **=MAX([Profit])**. Change the formulae for the minimum profit so that it becomes **=MIN([Profit])** and for the average profit so that it becomes **=AVG([Profit])**. In the final control to count the number of cars, change the formula so that it becomes **=COUNT([Profit])**. The controls should look like this.

In the **Property Sheet** pane for the final **Text Box**, change the format back from **Currency** to a **Standard** number. Set this control to 0 decimal places. Check the layout and calculations in **Report View**. The completed calculations look like this. Save the report.

Alloy W	Yes	£2,700.00	11%
m	No	£2,705.00	11%
Total profit		£86,920.00	
Maximum profit		£2,705.00	
Minimum profit		£600.00	
Average profit		£1,278.24	
Number of cars		68	

If you need to show evidence of the formulae that you used for the practical examinations, use screenshot evidence of the calculated controls.

Hint

If you are using screenshot evidence of calculated controls, make sure that each control is wide enough to show all of the formulae in full. If you do not show all the formulae, marks will not be awarded.

Activity 11j

Open the file saved in Activity 11i. Produce a new report from all the data which:

● displays at the bottom of the report the maximum and minimum percentage profit for all the items in stock
● displays at the bottom of the report the average profit per item
● displays the number of items in stock
● uses appropriate formatting for all data.

11.8 Sorting data

Although *Access* has the ability to sort your data in both tables and queries, it is easier to save the sorting until the data is produced in an *Access* report.

Task 11r

Open the database that you saved at the end of Task 11q. Produce a report which:

● displays all the data for the cars made by Ford or Vauxhall
● fits within the width of a single page
● is sorted into ascending order of make and model, then into descending order of sales price
● has your name in the report header followed by 'Ford or Vauxhall'.

You created the query in Task 11f. To produce this report, select the **Create** tab and click on the **Report Wizard** icon. In the **Tables/Queries** box select the Ford or Vauxhall query. Select all fields using the double arrow key and then click on Next > twice to obtain this view.

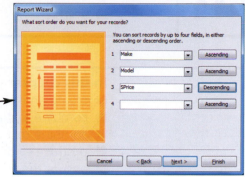

Use the drop-down lists to select the **Make** field, then the **Model** field and finally the **SPrice** field. For the **SPrice** field, click on Ascending to the right of this field and it will toggle (change) to Descending . When these field have been set as shown, click on Next > . Set the **Orientation** to **Landscape** and run through the final stages of the wizard, giving this report a suitable name. This process is the same for other data types such as dates.

Activity 11k

Open the file saved in Activity 11j. Produce a new report from all the data which:

● displays all the blue or black items
● fits within the width of a single page
● is sorted into ascending order of colour and type and then into descending order of description
● has your name in the report header followed by 'Black or blue items'.

CHAPTER 12

Integration

In this chapter you will learn how to:
- create an integrated document
- combine text and database extracts
- combine text and graphs or charts
- produce evidence of your methods
- ensure the consistency of display
- use precision framing.

For this chapter you will need these files from the CD:
- MEMO.RTF
- LETTER.RTF

For this chapter you will also need your worked copies of:
- Task 11e
- Task 11q
- Activity 10a
- Activity 10b
- Activity 10c
- Activity 10d
- Activity 10e
- Activity 10f
- Activity 10g
- Activity 10h
- Activity 10i
- Activity 10j
- Activity 10k
- Activity 10l
- Activity 10m
- Activity 10n
- Activity 11c
- Activity 11k

12.1 What is an integrated document?

In the examination you may be asked to create a document that contains text and other objects. These may include:
- images including screenshots of your work
- data taken from a database or spreadsheet
- graphs or charts
- short pieces of html
- cascading stylesheets.

If you are asked to create a document, select your word processor, in this case *Microsoft Word*. Sometimes the word report is used instead of document, as mentioned in Section 11.5. This means 'a document that gives information'. It does not mean a report created in *Microsoft Access* (although there are times when it might be appropriate to use this) and will usually mean a report created using a word processor.

12.2 Importing objects

In Chapter 10 you learnt how to import and edit text from a file, clip art and images from a variety of different sources. Many of these skills will be needed in any integrated document that you produce.

Hint

Keyboard shortcuts: You can use <Ctrl> and <C> to copy to the clipboard and <Ctrl> and <V> to paste the current contents of the clipboard.

To import text from a website, open the webpage in a web browser, in this case *Internet Explorer*, and highlight the text that you wish to use. Right click the mouse within this highlighted text and select **Copy** from the drop-down menu. Move into the word processor and right click the mouse in the position you want to place the copied text. Select **Paste** from the drop-down menu.

The same method is used to copy an image into your document from a webpage. However, note that in most countries, **copyright** laws mean that it is illegal to copy any text or image from a website without the permission of the owner of the copyright. For the practical examinations, copyright of the material on the websites that you will be asked to use will be owned by CIE, or permission to use the material for the examination will have been obtained by CIE.

12.3 Showing evidence of your methods

In the practical examinations, you may need to show the examiners how you answered the question. Using a series of **screenshots** is the quickest and easiest way of doing this. A screenshot is where you 'capture' an image of what is displayed on the screen at the time. This is copied and stored temporarily in the **clipboard** of the computer and can be pasted into a document. As well as using these basic tools provided within the *Windows* environment, there are other ways of doing this. There are a number of packages available that will produce screenshots, some of which are available as freeware. If you are already know how to use one of these packages, using them may save time in the practical examination. Because there are so many different packages available and each works in a different way, they are not covered in this book.

Hint

Make sure that the image you have captured can be seen clearly by the examiner.

To take a screenshot and capture an image of everything that is displayed on the screen at any time press the <Prt Scr> (or <Print Screen>) key on your keyboard. If you have more than one window open and wish to capture only the current window hold down the <Alt> key and press <Prt Scr>. Paste the contents of your clipboard into the word processor and edit the image (cropping and/or resizing, as described in Sections 10.7 and 10.8) to show only the sections that you require.

12.4 Showing evidence from Access

You have already produced queries, reports and calculated controls in *Access* in Chapter 11, but it is not always easy to produce the evidence of this for the practical examinations. If you have created a report containing a tick box, always print this directly from the report or use screenshot evidence. If you try to export a report containing tick boxes in rich text format for example, the tick boxes will not be included in the exported document. If you use screenshots and the evidence is in more than a single screen, make sure that you take a number of screenshots showing all of the evidence.

Task 12a

Open the file saved in Task 11q.

Show evidence of the formula and formatting used for the calculated controls for the 'Average profit' and 'Number of cars' within the report.

Open the report for Task 11q in **Design View**. Click the left mouse button on the **Text Box** containing the calculation for the average profit. If the **Property Sheet** pane is not visible, click the right mouse button on this control and select **Properties** from the drop-down menu. Select the **All** tab in the **Property Sheet** pane.

Screenshot the window using the <Prt Scr> key and paste this into a word-processed document. Crop the image so that the relevant sections can be seen. Enlarge the image so that the text can easily seen, like this.

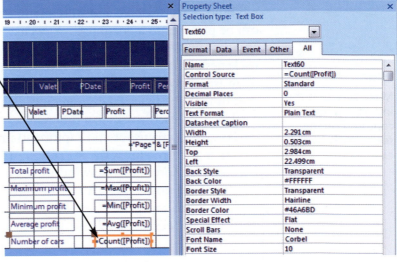

Repeat for the control for the number of cars. Left click on the **Text Box**, take another screenshot and paste this into your word-processed document. Again, crop and resize the image so that the relevant sections can be easily seen. Remember to add your name to the document before saving it.

Hint

If you need to include an *Access* report in the document, perhaps because calculated totals are also required, export the report in .rtf format and insert this into the word-processed document using the techniques shown in Section 10.1.

Activity 12a

Open the file saved in Activity 11k.
Show evidence of the formatting used for the Quantity and PPrice fields within the report to display the black or blue items.

12.5 Combining your document and a database extract

In the practical examinations you may need to take a database extract and place this into a word-processed document. Using an *Access* query rather than an *Access* report is often the easiest method of combining this information. Copying the query and pasting it into the document (as described below) gives instant results. Be careful to format the new text to match the existing document, to ensure the table fits within the margin (or column) settings and to maintain consistency of line spacing with the original document.

Task 12b

Open the file MEMO.RTF and place only the Make, Model, Colourv Year, Extras and Valet fields of all the Ford cars that need valeting as a table after the text '… that need to be cleaned:'.

Open the database that you saved in Task 11e. Open the query for the Ford cars and valeting is Yes in **Design View**. In the **Show:** row of the query, click on the tick boxes to remove the ticks from the fields that you do not need in the extract.

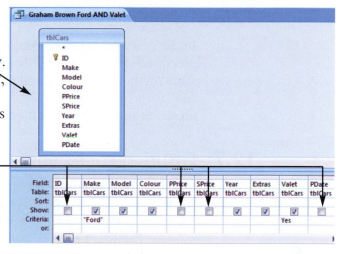

Save the changes to the query and close the query. In the **Navigation** pane, right mouse click on this query and use the drop-down menu to select **Copy**.

Open the document MEMO.RTF in your word processor. Move the cursor to the end of the text '… that need to be cleaned:' and click the right mouse button. Select **Paste** from the drop-down menu.

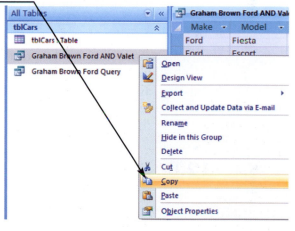

The document now looks like this.

Delete the top row from the table, and move the table so that it aligns with the left margin of the document. To do this, click in the table and adjust the ruler settings for the table. Set the font style in the table so that it matches the text in the paragraphs. The document now looks like this.

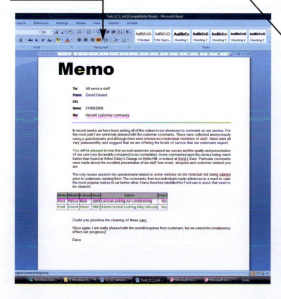

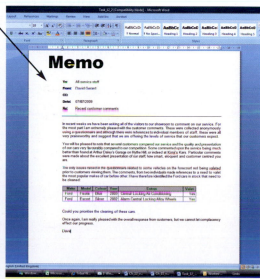

12.6 Combining your document and a graph or chart

In the practical examinations, you may need to insert a graph or chart into a word-processed document. You should treat the graph or chart as an image and use the same methods, like copy and paste. Make sure that you have displayed all of the data and labels in full in your graph before copying it into the document. This will be shown in more detail in Chapter 14.

12.7 Ensuring consistency of display

It is very important that the finished integrated document looks like a single piece of work. Every part of a finished document should look the same in terms of font style, line and paragraph spacing, paragraph settings, margin settings and headers and footers. The headers and footers should align with the margin settings of the page, not the default settings for your word processor. When you include tables or database extracts in your document these should have the same margin setting and font styles as the body text. All bulleted and numbered lists should also appear in the same style. In the practical examination, if you are not very careful about this you are likely to lose a large number of marks. This can be relevant in a question that is assessing your knowledge and understanding, if a question asks you to prepare a report, document or presentation on a topic; you are likely to be marked on both the subject content and on the quality of the document that you produce.

12.8 Precision framing

Make sure that objects like tables and charts always fit precisely into the column or page margins, unless you are told in the question to do something different. Examiners are unlikely to allow more than 1 or 2 millimetres overlap if images or other objects fit outside the column width or margins.

Output data

In this chapter you will learn how to:
- use sequential numbering to save files
- save files in different formats
- print a draft copy of the final version of a document
- print e-mails with a file attachment
- print a table, query or report in a database
- print a graph or chart.

For this chapter you will need no additional materials.

13.1 Saving documents

Version numbering

It is always wise to save each piece of work as you are producing it. You should save every 5 to 10 minutes, so that if there is a problem – a hardware fault or power cut for example – you only lose a few minutes' work.

It is always sensible to name your files with sequential numbers. For example, as each chapter of this book was being written, each was saved with a different version number so that different versions can be identified. When producing your work, if you want to go back to something from an earlier version, it is always available.

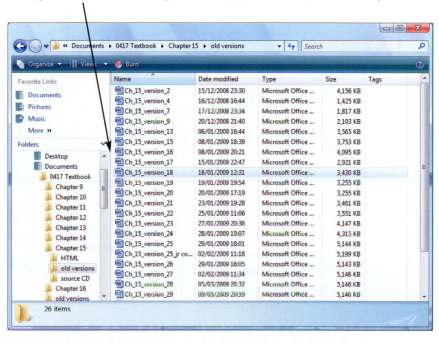

Saving a document in different formats

Documents and data can be saved in different formats. In earlier chapters, you have learnt how to import different file types, and how to export using different data types in *Access*. Saving a document has already been covered in earlier chapters, but to save a document in a different file format, click on the **Office** button followed by **Save As** and select **Other Formats**.

This will open the **Save As** window and you can choose the file type using the **Save as type:** drop-down list. This list may vary from the one shown, depending upon the configuration of your software.

The most common formats that you may need to use are text format (listed as **Plain Text**), and **Rich Text Format**. Select the one that you require and click on Save.

13.2 Printing data and documents

For all of the different applications used for the practical examinations, you can use the **Office** button followed by **Print** and **Print Preview** to check that the object that you want to print is correct before sending it to the printer. Please note that *all* documents, data, graphs, charts, presentations, etc. must be clearly labelled with your name, centre number and candidate number in order for it to be marked.

Printing any document created in colour on a black-and-white printer can cause problems. This book has sections of coloured text designed to outline key elements; for example, words in the glossary are shown in red, instructions are in blue and

Hint

Not all property windows have these settings. Each will depend upon the printer that you have installed. In this case, the **Document Properties** window can also used to change between **Color** and **Black & White** printing.

Hint

Always check that that the document that you are printing is free from errors before sending it to the printer. Use the **Print Preview** feature to help you.

fieldnames are in orange. If a page containing these three colours was printed on a black-and-white printer, each of the three colours would appear as a similar shade of grey. It would be impossible to identify which words were glossary terms, instructions or fieldnames. The use of colour in images is equally important; some colours appear identical in greyscale, particularly colours like red and green. You must be able to change the colour settings within your documents, diagrams and charts to enable the different sections to be distinctive when they are printed in black and white.

Printing a draft copy or final version of a document

You have already practised many of the skills needed for this chapter. There is often no difference between a draft copy and a final copy of a document in terms of the way that it is laid out. In some cases, draft documents may be produced to a lower quality than final copies, so you do not waste expensive printer consumables. In the practical examinations, there will be no need to change your printer settings or include watermarks on your documents, unless you are asked to do so in the question paper. If the question paper asks you to show how to set a draft copy, click on the **Office** button followed by **Print** and select **Print** again from the new list to open the **Print** window. Click on **Properties** to show the **Document Properties** or **Printing Preferences** window.

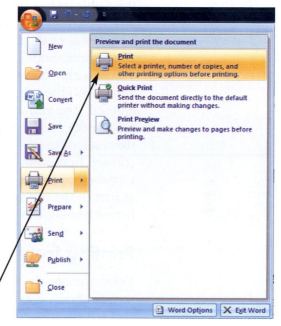

In the **Document Properties** window you can change the **Quality Settings** from the current value (in this case **Normal**) to **Draft**. You may need to screenshot this process as evidence for the examination.

Although this feature has been demonstrated using a document in the word processor, similar settings can be changed in other packages.

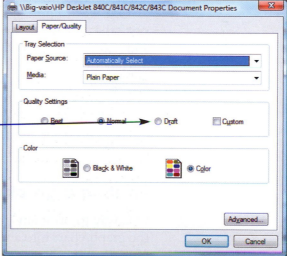

Printing emails with a file attached

Open your email browser or editor. Enter the address of the person that you are sending the message to in the **To:** box, and any copies in the **Cc:** and **Bcc:** boxes. Add the subject in the **Subject:** box and attach the file to the email. The details of the file attachment should be visible within the window, along with the other items entered. The examiners will check very carefully that each of these items is

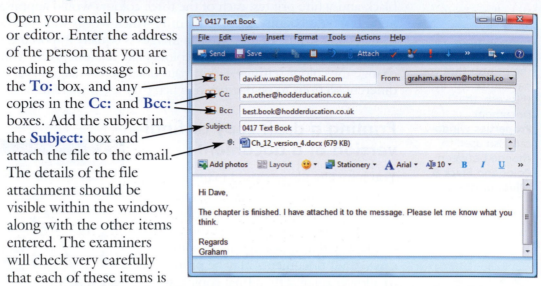

correct. In this email the address, subject and attachment are all clearly visible. Check that there are no errors in the text of the email. If you need to send evidence of this as part of the practical examination, copy the screen using <Alt> and <Prt Scr>, before pasting this into a word-processed document.

Printing from *Microsoft Access*

You have already covered many of the skills required for this in Chapter 11. This section shows you how to produce printouts of each area in *Access*. Do not forget that screenshots can be very useful as evidence, although documents containing a number of screenshots can be very large files and take a long time to print.

One way to print a table or query is to open the table or query, and copy and paste the data into a word-processed document. This document can be edited (to add your name and other details), saved and printed. A table or query can be printed directly from *Access* by double clicking on the table name or query name in the **Navigation** pane to open it and clicking on the **Office** button followed by **Print**.

Use a report in *Access* if you need to show calculated controls and improved page layout. Printing a report uses the same method as printing tables and queries. The report can be opened and printed using the **Office** button followed by **Print**. Reports can be exported for inclusion in a word-processed document as outlined in Chapter 11.

Printing a graph or chart from *Microsoft Excel*

One way to print any graph or chart is to open the graph/chart, and copy and paste the graph/chart into a word-processed document. You can add your name, candidate number and centre number and any other text that you require before saving and printing. A graph or chart can be printed directly from *Excel* by opening the graph/chart and clicking on the **Office** button followed by **Print**.

CHAPTER 14

Data analysis

In this chapter you will learn how to:

- create the layout for a spreadsheet model
- enter text and numeric data into a spreadsheet
- use editing functions such as cut, copy and paste
- enter formulae and simple functions into a spreadsheet
- replicate formulae and functions in the spreadsheet
- test the data model
- select subsets of data within a spreadsheet
- sort the data within the spreadsheet
- change the display and format of cells within a spreadsheet
- change the size of rows and columns within a spreadsheet
- adjust the page orientation
- save a spreadsheet
- print a spreadsheet displaying formulae or values
- create a graph or chart
- label a graph or chart
- extract segments from a pie chart
- add a secondary axis
- set axis scales
- change chart colours to print in black and white
- create, rename and delete files using an operating system
- access folders/directories within an operating system.

For this chapter you will need these source files from the CD:

- CLASSLIST.CSV
- CLIENT.CSV
- CLUBS.CSV
- COSTS.CSV
- EMPLOYEES.CSV
- ITEMS.CSV
- JOBS.CSV
- OPERATORS.CSV
- PROJECT.CSV
- RAINFALL.CSV

- ROOMS.CSV
- SALARY.CSV
- SALES.CSV
- STAFF.CSV
- TASKS.CSV
- TEACHERS.CSV
- TUCKSHOP.CSV
- TUTORS.CSV
- WEBHITS.CSV

14.1 What is a data model?

For data analysis, you will use a **spreadsheet model** to explore different possible answers. These models are often financial, mathematical or scientific. It is sometimes called using a 'what if' scenario or 'what if' modelling. It lets you change data in the spreadsheet to see what will happen to the results. In the practical examinations, you may be asked to build a simple spreadsheet model and change data within the model, or even change the model itself, to produce different results.

Hint

Remember that a column holds up the roof and you can see a row of houses.

Spreadsheet basics

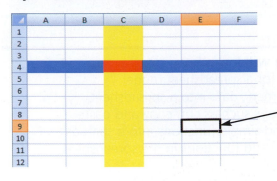

You will use the spreadsheet *Microsoft Excel* to create your data model. A spreadsheet is a two-dimensional table split into rows and columns. It looks like this.

It is made up of a number of individual cells, like this. This cell (with the darker outline) is the cell that has the cursor within it. To help us to use individual cells in a spreadsheet, each cell has an address. In this example the cell with the cursor in it is called cell E9 and the cell that has been coloured red is called cell C4. The red cell and all of the yellow cells are in column C, and the red cell and all of the blue cells are in row 4.

Task 14a

Create a spreadsheet to multiply any two numbers together and display the result.

Each cell in a spreadsheet can hold one of three things. It can contain:

- a **number**
- text, which is called a **label**
- a **formula**, which always starts with an = sign.

Move the cursor into cell A1 and click the left mouse button. Type in the label 'Multiplying two numbers'. Move the cursor down into cell A2 and enter a number. Repeat this for cell A3. In cell A4, enter the formula **=A2*A3** so that the spreadsheet looks like this.

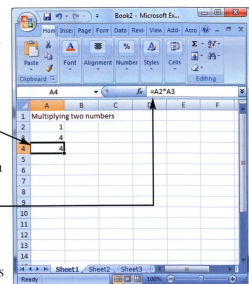

You will see that the formula is not visible in the sheet and that the cell A4 only contains the answer to the calculation within this cell. The formula for the cell containing the cursor can be seen in the formula bar.

If you have created the spreadsheet as shown, you should be able to change the contents of cells A2 and A3 to multiply any two numbers together. The changing of cells to see the results is called **modelling**.

If you enter large numbers into cells A2 and A3 the result in cell A4 may not appear as you expect it to. It may look like this.

This tells you that the number is too large to fit into the column. To expand the width of column, move the cursor to the end of the column heading for column A like this.

Double click the left mouse button to expand the column width to fit the longest item stored in this column. The spreadsheet now looks like this. You can see how the label and all of the data are fully visible.

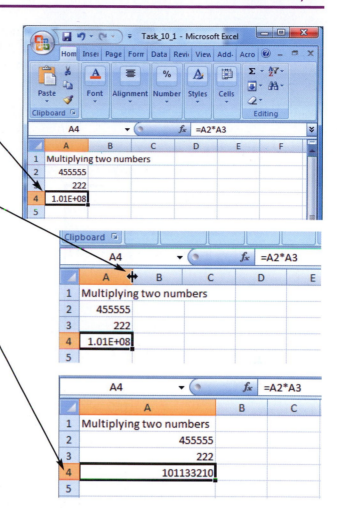

14.2 Creating a data model

Task 14b

Create a spreadsheet to display the times table for any number you choose to enter. Print your spreadsheet, showing values and formulae.

For this task, you need to design and create the data model to calculate and display the times table for any number that you choose. You must therefore have a single cell that contains the number to use for all the calculations. In this model you can place a simple number like 2 in cell A1, so that you can easily tell if you have made a mistake with your formulae later on. Type the label 'Times Table' in cell B1.

You are going to create the times table in cells A3 to B12, with those cells in column A holding the number to multiply by and those cells in column B holding formulae to calculate the answer. Move the cursor into cell A3 and enter the number 1. Move into cell A4 and enter the number 2. Rather than repeating this process another eight times for the numbers 3 to 10, highlight the cells A3 and A4, as shown here. Move the cursor to the drag handle in the bottom right corner of these cells.

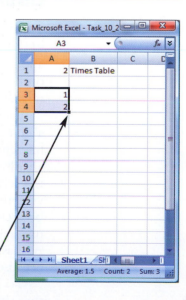

Click and hold the left mouse button on the drag handle, dragging it down to the bottom right corner of cell A12. This replicates (copies) the cell contents. *Excel* realises that the numbers in cells A3 and A4 increase by 1, so uses this pattern as it replicates the cells down.

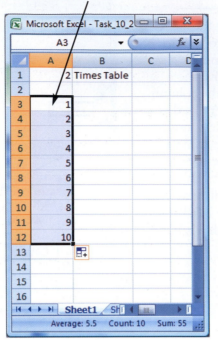

Move the cursor into cell B3 and enter the formula **=A3*$A$1**. The $ symbols in the reference to cell A1 will be used by *Excel* to keep that cell reference the same when this cell is replicated into cells B4 to B12. Use the drag handle in cell B3 to replicate this formula into the cells down to B12. The results should look like this.

Without checking the formulae, you can see that this has produced the correct results for the two times table. Change cell A1 to another number to check that the formula works correctly. Print this values view of the spreadsheet using the **Office** button, followed by **Print** and then **Print** again.

Displaying formulae

To display (and then print) the formulae used in the spreadsheet, select the **Formulas** tab and find the **Formula Auditing** section. Click on the **Show Formulas** icon. The spreadsheet now looks more like this.

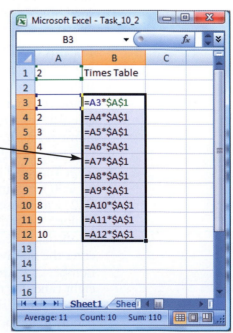

Each of these formulae contains both absolute and relative referencing. In cell B3, the reference to cell A1 (with the $ symbols) is an **absolute reference** and the reference to cell A3 is a **relative reference**. You can see from this view that the reference in cell B3 to cell A3 has been changed as the cell has been replicated, as it uses relative referencing, but the reference to cell A1 has not been changed during the replication, because absolute referencing has been used.

To return to the view of the spreadsheet that shows the values, click on the **Show Formulas** icon again.

More editing tools

Other standard *Windows* editing tools can be used in *Excel*, like cut, copy and paste. These can be used to copy the contents of one cell into another cell. An alternative method of replicating cell B3 into cells B4 to B12 is to enter the formula in cell B3, right mouse click on this cell and select **Copy** from the drop-down menu. Highlight the cells B4 to B12 and right mouse click, selecting **Paste** from the drop-down menu. This will paste the formulae, adjusting the cell references for A3 as this is a relative reference but retaining the absolute reference. The result is identical.

Accuracy of the data entry

When you are asked to 'create a data model that looks like this', make sure that you copy the model in the question paper exactly as shown. Do not try to make improvements or add enhancements (like colour and formatting) unless asked to do so. This is very important. Some students loose marks by trying to 'improve' the spreadsheet, for example by trying to left align a column containing numbers. *Excel*, quite correctly, should automatically right align numbers, so by left aligning this data it is now formatted incorrectly. Do not insert rows or columns, or remove rows or columns containing blank spaces, unless instructed to do so.

When you type data into a spreadsheet (or any other form of document) you must make sure that the data that you have entered is identical to the original source document or examination question paper. A large number of marks can be lost by rushing the data entry and not checking that it has been entered with 100 per cent accuracy. This is even more important when working in a spreadsheet because one error, for example a mistyped number or decimal point in the wrong place, could cause all of the data in the spreadsheet to be incorrect. Care must also be taken when entering a formula, as one small error is likely to stop the spreadsheet working as it is expected to.

Using formulae

Simple mathematical operators can be used to add, subtract, multiply, divide and calculate indices (powers) of a number. Each mathematical operator is placed in a formula, as you did in Tasks 14a and 14b. For addition use the + symbol, for subtraction use the – symbol, for multiplication use the * symbol and for division use the / symbol. Indices are calculated using the ^ symbol, so the contents of cell A2 squared (x^2) would be typed as **=A2^2**.

Task 14c

Open the file OPERATORS.CSV. Place two numbers of your choice in cells B1 and B2. Calculate in cell:

- B4, the sum of the two numbers
- B5, the difference between the two numbers
- B6, the product of the two numbers
- B7, the contents of cell B1 divided by the contents of cell B2
- B8, the contents of cell B1 to the power of the contents of cell B2.

Check that the formulae have worked before printing your spreadsheet showing the values and again showing the formulae used.

Open the file OPERATORS.CSV in *Excel*. Extend the width of column A so that all the labels are fully visible (see Task 14a). Move the cursor into cell B1 and enter the number 4, then into cell B2 and enter the number 2. These numbers have been chosen so that you can easily check your calculations. It is wise to perform all calculations by hand before entering the formulae, to make sure that you understand the formulae that you are using and to see the results of the calculation before the computer has shown you its results. These calculations may look like this.

Number X	4
Number Y	2

X + Y	4 + 2 = 6
X − Y	4 − 2 = 2
X * Y	4 * 2 = 8
X/Y	4/2 = 2
X ^ Y	4 ^ 2 = 16

- **Addition**: Move the cursor into cell B4. The sum of the two numbers is needed in this cell, which means to add the contents of the two cells. There are two ways of doing this: one method uses the + operator and the second uses a function. You will be shown how to use the SUM function later in this chapter, but the formula needed to enter in this cell for the + operator is **=B1+B2**. This can be typed in followed by the <Enter> key, or you can type the = sign, click the cursor into cell B1, type + and click in cell B2 before pressing the <Enter> key.
- **Subtraction**: Move the cursor into cell B5. The difference between two numbers is needed in this cell. Enter (using either of the methods described in the addition section above) the formula **=B1–B2**, followed by the <Enter> key.
- **Multiplication**: Move the cursor into cell B6. The product of two numbers means to multiply the two numbers together and you need to enter the formula **=B1*B2**, followed by the <Enter> key.
- **Division**: Move the cursor into cell B7. This cell needs a calculation to divide the contents of cell B1 by the contents of cell B2 using the formula **=B1/B2**, followed by the <Enter> key.
- **Indices**: Move the cursor into cell B8. This cell needs to calculate the contents of cell B1 to the power of the contents of cell B2 using the formula **=B1^B2**, followed by the <Enter> key.

Hint

The ^ symbol is often found using <Shift> and '6'.

To check that the formulae have worked correctly, compare your original paper-based calculations with the values in the spreadsheet.

You will notice that the values chosen earlier in this task were carefully selected to make the maths easy. The more difficult calculations are likely to be the division and indices. These numbers were selected so that the 4 divided by 2 gives an easy result and the 4 to the power of 2 is reasonably easy (4*4).

Print the values, making sure that your name is fully visible on the printout. Select the **Formulas** tab, then click on the **Show Formulas** icon in the **Formula Auditing** section to change the display to show the formulae, which should appear like this. Save and print the spreadsheet.

	A	B	C
1	First number - X	4	
2	Second number - Y	2	
3			
4	Sum of X and Y	6	
5	Difference between X and Y	2	
6	Product of X and Y	8	
7	X divided by Y	2	
8	X to the power Y	16	

	A	B
1	First number - X	4
2	Second number - Y	2
3		
4	Sum of X and Y	=B1+B2
5	Difference between X and Y	=B1-B2
6	Product of X and Y	=B1*B2
7	X divided by Y	=B1/B2
8	X to the power Y	=B1^B2
9		

med cells and ranges

individual cell or an area of a spreadsheet is going to be used a number of
the formulae of a spreadsheet, it is often a good idea to give it a name.
should be short and meaningful. In the case of a large spreadsheet, it is
remember the name of a cell, for example VAT or AveMiles, rather than
to remember the cell reference, for example AC456 or X232. Once a cell or a
range of cells has been named, you use this name in all your formulae.

> **Task 14d**
>
> Open the file SALES.CSV. This spreadsheet will be used to calculate bonus payments to sales
> staff for a small company.
> Name cell B1 'Unit'. Name cells A5 to C7 'Rate'. Name cells B11 to G18 'Sold'.

Open the file and find cell B2. You must name this cell 'Unit'. Right click on the
mouse in this cell to get the drop-down
menu. Select the option to **Name a
Range...** which will open the **New Name**
window. In the **Name:** box, *Excel* will
suggest a name for the range. It uses the
layout of your spreadsheet to do this. For
the practical examinations, ignore this
suggestion (in this case the name that it
suggests is too long to be used) and
overtype it with the word **Unit**, as
instructed in the question. Add suitable
text in the **Comment** box so that the
window looks like this. To name the
range click on OK .

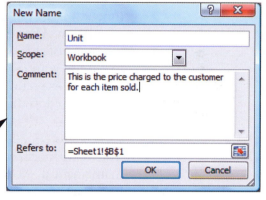

When you move the cursor into cell
B1, you will see in the **Name Box** that it
is now called **Unit**.

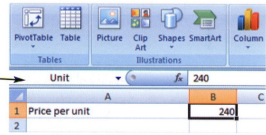

To create the named range for the rate, you must
highlight the cells between A5 and C7. Do this
by clicking on cell A5 and whilst holding down
the left mouse button, dragging the cursor to cell
C7. Click the right mouse button within the
highlighted range to get the drop-down menu.
Change the contents of the **Name:** box to **Rate**.
Check that the **New Name** window looks like
this before clicking on OK . The name of the
range is only visible in the **Name Box** if only the
cells in the range are highlighted.

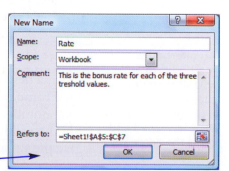

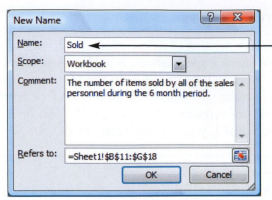

The final named range can be created in a similar way. Highlight cells B11 to G18, then name this range **Sold**. Each of these named cells and ranges will be used in other tasks. Save this spreadsheet as Task_14d as an *Excel* spreadsheet.

Using functions

A formula in *Excel* starts with an = sign. It could be a simple formula using mathematical operators like **=B1+B2**, a complex formula using nested statements (this will be explained later in this chapter) or a formula including functions. A function has a pre-defined name like **SUM** or **AVERAGE** that perform a particular calculation. There are many of these functions in *Excel*, many of which are beyond the scope of this book, but each has a reserved function name. If a question asks you to choose your own name for a cell or range, try to avoid using these function names. This section does not contain all of the functions available or all those that may be used in the examinations.

SUM

The SUM function adds two or more numbers together. In Task 14c, you used the mathematical + operator and the formula **=B1+B2** to add the contents of two cells together. With only two cells to be added, this was the most efficient way of doing this. If there had been more figures to add, particularly if they were grouped together in the spreadsheet, using the SUM function would have been more efficient.

Task 14e
Copy this spreadsheet model and calculate:
• the total number of hours worked by all of these five people
• the average number of hours worked per person
• the maximum number of hours worked by any of these five people
• the minimum number of hours worked by any of these five people.

	A	B
1	**Rate of Pay**	£12.80
2		
3	**Name**	**Hours**
4	David Watson	26
5	Graham Brown	20
6	John Reeves	17
7	Brian Sargent	4
8	Dan Bray	13
9	**Total**	
10	**Average**	
11	**Maximum**	
12	**Minimum**	

Hint

An alternative method is to enter =SUM(then drag the cursor to highlight cells B4 to B8, then type) and press the enter key.

Open a new sheet and copy the labels and values exactly as shown in the task. Select the **Home** tab and use the (bold) icon to embolden the cells shown. To find the total number of hours worked you will need to click the cursor into cell B9 and use SUM to add up the list of numbers. Enter the formula **=SUM(B4:B8)**. This should give the value 80.

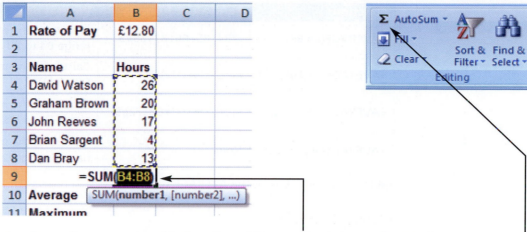

An alternative way to use this function without typing it into cell B9 is for you to use **AutoSum**. Move the cursor into cell B9, select the **Home** tab and find the **Editing** section. Click on the **AutoSum** icon. This will place the SUM function into cell B9 and attempt to work out which cells you wish to add up (by looking at the layout of your spreadsheet). It does not always get this range correct, so check carefully. If the range is correct (as it is in this case) press the <Enter> key to accept the **AutoSum**. If it is not correct, you can highlight the cells to be added before pressing the <Enter> key.

There are many ways of using the SUM function, some of which are shown in Table 14.1.

Function	Equivalent formula	What it does
=SUM(B4:B8)	=B4+B5+B6+B7+B8	Adds up the contents of all the cells in the range B4 to B8
=SUM(D3,D8,D12)	=D3+D8+D12	Adds up the contents of the cells D3, D8 and D12
=SUM(D5:D8,F2)	=D5+D6+D7+D8+F2	Adds up the contents of the cells in the range D5 to D8 and the contents of cell F2
=SUM(MyRange)	None	Adds up the contents of all the cells within a named range called MyRange; this can be used with any named range

Table 14.1 Ways of using the SUM function

As you can see, the range of cells selected within these functions can include a number of individual cells, ranges of cells, named ranges, named cells or a combination of these. The average, maximum, minimum and count functions also work like this.

AVERAGE

To find the average number of hours worked, click the cursor into cell B10 and use AVERAGE to calculate the mean (average) of a list of numbers. Enter the formula **=AVERAGE(B4:B8)**. This should give the value 16. There are many ways of using the AVERAGE function, some of which are shown in Table 14.2 overleaf.

Function	Equivalent formula	What it does
=AVERAGE(B4:B8)	=(B4+B5+B6+B7+B8)/5	Calculates the mean of the cells in the range B4 to B8
=AVERAGE(D3,D8,D12)	=(D3+D8+D12)/3	Calculates the mean of the cells D3, D8 and D12
=AVERAGE(D5:D8,F2)	=(D5+D6+D7+D8+F2)/5	Calculates the mean of the cells in the range D5 to D8 and cell F2
=AVERAGE(MyRange)	None	Calculates the mean of the cells in a named range called MyRange

Table 14.2 Ways of using the AVERAGE function

MAX

To find the person who worked the most hours, click the cursor into cell B11 and use **MAX** to select the largest (maximum) figure within the list of numbers. Enter the formula **=MAX(B4:B8)**. This should give the value 26.

MIN

To find the person who worked the least number of hours, click the cursor into cell B12 and use **MIN** to select the smallest (minimum) figure from the list. Enter the formula **=MIN(B4:B8)**. This should give the value 4. The finished spreadsheet should look like this. Save this spreadsheet as Task_14e.

	A	B
1	**Rate of Pay**	£12.80
2		
3	**Name**	**Hours**
4	David Watson	26
5	Graham Brown	20
6	John Reeves	17
7	Brian Sargent	4
8	Dan Bray	13
9	**Total**	**80**
10	**Average**	**16**
11	**Maximum**	**26**
12	**Minimum**	**4**

Activity 14a

Open the file TUCKSHOP.CSV.
In cells B14 to B17, calculate the total number of days that all the students worked in the school shop, the average number of days worked, and the maximum and minimum values. Place your name on the spreadsheet. Print your spreadsheet showing the values. Print your spreadsheet showing the formulae used.

Hint

Setting a cell as an integer value will truncate the contents of a cell to remove the decimal/fraction part of the number. This is *not* the same as formatting a cell to 0 decimal places which stops the decimal/fraction part from being displayed but not from being used in a calculation.

Task 14f

John Reeves did an extra four hours' work. Change the spreadsheet that you created in Task 14e to show the new figures. The manager wants to see the average number of hours worked displayed as:

● an integer value

● rounded to the nearest whole hour.

Print two copies of the spreadsheet showing these values.

Open the file Ch_14_Task_14e. Change the contents of cell B6 to 21 to add the four extra hours that he worked. This gives an average value of 16.8 hours. Move the cursor into cell C9 and enter the text 'Integer', then move into cell D9 and enter the text 'Rounding'. To get the first value requested by the manager, we have to set cell B10 to hold an integer value.

INT

In mathematics, an integer is the word used to describe a whole number (with no decimals or fractions). Within *Excel*, the **INT** function takes the whole number part of a number and ignores all digits after the decimal point. Move the cursor into cell C10 and enter the formula **=INT(B10)**. This should give the value 16.

ROUND

Move the cursor into cell D10 and enter the formula **=ROUND(B10,0)**. This uses the **ROUND** function which takes the content of cell B10 and rounds the number to 0 decimal places: if the next digit is five or more the number will be increased by one. For example, in cell B10 the value is 16.8, so the content of D10 is 17, as it has rounded the value to the nearest whole number. The spreadsheet should look like this.

	A	B	C	D
1	Rate of Pay	£12.80		
2				
3	Name	Hours		
4	David Watson	26		
5	Graham Brown	20		
6	John Reeves	17		
7	Brian Sargent	4		
8	Dan Bray	13		
9	Total	80	Integer	Round
10	Average	16	16	17
11	Maximum	26		
12	Minimum	4		

Rounding can be used with a number of decimal places, for example using rounding for currencies with 2 decimal places can avoid calculation errors. Table 14.3 shows more examples of how you can use the ROUND function, using cell A1 which contains the number **62.5512**.

Function	Result of rounding	What it does
=ROUND(A1,2)	62.55	Rounds the contents of A1 to two decimal places
=ROUND(A1,1)	62.6	Rounds the contents of A1 to one decimal place. Note that the figure 5 in the 62.5512 has forced the previous figure to be rounded up
=ROUND(A1,0)	63	Rounds the contents of A1 to no decimal places. Note that the figure 5 in the 62.5512 has forced the previous figure to be rounded up
=ROUND(A1,-1)	60	Rounds the contents of A1 to the nearest 10. The negative value for decimal places allows this function to round numbers in tens, hundreds, etc.
=ROUND(A1,-2)	100	Rounds the contents of A1 to the nearest 100. Note that the figure 6 has forced the previous figure to be rounded up from 0 to 1

Table 14.3 Ways of using the ROUND function

Save and print a copy of the spreadsheet showing the average number of hours worked displayed as an integer value. Print a copy of the spreadsheet showing the average number of hours worked rounded to the nearest whole hour.

Activity 14b

Create a new spreadsheet model to calculate:

- the whole number part of 375.56411
- 375.56411 rounded to two decimal places
- 375.56411 rounded to the nearest whole number
- 375.56411 rounded to the nearest ten
- 375.56411 rounded to the nearest hundred
- 375.56411 rounded to the nearest thousand.

COUNT

For this task you will need to use functions that count different values. It is possible to count the number of numeric (number) values in a list using the **COUNT** function. Open the file, place the cursor in cell A22 and enter the formula **=COUNT(A2:A19)**. This will look at the range A2 to A19 (notice that you have not counted cell A1 which contains the title, nor cell A20 that may be used for something else later) and count only the cells with numbers in them. It will not count any blank spaces and should give the value 7.

COUNTA

The **COUNTA** function works in a similar way to the COUNT function. Rather than counting just the number of numeric values, this function counts the number of numeric or text values displayed in the cells. It will not count any blank cells within the range. In *Excel* there is not a count function for just text values, so the COUNTA and COUNT functions will both be used to calculate the number of workers on the project. Place the cursor in cell A24 and enter the formula **=COUNTA(A2:A19)-COUNT(A2:A19)**. This will look at the range A2 to A19 and count the cells with text or numbers in them, then subtract the number of cells with numbers in to leave only the cells with text in them, in other words the names of the employees. It should give the value 9 and look like this.

	A
1	Project 142
2	Laila Aboli
3	4
4	Sri Paryanti
5	7
6	David Watson
7	2
8	Graham Brown
9	12
10	John Reeves
11	
12	Brian Sargent
13	6
14	Dan Bray
15	
16	Thirumalar Asokmani
17	3
18	Lea Cabusbusan
19	2
20	
21	Number of workers who have not finished
22	7
23	Number of workers on the project
24	9

A
Number of workers who have not finished
=COUNT(A2:A19)
Number of workers on the project
=COUNTA(A2:A19)-COUNT(A2:A19)

COUNTIF

For this task, you need to count how many people have each type of job. Open the file and place the cursor in cell B24. The function needed for this task is **COUNTIF**, which looks at the cells within a given range and counts the number of cells in that range that meet a given condition. The condition is placed in the function and can be a number, a string, an inequality or a cell reference. There are a number of ways the COUNTIF function can be used: any of the formulae given in Table 14.4 can be entered in cell B24 and will give the correct result.

Replicate this formula into cells B25 to B28. As these cells are to be replicated, methods three and four in Table 14.4 are the most efficient, as you do not have to edit each formula with a different name for each row. If an examination question asks you to show evidence of absolute and relative referencing, then method three would be the most appropriate. If named ranges are required or absolute and relative referencing are not asked for in the question method four is the most efficient.

Hint

Note in examples one and three in Table 14.4 that the range $B$3:$B$21 has been set as an absolute reference so that this range is always in the same place if the formula is replicated. Also note that examples three and four have cell A24 set as a relative reference so that it will look for the next job title when the formula is replicated. Named ranges are absolute references, but you must show screenshot evidence that you have named the range correctly in the practical examinations.

Function	What is does?
=COUNTIF($B$3:$B$21,"Director")	Counts the number of cells in the range B3 to B21 that contain the word 'Director'
=COUNTIF(Job,"Director")	Counts the number of cells in the named range Job (B3 to B21) that contain the word 'Director'. This only works if cells B3 to B21 have been named 'Job'
=COUNTIF($B$3:$B$21,A24)	Counts the number of cells in the range B3 to B21 that contain the same text as the contents of cell A24
=COUNTIF(Job,A24)	Counts the number of cells in the named range Job (B3 to B21) that contain the same text as the contents of cell A24. This only works if cells B3 to B21 have been named 'Job'

Table 14.4 Alternative formulae using the COUNTIF function

To count the number of employees with less than five years' experience, place the cursor in cell B31 and enter the formula **=COUNTIF($C$3:$C$21,"<5")**. This will look at the range C3 to C21 and count the cells with a number value of less than five. The speech marks around the <5 are needed to tell *Excel* that it is dealing with another formula (in this case an inequality), rather than searching for the symbols <5. The spreadsheet should show the value 8.

To count the number of employees with ten or more years' experience, place the cursor in cell B32 and enter the formula **=COUNTIF($C$3:$C$21,">=10")**. The value calculated should be **5**. Save your spreadsheet as Ch_14_Task_14h.

IF

An **IF** function contains a pair of brackets and within the brackets three parts, each separated by a comma. An example of an IF function is **=IF(A1=5,A2*0.05,"No discount")**. The first part is a condition; in this example, it is testing to see if cell A1 contains the number 5. The other two parts are what to do if the condition is met, and what to do if it is not met. If the condition is met a number or label could be placed in the cell, or a reference to another cell, or even a calculation that needs to be performed. The same range of options applies if a condition is not met. In this example, if the condition is met, the result of multiplying the contents of cell A2 by the figure 0.05 is displayed in this cell. If the condition is not met this cell will display the text 'No discount'.

Open the file and place the cursor in cell D2. Enter the label 'Category'. Place the cursor in cell D3 and enter the formula: **=IF(C3>=10,"Very experienced","Not experienced")**. The reason that C3>=10 is used rather than C3>9 (which in many circumstances would be a more efficient formula), is because one employee has 0.2 years' experience. As the data does not all contain whole numbers, there could be an employee with 9.5 years experience so this would not work for all data. Do not use absolute referencing in this formula as the reference to cell C3 needs to change when you replicate the formula. Replicate this formula so it is copied into cells D4 to D21. Your spreadsheet should look similar to this.

Save your spreadsheet as Ch_14_Task_14h.

	A	B	C	D
1	**Project 153**			
2	**Name**	**Job**	**Years exp**	**Category**
3	Laila Aboli	Programmer	3	Not experienced
4	Greg Mina	Programmer	2	Not experienced
5	Sri Paryanti	Analyst	12	Very experienced
6	Bishen Patel	Sales	5	Not experienced
7	Rupinder Singh	Engineer	7	Not experienced
8	Sergio Gonzalez	Programmer	5	Not experienced
9	Rupinder Vas	Sales	6	Not experienced
10	Henri Ramos	Sales	10	Very experienced
11	John Mortlock	Programmer	14	Very experienced
12	Cameron Garnham	Analyst	7	Not experienced
13	Brian Guthrie	Director	3	Not experienced
14	Julia Frobisher	Engineer	6	Not experienced
15	Dan McNevin	Programmer	9	Not experienced
16	Patrick O'Malley	Engineer	11	Very experienced
17	Thirumalar Asokmani	Sales	10	Very experienced
18	Sean O'Byrne	Programmer	2	Not experienced
19	Lea Cabusbusan	Programmer	1	Not experienced
20	Brian O'Driscoll	Programmer	0.2	Not experienced
21	Wim Van Hoffmann	Engineer	2	Not experienced

Nested formulae and functions

A nested formula or function is having one formula or function inside another one. Sometimes nested formulae could contain several formulae nested within each other. If the nested functions include a number of IF statements, be careful to work in a logical order, either from smallest to largest or vice versa (depending upon the question). Do *not* start with middle values, this will give incorrect results.

Hint

Note that as the conditions are all 'greater than', they have been placed in reverse order. For example, if the value for experience was 40 and the condition <5 was first, then >=5 next and then >=10: the first condition <5 would be not true, so it would go to the next condition; >=5 would be true, so the result displayed would be 'Experienced'; it would never get as far as the test for >=10.

Task 14j

Open the file that you saved in Task 14i.
Change the formulae in cells D3 to D21to display 'Not experienced' if they have less than five years' experience, 'Experienced' if they have five or more years' experience and 'Very experienced' for employees with ten or more years' experience.

For this task, three conditions exist. If the value for experience is:
- >=10 then display 'Very experienced'
- >=5 then display 'Experienced'
- <5 then display 'Not experienced'.

Place the cursor into cell D3 and change the formula so that it becomes:
=IF(C3>=10,"Very experienced", IF(C3>=5,"Experienced","Not experienced"))

Notice how the second formula (highlighted in yellow) has been placed as a 'No' condition within the first formula. Be very careful to get the brackets correct, each condition has one open and one close bracket. When you work through this formula, it checks whether the value is greater than or equal to ten first; if so, it displays the correct text. Then if it was not true it would check if the value is greater than or equal to five next, if so it displays the correct text. As there are no other conditions that could occur, rather than having another nested statement the resulting text has been placed.

Replicate this formula into cells D4 to D21. Your spreadsheet should look similar to this. Save your spreadsheet as Ch_14_Task_14j.

Activity 14f

Open the file that you saved in Activity 14e.
Change the formulae in cells F2 to F6 to display 'Add to this house' if the number of students in this house is fewer than six, 'Ideal number' if there are between six and ten students and 'Full' if the number is more than ten.

	A	B	C	D
1	Project 153			
2	Name	Job	Years exp	Category
3	Laila Aboli	Programmer	3	Not experienced
4	Greg Mina	Programmer	2	Not experienced
5	Sri Paryanti	Analyst	12	Very experienced
6	Bishen Patel	Sales	5	Experienced
7	Rupinder Singh	Engineer	7	Experienced
8	Sergio Gonzalez	Programmer	5	Experienced
9	Rupinder Vas	Sales	6	Experienced
10	Henri Ramos	Sales	10	Very experienced
11	John Mortlock	Programmer	14	Very experienced
12	Cameron Garnham	Analyst	7	Experienced
13	Brian Guthrie	Director	3	Not experienced
14	Julia Frobisher	Engineer	6	Experienced
15	Dan McNevin	Programmer	9	Experienced
16	Patrick O'Malley	Engineer	11	Very experienced
17	Thirumalar Asokmani	Sales	10	Very experienced
18	Sean O'Byrne	Programmer	2	Not experienced
19	Lea Cabusbusan	Programmer	1	Not experienced
20	Brian O'Driscoll	Programmer	0.2	Not experienced
21	Wim Van Hoffmann	Engineer	2	Not experienced

SUMIF

SUMIF works in a similar way to COUNTIF. It compares each value in a range of cells and if the value matches the given condition it adds another related cell to form a running total.

Add the labels as required by the task into cells A34, A35 and A36. Move the cursor into cell B35 and enter the formula **=SUMIF($B$3:$B$21,A35,$C$3: $C$21)**. The total for this cell starts at zero. This looks at the contents of each row in the range B3 to B21 and compares the value in each cell to the contents of cell A35 (which contains the text 'Programmer'). If these two items are identical it adds the value from the same row within the range C3 to C21 to the total. When all rows in this range have been checked the total is displayed in this cell. This happens within a fraction of a second as you press the <Enter> key or change any value within these ranges.

	A	B
34	Total experience for:	
35	Programmer	36.2
36	Engineer	26
37		

To total the hours for the engineers, place in cell B36 the formula **=SUMIF($B$3:$B$21,A36,$C$3:$C$21)**. The results of these formulae should look like this. Save the spreadsheet as Ch_14_Task_14k.

Using lookups

The term 'look up', as used in the practical examinations, means to look up from a list. It does not mean that you should use the LOOKUP function, as there are three variations of the LOOKUP function that can be used within *Excel*. These are: **LOOKUP**, **HLOOKUP** and **VLOOKUP**.

LOOKUP

LOOKUP is used to look up information using data in the first row or the first column of a range of cells and returns a relative value. For the purpose of the practical examinations, this is probably the least useful of the three formulae.

HLOOKUP

HLOOKUP is a function that performs a horizontal look-up of data. This should be used when the values that you wish to compare your data with are stored in a single row. The values to be looked up are stored in the rows below these cells.

Task 14l

Open the file JOBS.CSV.
Insert formulae in the Description column to look up and display the JobTitle using the JobCode as the look-up value.

Open the file JOBS.CSV and click the left mouse button to place the cursor in cell C6. Enter the formula **=HLOOKUP(B6,$B$2:$H$3,2)** into this cell. This formula will look up and compare the contents of cell B6 with the contents of each cell in the top (horizontal) row of the range B2 to H3. When it finds a match, it will take the value or label stored in the second row which is directly under the matched cell. The two at the end of the formula tells *Excel* to look in the second row of the given range. Replicate this formula into cells C7 to C27. The results should look similar to this. Save the spreadsheet as Ch_14_Task_14l.

	A	B	C	D	E	F	G	H
1	Project 160							
2	JobCode	1	2	3	4	5	6	7
3	JobTitle	Director	Engineer	Analyst	Sales	Programmer	Tester	Clerical
4								
5	Name	JobCode	Description					
6	Laila Aboli	5	Programmer					
7	Greg Mina	5	Programmer					
8	Sri Paryanti	3	Analyst					
9	Bishen Patel	4	Sales					
10	Rupinder Singh	2	Engineer					
11	Sergio Gonzalez	5	Programmer					

VLOOKUP

VLOOKUP is a function that performs a vertical look-up of data. This should be used when the values that you wish to compare your data with are stored in a single column. The values to be looked up are stored in the columns to the right of these cells. The look-up data can be stored either in the same file or in a different file.

Task 14m

Open the file TASKS.CSV.
Insert formulae in the CurrentTask column to look up the client, using the TaskCode for the look-up value and the file CLIENT.CSV. Make sure that you use both absolute and relative referencing within your function.

Hint

Experiment with these settings. Change the value in cell B24 to 5.2 See the result of this change. Now change the exact match condition from False to True in cell C24. See the result of this change. Try other numbers like 5.9 in B24 to see what happens

Open the file TASKS.CSV and click the left mouse button to place the cursor in cell C3. The Task instructs you to use the file CLIENT.CSV for the lookup. Examine this file by opening it in a new spreadsheet. Look at the layout of this file to decide which type of look up formula to use. CLIENT.CSV looks like this. ———→

	A	B
1	TaskCode	Client
2	1	Rootrainer
3	2	Quattichem
4	3	Hothouse Design
5	4	Avricom
6	5	Binnaccount
7	6	LGY
8	7	Rock ICT

Because it is stored with the look up data in vertical columns, a VLOOKUP is the most appropriate formula to use. Enter the formula **=VLOOKUP(B3, Client.csv!$A$2:$B$8 ,2,FALSE)** into this cell. This formula will look up and compare the contents of cell B3 with the contents of each cell in the left (vertical) column of the range A2 to B8 within the file CLIENT.CSV. When entering this formula, you can add the yellow highlighted section of the formula by moving the cursor into this file and dragging it to highlight all of the cells in both columns, so it includes the look-up value and the result. The number 2 in the formula tells *Excel* to look in the second column of this range. The 'False' condition

in the formula tells *Excel* to only display the match if it is an exact match. If you set this to True it will find the nearest approximate match. When it finds a match, it will take the value or label stored in the second column which is to the right of the matched cell. Replicate this formula into cells C4 to C24.

The results should look similar to this. Save the spreadsheet as Ch_14_Task_14m.

	A	B	C
1	**Current client list**		
2	**Name**	**TaskCode**	**CurrentTask**
3	Laila Aboli	6	LGY
4	Greg Mina	4	Avricom
5	Sri Paryanti	6	LGY
6	Bishen Patel	6	LGY
7	Rupinder Singh	3	Hothouse Design
8	Sergio Gonzalez	5	Binnaccount
9	Rupinder Vas	1	Rootrainer
10	Bryan Revell	1	Rootrainer
11	Henri Ramos	7	Rock ICT

Activity 14h

Open the file TUTORS.CSV. This lists a number of students and the initials for their personal tutor.
Insert formulae in the Tutor Name column to look up the tutor's name using the file TEACHERS.CSV. Insert formulae in the Room Number column to look up the room number using the file ROOMS.CSV. Make sure that you use both absolute and relative referencing within all of your functions. Save your spreadsheet.

14.3 Testing the data model

Designing a test plan and choosing your test data are the most important parts of testing the data model. Choose data that will test every part of a condition. Be careful to test each part of the spreadsheet with **normal data** that you would expect to work with your formulae, with **extreme data** to test the boundaries and with **abnormal data** that you would not expect to be accepted. Carefully check that each formula and function works as you expect it to by using simple test data.

For example, to test the look-up used in Task 14m:
- make sure that each number between 1 and 7 (normal data) is used in the TaskCode
- use 0 and 8 and other abnormal data
- use decimal values between 1 and 7.

Write down each number and the expected results, before trying each number in the TaskCode column. Check that the actual result matches the expected result for every entry. If not, change the formula before starting the whole test process again. A test plan for this formula would be similar to that shown in Table 14.5.

Formula in cell C3 using data from cell B3:

Data entry in B3	Data type	Expected result	Actual result
1	Extreme/Normal	Rootrainer	
2	Normal	Quattichem	
3	Normal	Hothouse Design	
4	Normal	Avricom	
5	Normal	Binnaccount	
6	Normal	LGY	
7	Extreme/Normal	Rock ICT	
0	Abnormal	Error – value not available	
8	Abnormal	Error – value not available	
1.3	Abnormal	Error – value not available	
5.6	Abnormal	Error – value not available	
7.2	Abnormal	Error – value not available	
94	Abnormal	Error – value not available	

Table 14.5 Sample test plan for Task 14m

Many marks are lost in practical examinations by careless use of ranges within formulae and functions. Check that everything works before using real data in your model.

14.4 Selecting subsets of data

This means getting *Excel* to search through data held in a spreadsheet to extract only rows where the data matches your search criteria.

Searching using text filters

Task 14n

Open the file that you saved in Task 14m.
Select from all the data only the employees who are currently working on jobs for Binnaccount.

Open the file that you saved in Task 14m and highlight cells A2 to C24. Select the **Data** tab and find the **Sort & Filter** section. Click on the **Filter** icon to display an arrow in the top right corner of each column, like this.

For this task, you need to use this arrow to select the people working on the Binnaccount task. When you click on the CurrentTask arrow, a small drop-down menu appears like this.

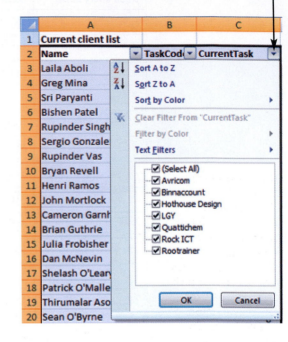

	A	B	C
1	Current client list		
2	Name	TaskCode	CurrentTask
8	Sergio Gonzalez	5	Binnaccount
15	Julia Frobisher	5	Binnaccount
18	Patrick O'Malley	5	Binnaccount
19	Thirumalar Asokmani	5	Binnaccount
24	Wim Van Hoffmann	5	Binnaccount

Hint

To remove the AutoFilter, either click on the tick box for (Select All), or use select **Clear Filter** in the drop-down list.

In the **Text Filters** section of the menu, click on the tick box for (Select All) to remove all of the ticks from every box. Then tick only the Binnaccount box, before clicking on ⊙ OK. This will display only the five selected rows like this.

The same method can be use to select more than one company from the list. By selecting different drop-down menu options, searches can be made using different criteria in different columns. Save the spreadsheet as Ch_14_Task_14n.

Searching using number filters

Task 14o

Open the file that you saved in Task 14m.
Select from all the data only the employees where the task code is between three and six inclusive.

Open the file and set the **AutoFilter** arrows for cells A2 to C24 as in the previous task. This time the search will be performed on the TaskCode column. Select the drop-down menu for this column using the arrow. Select **Number Filters** to get a sub-menu. Select **Custom Filter...** to get the **Custom AutoFilter** window.

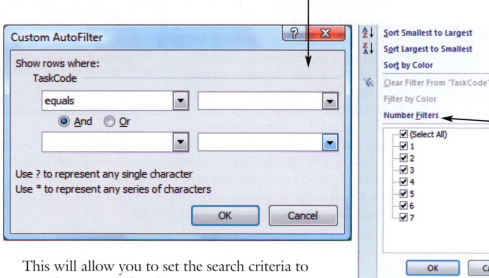

Hint

The method shown here is an alternative to selecting only the boxes for three, four, five and six. Even though it may seem easier to click on the tick boxes for this question, you will need to use the Custom AutoFilter window where a number of options are required. The Custom AutoFilter window also allows you to select is not equal to and to perform wildcard searches.

This will allow you to set the search criteria to greater than or equal to 3.

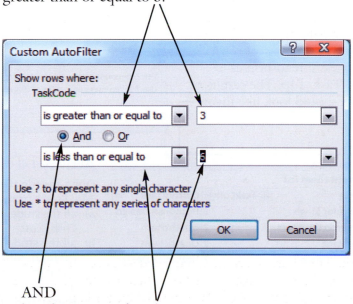

AND
less than or equal to 6.

The drop-down options in each box of the **Custom AutoFilter** window can be used to select equals to, not equal to, less than, or greater than, as well as the options shown. Save the spreadsheet as Ch_14_Task_14o.

Searching using more than one criteria

Task 14p

Open the file that you saved in Task 14m.

Select from all the data all the employees except John Mortlock and Sean O'Byrne who are currently working on jobs for Quattichem or Hothouse Design.

Open the file and set the **AutoFilter** arrows for cells A2 to C24 as in the previous task. This time the search will be performed on both the Name and CurrentTask columns. Select the drop-down arrow for the Name column, **Text Filters** and then select **Does Not Equal** from the sub-menu. This opens the **Custom AutoFilter** window, enter the initial letter 'J' in the right box

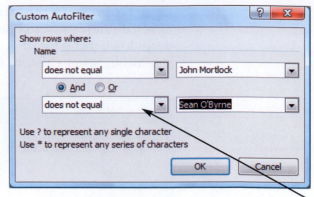

(this speeds up the search). When you click on the arrow for the drop-down list it will show you all the Names starting with 'J', so select 'John Mortlock' from the list. Select the AND operator and repeat the process for Sean O'Byrne, selecting **does not equal** in the left box and typing 'S' to find Sean O'Byrne, selecting his name from the list in the right box. Click on OK.

Select the search arrow for the CurrentTask column. Select from this menu only the two tick boxes for 'Hothouse Design' and 'Quattichem', or select **Text Filters** and set up the OR search like this.

Save the spreadsheet as Ch_14_Task_14p. The results of this task should look like this.

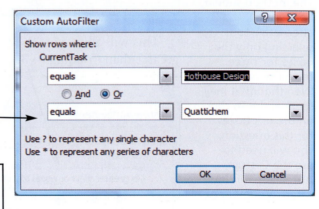

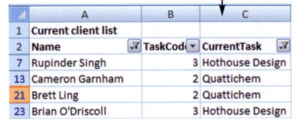

	A	B	C
1	**Current client list**		
2	**Name**	**TaskCode**	**CurrentTask**
7	Rupinder Singh	3	Hothouse Design
13	Cameron Garnham	2	Quattichem
21	Brett Ling	2	Quattichem
23	Brian O'Driscoll	3	Hothouse Design

Activity 14i

Open the file that you saved in Task 14h. Select from all the data:
a) all the students with a tutor called Chris Scott
b) all the students who will be using rooms numbered between 22 and 74 inclusive
c) all the students except Kiah and Hartati with a tutor called Kate Morrissey or Mike Arnott.

Searching using wildcards

A wildcard is a character that is used as a substitute for other characters. The * (asterisk) character is often used to show a number of characters (including 0) and the ? (question mark) is often used to show a single character. *Excel* uses these wildcard characters, but AutoFilter also contains other features that simplify some of these searches.

Task 14q

Open the file that you saved in Task 14m.
Select from all the data only the employees who have a name that starts with the letter 'S'.

Open the file and set the AutoFilter arrows for the cells A2 to C24 as in the previous task. This time the search will be performed on the Name column. Click on the drop-down arrow for this column and select **Text Filters** followed by **Begins With...** from the sub-menu. This opens the **Custom AutoFilter** window. Enter the initial **S** in the right box like this and click on OK . You should find these four rows. Save the spreadsheet as Ch_14_Task_14q.

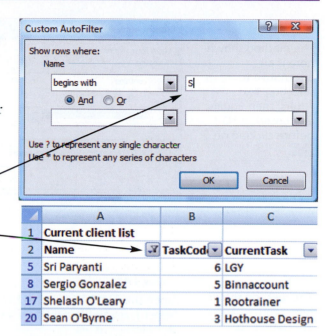

⊿	A	B	C
1	Current client list		
2	Name	TaskCod	CurrentTask
5	Sri Paryanti	6	LGY
8	Sergio Gonzalez	5	Binnaccount
17	Shelash O'Leary	1	Rootrainer
20	Sean O'Byrne	3	Hothouse Design

Task 14r

Open the file that you saved in Task 14m.
Select from all the data only the employees who have a name that ends with the letter 'a'.

This is a similar process to the previous task. Use the same process, this time selecting the **Text Filters** from the menu, then the **Ends With...** option to obtain the **Custom AutoFilter** window. Enter the letter **a** in the right box like this and click on OK . You should find this single row. Save the spreadsheet as Ch_14_Task_14r.

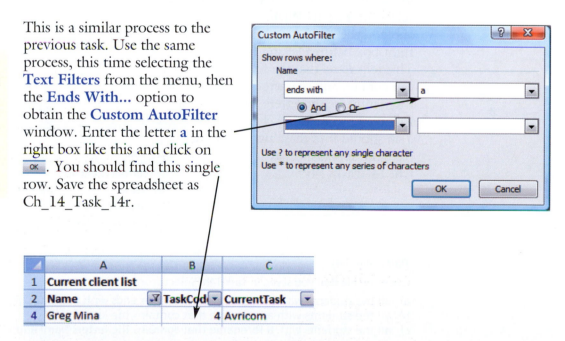

⊿	A	B	C
1	Current client list		
2	Name	TaskCod	CurrentTask
4	Greg Mina	4	Avricom

Task 14s

Open the file that you saved in Task 14m.
Select from all the data only the employees who have a name that contains the characters 'O''.

Hint

The method shown
here is an
alternative to
selecting Text
Filters, then Equals
and entering *O*
before clicking on
OK .

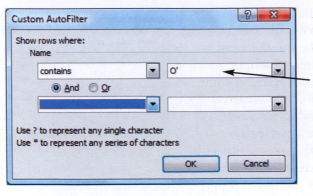

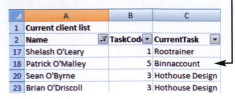

Again, select the **Text Filters** from
the drop-down menu in the Name
column. This time select the
Contains… option, enter the letter
O followed by an apostrophe to the
right box and click on OK . You
should find these four rows. Save
the spreadsheet as Ch_14_Task_14s.

Hint

The method shown
here is an
alternative to
selecting Text
Filters, then Equals
and entering ?ea*
then OK .

Task 14t

Open the file that you saved in Task 14m.
Select from all the data only the employees who have a first name that has the second and
third letters as 'ea'.

Using the same methods as the
previous searches, select the **Text
Filter** from the drop-down menu
in the Name column. This time
select the **Begins With…** option
and add the characters **?ea** to the
right box before clicking on OK .
This tells *Excel* that the first letter
can contain any character. Then
there must be the letters 'ea'
followed by any other characters.
You should find these two rows.
Save the spreadsheet as
Ch_14_Task_14t.

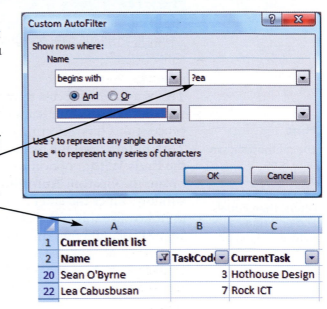

Activity 14j

Open the file that you saved in Task 14h. Select from all the data:

a) all the students with a forename that starts or ends with the letter 'R'
b) all the students with a forename that contains the letters 'eth'
c) all the students with a forename that contains the letters 'Jam' and who have a tutor
who uses room 60.

14.5 Sorting data

Before you try to sort any data, make sure that you select all of the data for each
item to be sorted. One common error in practical examinations is to select and sort
on a single column. If you were to do this, the integrity of the data would be lost.

Table 4.6 gives an example showing correct and incorrect sorting on the student's name for a spreadsheet containing their test results in Maths and English. The yellow shaded cells show the areas selected for the sort. Note how the results for each person have been changed when sorting without highlighting all the data.

Original data			Sorted correctly with all data selected			Sorted with only the name column selected		
Name	Maths	English	Name	Maths	English	Name	Maths	English
Shelia	72	75	Karla	52	75	Karla	72	75
Marcos	64	34	Marcos	64	34	Marcos	64	34
Vikram	61	44	Shelia	72	75	Shelia	61	44
Karla	52	75	Vikram	61	44	Vikram	52	75

Table 4.6 Correct and incorrect data selection for sorting

Task 14u

Open the file SALARY.CSV.
Sort the data into ascending order of surname, then ascending order of forename.

Open the file SALARY.CSV. Highlight all the cells in the range A2 to C43. Do not highlight row 1 or the column headings would also be sorted within the employee names. Select the **Home** tab and find the **Editing** section. Click on the **Sort & Filter** icon to obtain the drop-down menu. Select **Custom Sort...** to open the **Sort** window. In the **Sort by** box select **Surname** from the drop-down list. This will be the primary sort for this task. Make sure that the **Order** box contains **A to Z** to sort the data into ascending order.

To add the secondary sort to this data you need to add a second level to the **Sort** window. Click on **Add Level** to add the second sort level. In the **Then by** box select **Forename** from the drop-down list. Again, make sure that the

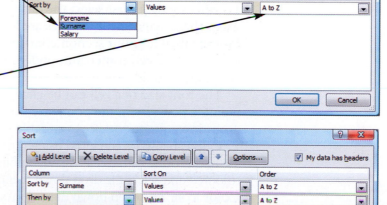

Hint

You can sort into descending order rather than ascending order by selecting Z to A rather than A to Z in the Order box.

Order box contains **A to Z** to sort the data into ascending order. Click on OK to perform the sort.

The data should look like this. ──────

	A	B	C
1	**Forename**	**Surname**	**Salary**
2	Laila	Aboli	25000
3	Thirumalar	Asokmani	10000
4	Lea	Cabusbusan	28000
5	Liam	Chi	8500
6	Dan	Dare	14000
7	Julia	Frobisher	16500
8	Cameron	Garnham	36000
9	Jake	Garnham	12500
10	Lauren	Garnham	6200
11	Jack	Gonzalez	8200
12	Sergio	Gonzalez	26000
13	Brian	Guthrie	43000
14	Lilik	Kaznica	9000
15	Jamal	Khan	8000
16	Kristy	King	12300
17	Brett	Ling	8200
18	Holly	Ling	27000

Activity 14k

Open the file that you saved in Activity14h. Sort the data into descending order of tutor name, then ascending order of forename.

14.6 Using display features

Many of the features described in this section can be applied to an individual cell, a range of cells, to one or more rows or columns, or to the entire spreadsheet. To apply the feature to the entire spreadsheet, click in the top left-hand corner of the sheet.

To select a row or rows, click on the number or numbers to the left of the row and it will select all the cells in that row.

To select a column or columns, click on the column letter or letters to select all the cells in the column or columns. To select a single cell, click in that cell. To select a range of cells, drag the cursor to highlight a range of cells. If you need to select different cells or ranges from different parts of the sheet at the same time, hold down the <Ctrl> key whilst making your selections.

Enhancing data

To enhance data, first select the data to be enhanced. All of the enhancement features are located using the **Home** tab. The **Font** section contains icons to allow you to set the cell contents to <u>underlined</u>, *italic* (sloping) or bold. ──────

The font size of a cell can be changed by either typing a new size in the point size box or using the drop-down menu to select a suitable size.

Cells can also be enhanced using different colours for the background of the cell. Again, highlight the area to be coloured and select the drop-down menu from the **Fill Color** icon. The drop-down menu looks like this. There are a number of standard colours as well as colours selected by *Excel* for the current colour schemes. If the colour that you want is not there, click on the colour palette icon. ──────

If you are selecting colours, ensure that the foreground and background colours contrast and can be easily seen when printed. The foreground colour of a cell (the font colour) can be selected in the **Font** section. The **Font Color** icon is to the right of the **Fill Color** icon. The drop-down menu from this icon is the same as the menu for the background colour.

Formatting cells

Formatting cells containing numbers changes the way a cell is displayed, but does
not change the values held within it.

Task 14v

Create a spreadsheet model that looks like this. Place
a formula in cell C2 that multiplies the contents of cell
A2 by the contents of cell B2.
Format cell A2 as an integer.

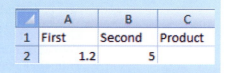

	A	B	C
1	First	Second	Product
2	1.2	5	

Create this spreadsheet as shown. In cell C2 enter
the formula **=A2*B2**. The spreadsheet will look
like this. ⟶

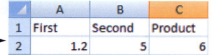

	A	B	C
1	First	Second	Product
2	1.2	5	6

To format cell A2 as an integer, place the cursor
in this cell and select the **Home** tab. In the **Number** section, click on the arrow in
the bottom right corner to open the **Format Cells** window.

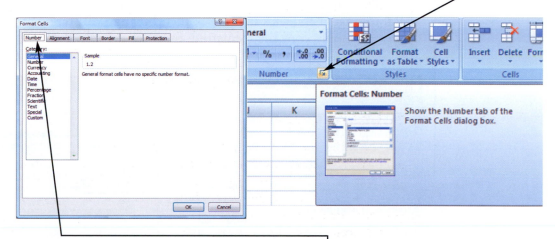

Format Cells: Number

Show the Number tab of the
Format Cells dialog box.

When this window opens, it should have the **Number** tab selected. The **Format
Cells** window will allow you to format cells in different currencies, into percentages
or even as dates or times.

For this task, you need to format this cell as
a number. Select the **Number** option in the
Category: section. Change the cell formatting
to 0 **Decimal places:**. Click on OK to set
the formatting. The spreadsheet will now look
like this.

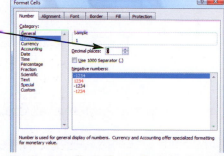

	A	B	C
1	First	Second	Product
2	1	5	6

If you compare the two views of the spreadsheet, you can see that cell A2 has changed. The contents still remain 1.2 but in the second view the answer for the product appears to be incorrect. To change the contents of cell A2 to a whole number, use the INT function.

Original

◢	A	B	C
1	First	Second	Product
2	1.2	5	6

Formatted

◢	A	B	C
1	First	Second	Product
2	1	5	6

Task 14w

Open the file COSTS.CSV. Format cells A1, D1, D3 and G3 as a bold 14 point font.
Format all numeric cells in row 2 into their respective currencies to 3 decimal places.
Format all numeric cells in columns C and D into pounds sterling with 2 decimal places.
Format the cells E5 to E15 into Euros with 2 decimal places.
Format the cells F5 to F15 into Japanese Yen with 0 decimal places.
Format all cells between G5 and G15 into percentage values with no decimal places.

Open the file COSTS.CSV. Click in cell A1. Select the **Home** tab, find the **Format** section, then use the drop-down list to change the size of this cell to 14 point. Click the mouse on the **Bold** icon to set this cell to bold.

Click on the **Format Painter** icon and click in cell D1. Click on the **Format Painter** again and click in cell D3, then **Format Painter** again and cell G3. This process should copy the formatting from cell A1 into these other three cells.

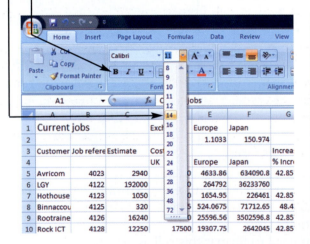

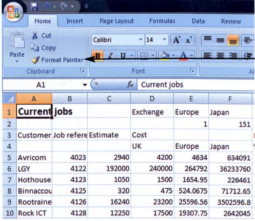

Move the cursor into cell E2. In the **Number** section, click on the arrow in the bottom right corner to open the **Format Cells** window in the **Number** tab. In the **Category:** section, select **Currency**.

Set the number of decimal places to three. Although this is not the correct number of decimal places for Euros, it was specified in the task.

In the **Symbol:** section, select an appropriate Euro format from the list. You may need to scroll down the list of available currencies to find it. The **Sample** area will show you what the formatting of the cell will look like when you click on [OK]. When you have checked this formatting, click on [OK].

Repeat this process for cell F2, but this time selecting Japanese Yen. Some currencies like Japanese Yen have no decimal places and so would normally need to be formatted to zero decimal places, but in this task you were told to set this cell to 3 decimal places. The **Format Cells** window should look like this. Click on [OK].

To format all the numeric cells in columns C and D, highlight all cells in the range C5 to D15. Then open the **Format Cells** window and set the **Category:** to **Currency**, the number of **Decimal places:** to two and the **Symbol:** to pounds sterling (£). Repeat this process for cells E5 to E15, selecting Euros with 2 decimal places, and for cells F5 to F15 with Japanese Yen set to no decimal places (which are the appropriate formats for both of these currencies).

To format all cells between G5 and G15 into percentage values, highlight this range, then in the **Format Cells** window set the **Category:** to **Percentage**. Set the number of **Decimal places:** to 0. Resize columns as necessary. The finished spreadsheet should look like this.

Hint

If the currency symbol that you are looking for (e.g. ¥) may not appear in the drop-down list, there are a number of text options available. In this case you can select JPY which is the international standard code for Japanese Yen.

Hint

An alternative to this for percentage values with no decimal places is to highlight the cell/s, select the Home tab and click the Percent Style icon in the Number section.

	A	B	C	D	E	F	G
1	**Current jobs**			**Exchange**	Europe	Japan	
2					€1.103	¥150.974	
3	Customer	Job reference	Estimate	**Cost**			**Increase**
4				UK	Europe	Japan	% Increase
5	Avricom	4023	£2,940.00	£4,200.00	€4,634	¥634,091	43%
6	LGY	4122	£192,000.00	£240,000.00	€264,792	¥36,233,760	25%
7	Hothouse Design	4123	£1,050.00	£1,500.00	€1,655	¥226,461	43%
8	Binnaccount	4125	£320.00	£475.00	€524	¥71,713	48%
9	Rootrainer	4126	£16,240.00	£23,200.00	€25,597	¥3,502,597	43%
10	Rock ICT	4128	£12,250.00	£17,500.00	€19,308	¥2,642,045	43%
11	Quattichem	4129	£1,400.00	£2,000.00	€2,207	¥301,948	43%
12	LGY	4130	£10,800.00	£12,000.00	€13,240	¥1,811,688	11%
13	Hothouse Design	4131	£720.00	£720.00	€794	¥108,701	0%
14	Binnaccount	4132	£1,680.00	£2,400.00	€2,648	¥362,338	43%
15	Hothouse Design	4133	£4,500.00	£5,000.00	€5,517	¥754,870	11%

Activity 14m

Open the file that you saved in Activity 14g.
In cell A41, place the label 'Total'.
In cell B41, add the total number of students in all houses.
In cell C36, add the label 'Percent'.
In cells C37 to C40, calculate, using absolute and relative referencing, the percentage of students in each house. Format these cells as a percentage with 1 decimal place.

Activity 14n

Open the file ITEMS.CSV.
Format cells A4 and A5 so that they are bold, italic and 20 points high.
In cells C3 to F3, place current exchange rates for each currency shown. Use the internet (or exchange rates supplied by your teacher) to do this. Do not format these cells as currency.
For each cell in the range C8 to F22, calculate the price of each item in the correct currency.
Format each of the cells in the range B8 to F22 in the appropriate currency with the appropriate number of decimal places.

Adjusting rows and columns

In Section 4.2, you learnt how to expand column widths using the drag handle to make sure that all data is visible in the spreadsheet. Row heights can be adjusted in exactly the same way.

The settings for row heights can also be changed by right clicking the mouse button on the row number on the left to obtain this drop-down menu.

The row can be hidden from view by selecting the **Hide** option, or can have a different row height set using the **Row Height...** option. This option opens the **Row Height** window, where you can adjust the height setting before clicking on OK.

The column width can be hidden or adjusted in a similar way. To get the drop-down menu click the right mouse button on the column heading at the top of the column.

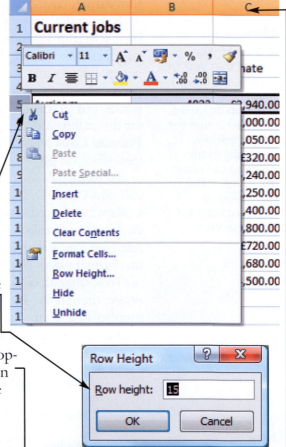

Adjusting page orientation

You may need to change the page orientation from portrait to landscape, especially when displaying the formulae that you have used. To change this select the **Page Layout** tab, and find the **Page Setup** section. Click on the **Orientation** icon, then select either **Portrait** or **Landscape** from the drop-down menu.

Hint

This window can be used as another way of changing the page orientation.

When preparing your spreadsheet for printing, you can adjust the layout of the spreadsheet on the printed page/s using **Print Preview**. To do this, select the **Office** button and then **Print** from the drop-down menu. Select the **Print Preview** option from the sub-menu. The print preview of the spreadsheet is shown. If you need to adjust how your spreadsheet appears, you can click on the **Page Setup** icon in the **Print Preview** tab to open the **Page Setup** window.

If you need to change the number of pages wide or tall in the printout use the **Fit to:** radio button in the **Scaling** section and select the number of pages.

Ensure that if you set a printout to a single page wide that all the formulae/ values and labels can be clearly seen. If the font size is so small that it is not clearly readable by an examiner, you may not be awarded the marks for that section. When you have changed the page settings click on OK .

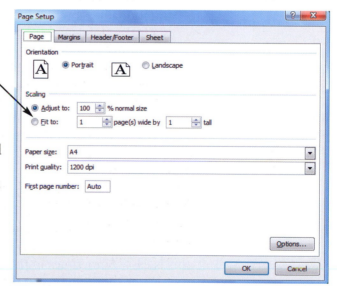

14.7 Save and print data

Save your work regularly. As recommended in Section 13.1, it is a good idea to save different versions, both in your work and in the practical examinations, each with a different version number. If you make a mistake and corrupt a file, you can always go back and redo a small part of the task without losing too much time.

When printing your spreadsheets, make sure that you have adjusted all column widths and row heights to ensure that all printouts show all:

- labels in full
- formulae in full
- data in full.

Remember that the examiner can only mark what can be seen. If you don't show that you have done, it will not get you any marks. Many candidates forget to submit printouts showing the formulae used – check that you have worked through how to display formulae in Section 14.2. You can use screenshots to show how you achieved your results. Make sure that all printouts contain your name, candidate and centre number. To print, select the **Office** button followed by **Print**.

You may be required to export your spreadsheet data into different formats. In *Excel*, this is done by selecting the **Office** button followed by **Save As**. This will allow you to export the data into common text formats like .txt (text format), .rtf (rich text format) and .csv (comma separated values). Although other export features exist, these should be sufficient for the practical examinations.

14.8 Produce a graph or chart

In the examination, you may be asked to select an appropriate chart for a purpose. Which chart is the most appropriate is often very difficult to work out. For the practical examination, the choice will be between a pie chart, a bar chart and a line graph.

- **Pie charts:** if you are asked to compare percentage values, a pie chart is often the most appropriate type because pie charts *compare parts of a whole*. An example would be comparing the percentage of children who preferred ice cream, jelly or trifle.
- **Bar charts:** these *show the difference* between different things. A bar chart is traditionally a graph with vertical bars, but is called a column graph in *Excel*. This is a little confusing but in the practical examinations to create a vertical bar chart you would need to use the 'column chart' and for a horizontal bar chart (with the bars going across the page) you would need to use the 'bar chart'. An example would be showing the number of items sold by five people in the same month.
- **Line graphs:** these are used to *plot trends* between two variables. An example would be plotting the temperature of water as it was heated against time. You could then find any point in time on the graph and be able to read the corresponding temperature, even if the temperature had not been taken at that time.

> **Hint**
>
> Do not used stacked column charts or stacked bar charts for the practical examinations

Creating a chart

To create a chart, you have to highlight the data that you wish to use. This is highlighted in the same way as before. If all the data is together (**contiguous data**) this is easy. Sometimes in the practical examinations you will need to highlight data that is not kept together in the spreadsheet (**non-contiguous data**). To do this, hold down the <Ctrl> key whilst making your selections.

> **Task 14x**
>
> Open the file EMPLOYEES.CSV. This shows the job types, the number of employees with that job type and the percentage of employees with that job type.
> Create an appropriate graph or chart to show the number of employees with that job type.

Open the file and highlight only cells A1 to B8. The highlighted data should look like this. This highlighted area will be the cells used to produce the graph. Notice that the cells containing the column headings (A1 and B1) have been included in this selection as these will be used as the labels in the chart (they can be changed later if the question asks for different labels).

	A	B	C
1	JobTitle	Number of staff	Percentage
2	Director	3	0.0483871
3	Engineer	12	0.19354839
4	Analyst	4	0.06451613
5	Sales	16	0.25806452
6	Programmer	9	0.14516129
7	Tester	5	0.08064516
8	Clerical	13	0.20967742
9		62	

Hint

Keep your charts simple – do not use 3D charts or add features that are not a necessary part of a task. A simple chart is more effective.

Decide what type of chart you will need for this task. Look at the data and decide if it compares parts of a whole; shows trends between two variables; or shows the difference. In this task, the data shows the different numbers of employees in each job type, so a bar chart is the most appropriate chart type and in this case you can use a vertical bar chart.

Select the **Insert tab** and find the **Charts** section. Then select a vertical bar chart (labelled **Column** in *Excel*) and select a **Clustered Column** chart from the drop-down options. The finished bar chart will look like this. Save this chart for later use.

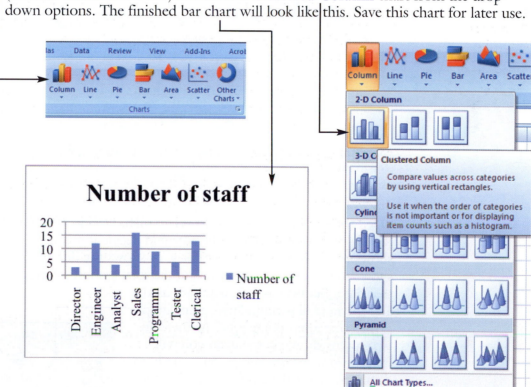

Task 14y

Open the file EMPLOYEES.CSV. Create an appropriate graph or chart to show the percentage of employees with that job type.

Open the file and, using the <Ctrl> key and the mouse, highlight cells A1 to A8 and C1 to C8. Do not highlight any other cells. The highlighted spreadsheet should look like this.

	A	B	C
1	JobTitle	Number of staff	Percentage
2	Director	3	0.0483871
3	Engineer	12	0.19354839
4	Analyst	4	0.06451613
5	Sales	16	0.25806452
6	Programmer	9	0.14516129
7	Tester	5	0.08064516
8	Clerical	13	0.20967742
9		62	

Decide what type of chart you will need for this task. Again, look at the data and decide if it compares parts of a whole; shows trends between two variables; or shows the difference. In this task, the data compares parts of the whole, so a pie chart is the most appropriate chart type. Select the **Insert tab** and find the **Charts** section. Then select a **Pie** chart and the **2-D Pie**. The finished pie chart will look like this. Save this chart for later use.

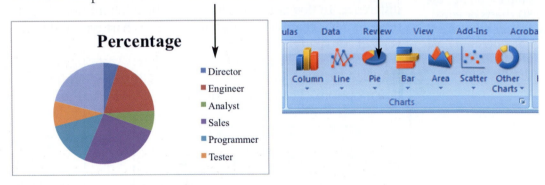

Task 14z

Open the file RAINFALL.CSV. Create an appropriate graph or chart to show a comparison of the monthly data for towns A and B.

Open the file and highlight cells A1 to C15. Decide what type of chart you will need for this task. Again, look at the data and decide if it compares parts of a whole; shows trends between two variables; or shows the difference. In this task, the data shows trends between the date and the total amount of rainfall that had fallen by that date. Because specific dates are used and the rainfall is cumulative, a line graph is the most appropriate type. As there are two towns shown in the data, you will make a comparative line graph using both data sets. Select the **Insert** tab and in the **Charts** section select a **Line** graph and the **2-D Line** (the top left icon).

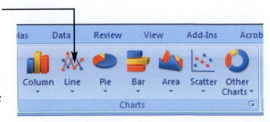

The finished line graph will look like this. Save this chart for later use. →

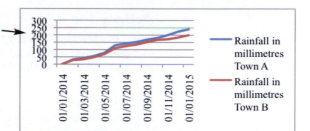

Modifying a chart

Open the chart that you saved in Task 14x. Move the cursor onto the chart title and click the left mouse button on the title to select it, like this. With the title selected, highlight the title and replace the text with the new title 'Employees'.

You have to add a new axis label to the category axis. To do this select the **Insert** tab, then in the **Text** section select **Text Box**. Click the left mouse button on the chart near the category axis and type in 'Job type'. Resize the text box and change the font style, size, etc. to match the rest of the chart. Move the text box if necessary. It should look similar to this.

You can repeat this process to add the value axis label 'Number of staff', but you may find it quicker to highlight the text box for 'Job type', copy and paste it, then edit and move it. This will save time formatting the new text box to match the existing one. You can rotate the text through 90 degrees using the green handle.

After rotating the text, move the chart and place the value axis label to the left of the axis. To remove the legend (the key), click the left mouse button on the legend and then press the <Delete> key. Again, edit the layout of the chart so that it looks like this. ——

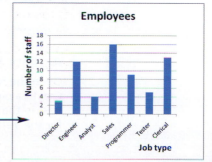

Activity 14o

Open the file that you saved in Activity 14a. Use this data to produce a vertical bar chart comparing the number of days worked for each person, except Aminat and Sukrit. Add an appropriate title and labels to the chart. Do not include a legend.

Activity 14p

Open the file WEBHITS.CSV. This contains data about the number of members for an online book club and the average number of website hits each week over a nine year period. Create and label an appropriate graph or chart to show a comparison of these two sets of data.

Hint

It is worth spending time browsing through each of these chart layouts to see what is available.

Task 14bb

Open the chart saved in Task 14y.
Display all segment labels and percentage values on the chart. Do not display a legend.
Extract the segment for engineers.

Open the chart saved in Task 14y, click on the chart with the left mouse button and select the **Design** tab. Select from the **Chart Layouts** one which displays the segment labels and percentage values. Other layouts display the segment labels and values, some include a legend. Selecting the first option changes the chart from this to this.

Chart Layouts

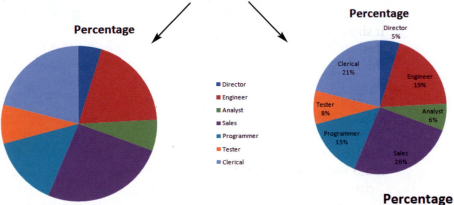

To extract the segment for engineers, click the left mouse button on the segment for engineers and then click again. Now click and hold the mouse button to drag the segment out from the pie in the direction of the red arrow shown in the diagram above. This pulls out the segment so that it looks like this. Save this chart for later use.

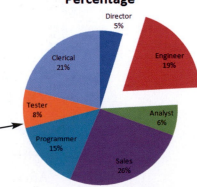

Activity 14q

Open the file that you saved in Activity 14m.
Create a pie chart showing the name of each house (the colours) and the percentage of the class in that house. Add the title 'Percentage of students in each house'. Extract the segment for the Yellow house.

Using secondary axes

Task 14cc

Open the file RAINFALL.CSV.
Create an appropriate graph or chart to show a comparison of the rainfall and average temperatures for each month in only town A. Add a second value axis to the chart for the temperature series and label and scale these axes appropriately.

Open the file RAINFALL.CSV and highlight the dates and data for Town A; this is in cells A1 to B15 and D1 to D15. Select the **Insert** tab and then in the **Charts** section select a **Line** graph. Use the top left option from those available (this will generally be the most frequently used choice). The line graph will look similar to this.

It is difficult to read the values for the temperature, so adding and scaling a second value axis will make it easier to read the graph.

Click the left mouse button on the data series for the temperatures (the red data line in this example), so that it shows each of the points plotted like this. Right click the mouse button on this data series to obtain the drop-down menu and select **Format Data Series…**. This opens the **Format Data Series** window.

Select the **Series Options** section on the left (it may already be selected), and use the radio button to change the axis type from a **Primary Axis** to a **Secondary Axis**. Click on Close. Your graph will now look similar to this.

The secondary axis is now visible. Excel has attempted to scale these axes but you are now going to adjust them further. You will change the primary axis so that it is set between 0 and 240 and the secondary axis so that it is set between −1 and 23. These values have been extracted from the original data: the total cumulative rainfall is 240 millimetres, and the temperature changes between −1 and 23 degrees. It would be acceptable to use values like −2 to 24 or even the −5 to 25 suggested by *Excel* for this.

To change the primary axis values click on the axis labels like this.

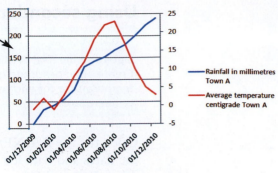

Right mouse click within the axis labels to obtain the drop-down menu and select **Format Axis...** to open the **Format Axis** window. In the **Axis Options** section, change the **Maximum** value to a **Fixed** value using the radio button. Change the value to 240.0 and click on Close.

Follow a similar procedure for the secondary axis. Click the left mouse button on the axis, then right mouse click and select **Format Axis...** to open the **Format Axis** window. In the **Axis Options** section, change the **Minimum** value to a **Fixed** value of −1 and the **Maximum** value to a **Fixed** value of 23.

It is important to label these axes appropriately. Label the primary axis 'Cumulative rainfall in millimetres' and the secondary axis 'Average temperature'. These changes should leave the chart looking like this.

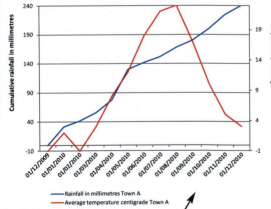

The legend has been moved so that all of the category axis labels are fully visible. In the earlier printout only every second label was visible. The category axis should also be labelled and the chart given a title before it is submitted for assessment. Save the file.

Activity 14r

Open the file that you saved in Activity 14p.
Add a second value axis to the chart for the number of members and set the maximum value for this axis to 3200.

Formatting graphs and charts

You have already learnt how to enhance a pie chart by extracting a segment or segments. Charts can also be enhanced using colour and/or shading. In some circumstances, the use of colour can be used to ensure that the person reading a document has their attention drawn to one specific part of a chart.

Task 14dd

Open the chart saved in Task 14bb. Change this chart so that the segments for 'Programmer' and for 'Engineer' attract a reader's attention.

Open the chart saved in Task 14bb and click the left mouse button on the segment for 'Programmer' and then click again, so that only that segment is selected. Select the **Home** tab and in the **Font** section click on the **Fill** icon. Select a bright colour, for example red, from the colour palette. Repeat this process for the 'Engineer' segment, this time selecting bright yellow (bright orange may be better if printing the chart). Now select other softer colours for the other segments. The chart should look similar to this. ─────

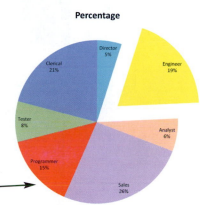

You can see that the brighter colours for the two segments stand out and the softer pastel colours are not as prominent.

Activity 14s

Open the file that you saved in Activity 14q. Change the segment colours to match the labels for each segment.

Using colour to enhance your charts is useful if you have a colour printer, but printing a document created in colour on a black-and-white printer can cause problems. This book has sections of coloured text designed to outline key elements, like words in the glossary shown in red, instructions to follow in blue and field names in green. If a page containing these three colours was printed on a black-and-white printer, each of the three colours would appear as a shade of grey. It would be impossible to identify which words were glossary terms, instructions or fieldnames.

With a black and white printer it is sometimes difficult to ensure that there is enough contrast between different parts of a graph or chart, for example this chart, appears like this if it is printed in greyscale (black and white).

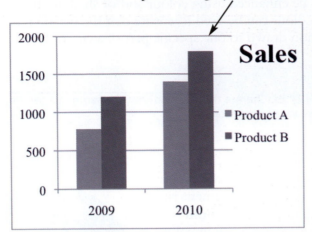

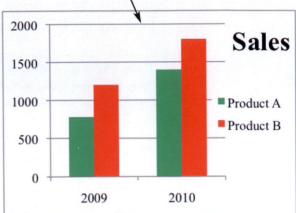

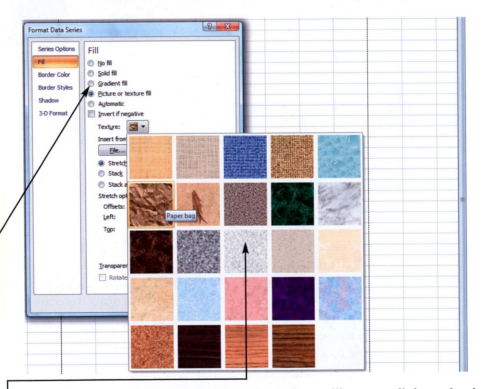

Hint

An alternative is to use gradient fills which are also in the Fill section of the Format Data Series window.

In this case, choose more contrasting colours, like a very light and a dark colour, or use a patterned fill for one of the columns. To choose a patterned fill, click the right mouse button on one of the bars, in this case the right-hand bar. From the drop-down menu, select **Format Data Series…**, then in the **Format Data Series** window select the **Fill** section. Select the radio button for **Picture or texture fill** and choose a pattern from those available in the drop-down menu from the **Texture:** box. Click on Close.

Texture fills can also be applied to pie charts. Select a segment and right click the mouse button, then select **Format Data Point…** to edit the fill type.

Activity 14t

Open the file you saved in Activity 14s. Change the background fills so that each segment is distinctive when printed in black and white.

CHAPTER 15

Website authoring

In this chapter you will learn how to:

- define and use HTML tags
- use a text editor to create a webpage
- display your webpages in a web browser
- format text using pre-defined styles
- align and enhance text
- create, edit and attach a cascading stylesheet
- create styles using specific and generic font families
- set font sizes using absolute and relative values
- use classes within a stylesheet
- annotate your markup with comments
- create numbered, bulleted and nested lists
- use colour names and hexadecimal colour codes
- apply colour to text and backgrounds
- use anchors and hyperlinks within a webpage, to external pages and to send email
- open a webpage in a new window
- design and create page layout using tables
- create and format tables, including header, footer and body sections
- insert, place and manipulate an image within a webpage
- manipulate an image in a graphics package
- create a hyperlink from an image.

For this chapter you will need these source files from the CD:

- ALIGN.CSS
- COLOUR_CODES.HTM
- CLASS1.CSS
- HTMLTIPS.HTM
- PCTC.JPG
- REMORA.HTM
- REMORA.JPG
- STYLE1.CSS
- STYLE2.CSS
- STYLE3.CSS
- SUBSCRIPT.HTM
- TURTLE.JPG
- WEBPAGE1.HTM
- WEBPAGE2.HTM
- WEBPAGE3.HTM
- WEBPAGE4.HTM
- WEBPAGE5.HTM
- WEBPAGE6.HTM
- WEBPAGE7.HTM

15.1 Introduction

What is a website?

A **website** is a collection of individual but related **webpages** that are usually stored together and hosted by a web server. These can be programmed or created using different languages including **HTML**, *Sun Microsystems Java* and *Microsoft ASP*. Each webpage can include a variety of different objects such as text, images (including moving images) and sound. You are going to develop your webpages in HTML.

What is HTML?

HTML is an abbreviation for HyperText Markup Language. It is a text-based language used to develop websites, and is often used within an intranet or on the Internet. Files are written in HTML using a simple **text editor** (or **web-authoring package** like *Macromedia Dreamweaver* or *Microsoft FrontPage*). Files are written in text format and are usually saved with an .htm file extension. These are file formats that are recognised as webpages by **web browsers** like *Microsoft Internet Explorer* or *Mozilla Firefox*. You are going to develop your webpages using a simple text editor.

Getting started

A good technique for working on webpages is to tile three windows on the screen at the same time: this means to fit them side by side like tiles. Whenever you do any work in HTML, it is recommended that you have a text editor, a web browser and a list of your files in their storage folder visible. Select the **Start** button, followed by **Documents**. This opens the **Documents** window, which will look similar to this.

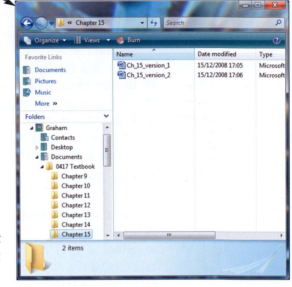

Place this window in the lower left of the screen and resize it to fill about a quarter of the screen.

Create a new folder for your HTML work in your user area by clicking the right mouse button on the background for the file list on the right and selecting **New** followed by **Folder**. Rename this **HTML**. The location of this will depend on the structure of the system you are using. Go into this folder and create new sub-folders for each task in this chapter. Call these folders **Task 15a** to **Task 15w**. For each task in this chapter you *must* save all the files for that task in the correct folder.

Make sure you are in the folder Task 15a. This is where all the work from the first part of this chapter will be stored. The window should look similar to this.

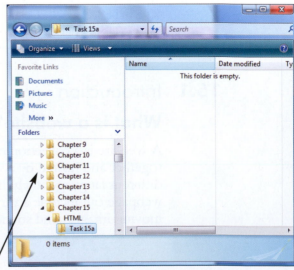

Open your text editor; in this case you are going to open *Notepad*. This can be opened by selecting the **Start** button, followed by **All Programs**, **Accessories** and selecting **Notepad** from the list of programs. Place this window in the top left of the screen and resize it so that it fills about a quarter of the screen. The text editor will be where we write the HTML markup to create each webpage.

Open your web browser and resize this window so that it fills the remaining half of your screen. Make sure that the windows fit together and do not overlap. The screen will look similar to this.

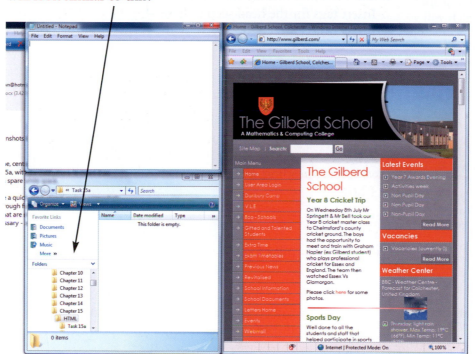

Hint

When using stylesheets later in this chapter you will have more than one copy of the text editor open and may need to tile these on the screen.

Hint

Note that all text in HTML tags should be in lower case so that if it is structured correctly it would need little editing to become XHTML.

Although many people refer to HTML as a programming language, that is not strictly true. It is a markup language that uses a set of markup **tags** to describe a webpage to the browser. HTML tags are shown using angle brackets around them like this:

```
<html>
```

The angle brackets tell the browser that this is a markup tag and not text to be placed on the webpage. The browser does not display the HTML tags, but uses the tags to display the content of the page. Most HTML commands have pairs of tags, one to open the command and one to close the command. Each tag has a pair of angle brackets around it.

The first tag that will usually appear in any webpage will be **<html>**. This tag tells the browser that everything following this tag will be written in hypertext markup language. The tag **</html>** tells the browser that this is the end of the markup language. The forward slash shows that it is a closing tag. All other HTML tags will appear between these tags.

Each webpage will have two clearly defined sections, the head and the body. The head section starts with **<head>** and closes with **</head>** and objects between these tags are not usually displayed by the web browser. Only a few tags are universally accepted within the head section of a webpage, these are: **<base>**, **<link>**, **<meta>**, **<title>**, **<style>** and **<script>**. The body section starts with **<body>** and closes with **</body>** and objects between these tags should be

Hint

If you look at other websites' HTML markup you may find a doctype definition before the <html> tag. This is normal but it is beyond the scope of this book. It will be needed if you wish to validate your webpages.

displayed by the browser. The body section should always contain a title. This is the name displayed in the browser toolbar. It is the page title if a page is added to **Favorites** and is the title displayed in search engine results. The basic structure of any webpage should therefore include these tags.

```
<html>
<head>
  <title>Webpage name</title>
</head>
<body>

</body>
</html>
```

Insert tags for the head section here.
Insert objects to be displayed by the browser in the body section here.

15.2 Format text using pre-defined styles

Hint

It is essential that the text is typed exactly as shown here. One typing error may cause the webpage not to function as expected.

All text added to a webpage should have a tag telling the browser what the text style should look like. There are a number of pre-defined styles available for use in a webpage. The normal paragraph style is obtained using **<p>** and ended with **</p>**. Likewise, six heading styles are available and are defined with the style names **<h1>** to **<h6>**.

Task 15a
Create and save a new webpage showing paragraph and heading styles.

Hint

It is acceptable to use capital letters in the text that is displayed on the page, but not in the tags.

Click the cursor into the text editor. Type this markup into the editor, replacing MY NAME HERE with your name. Remember to always add your name, centre number and candidate number to all of your printouts.

```
<html>
<head>
  <title>Task 15a/title>
</head>
<body>
   <p>My first webpage by MY NAME HERE</p>
   <h1>This is style h1, the largest heading style</h1>
   <h2>This is style h2</h2>
   <h3>This is style h3</h3>
   <h4>This is style h4</h4>
   <h5>This is style h5</h5>
   <h6>This is style h6, smallest heading style</h6>
   <p>This is style p, the paragraph style</p>
</body>
</html>
```

When this has been entered and carefully verified (by checking this original document with your typed copy), you must select **File** followed by **Save As...**, which will open the **Save As** window. Click on **Browse Folders** to expand the window. The expanded window will look similar to this.

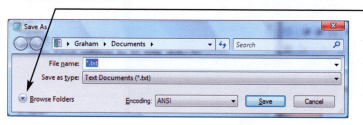

Click on the folder names until you find the Task 15a folder created earlier in this chapter.

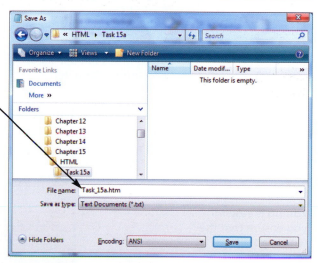

You need to enter a filename for the webpage. This filename *must* be saved with an .htm extension. If you do not use an .htm file extension, this will operate as a text file rather than as a webpage. Enter the filename **Task_15a.htm** and click on Save .

The file should appear in the **Documents** window and may look similar to this.

Make sure that the file displays the browser symbol 🅔 to show that this is a webpage and not the text document symbol. The text document 📄 symbol only

appears if you forget to add the .htm extension to the filename.

Select the file Task_15a from the **Documents** window and drag this file (holding the left mouse button down) into the browser window. The screen should now look similar to the screen shown overleaf. The browser view now contains your first webpage.

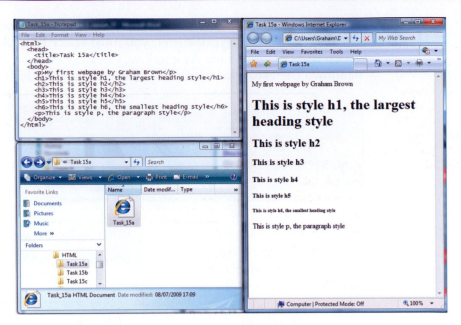

15.3 Opening existing webpages and enhancing text

To open an existing webpage in both the text editor and the web browser you must first find the website in the **Documents** window. For all webpage files, including those given in the examination, it is advisable to copy the files into a sub-folder of your HTML directory before starting.

> ### Task 15b
> Open the file WEBPAGE1.HTM and view this webpage in both the text editor and browser. Improve this webpage by emboldening the word 'bold', setting the word 'italic' to an italic font, setting the 3 in x3 as a superscripted character and setting the 2 in H2O as a subscripted character.

Copy the file WEBPAGE1.HTM into your Task 15b folder. Drag this file from the **Documents** window into your text editor. Drag another copy of this file from the **Documents** window into your browser. The screen should look like this.

Hint
Editing is easier if you ensure that the word wrap is selected in Notepad. To do this, use the Format menu and check that the Word Wrap option is ticked.

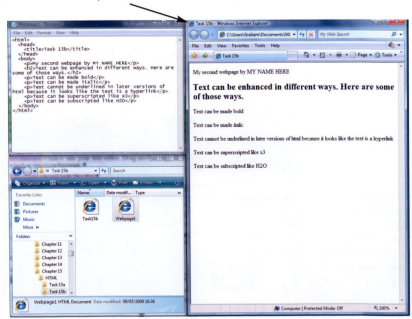

Hint

If you prefer you can click the mouse on the browser window and then press the function key <f5> to refresh the browser view each time you have saved the file.

Move the cursor into the text editor window and make the following changes to the markup.

Replace the word 'first' with 'second'.

Replace MY NAME HERE with your name.

Place the tags **** and **** around the word 'bold'.

Place the tags **<i>** and **</i>** around word 'italic'.

Place the tags **^{** and **}** around the number '3'.

Place the tags **_{** and **}** around the number '2'.

```
<html>
<head>
   <title>Task 15b</title>
</head>
<body>
   <p>My second webpage by Graham Brown</p>
   <h2>Text can be enhanced in different ways. Here are
some of those ways.</h2>
   <p>Text can be made <b>bold</b></p>
   <p>Text can be made <i>italics</i></p>
   <p>Text cannot be underlined in later versions of html
because it looks like the text is a hyperlink</p>
   <p>Text can be superscripted like x<sup>3</sup></p>
   <p>Text can be subscripted like H<sub>2</sub></p>
</body>
</html>
```

When you have made all these changes to the webpage, save the page by selecting the text editor, followed by **File, Save As...**, selecting the **Task 15b** folder and entering the filename **Task_15b.htm** before clicking on [Save].

Test the webpage works by dragging this new filename from the **Documents** window into the browser window. The new browser view should look like this.

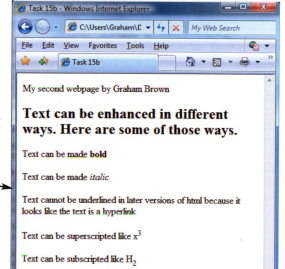

15.4   Working with styles

Hint

Remember to always add your name, centre number and candidate number to all of your printouts. You will not gain any credit in the practical examinations if there is nothing to identify the candidate on the printout.

Using **styles** in your webpages helps you to be consistent in the way the pages look. Using styles is much quicker and easier than applying individual settings, such as font face, font size, text alignment and font colours, to every piece of text in each webpage that you create.

You have already met the heading styles h1 to h6 and the paragraph style p earlier in the chapter. When you used these styles the web browser did not find any of these style definitions in your HTML markup so used its own default settings. However, you can set your own definitions for each style and the web browser will attempt to apply these styles to the page. Styles are not only set for text, but can also be used to define page layout, colour schemes and default settings for other objects and links on the page. Using consistent styles is often important to give a 'corporate feel' to a website. Particular elements like colour schemes, logos and font faces are sometimes used to aid recognition of well-known companies or brands.

Styles are always defined in the head section of a webpage. They may be defined in each webpage or defined in a **stylesheet**. If stylesheets are used, the stylesheet is attached to the webpage in the **head** section of the markup. Although styles can be applied individually to each page, it is more efficient to write, edit and attach one or more common stylesheet/s to all the pages in a website.

Using stylesheets

Hint

If you attach more than one stylesheet to a webpage at the same time, those attached later in the markup have priority over earlier ones.

You have already used different styles in your webpages, for example text set as a heading style (h1 to h6) or paragraph style. These styles are often gathered together and held in a stylesheet. This is a collection of styles saved in a different file in **cascading stylesheet** (.css) format.

One or more of these cascading stylesheets can be attached to a webpage, and the styles in the stylesheet will be applied to this page. Where more than one webpage is used, the styles only have to be defined once and attached to all webpages. This allows companies to develop different stylesheets for specific items like corporate colour schemes, corporate text styles and styles for a particular document or set of documents.

Hint

Copy all HTML exactly as shown, including any spaces.

Task 15c

Open a copy of the webpage that you saved in Task 15a.
Apply the stylesheet STYLE1.CSS to this page and save this webpage.
Change the attached stylesheet to STYLE2.CSS and save this with a new filename.

Select the folder called Task 15c in your **Documents** window. Copy the file Task_15a.htm into this folder. Rename this file as Task_15c.htm. Open this file in your text editor and in your web browser. Copy the files STYLE1.CSS and STYLE2.CSS into this folder.

Change the title of the webpage to Task 15c. To apply the styles from the stylesheet STYLE1.CSS you must attach it to the webpage. Move the cursor to the text editor containing the HTML and add this line of text below the title tags in the head section of the markup.

This defines the relationship of this link as a stylesheet, in cascading stylesheet format and searches for the file style1.css and applies this to the page. Your finished markup should look like this. Save this webpage. View this webpage in your browser.

```
<link rel="stylesheet" type="text/css" href="style1.css">
```

```
<html>
<head>
  <title>Task 15c</title>
  <link rel="stylesheet" type="text/css" href="style1.css">
</head>
<body>
  <p>My first webpage by MY NAME HERE</p>
  <h1>This is style h1, the largest heading style</h1>
  <h2>This is style h2</h2>
  <h3>This is style h3</h3>
  <h4>This is style h4</h4>
  <h5>This is style h5</h5>
  <h6>This is style h6, the smallest heading style</h6>
  <p>This is style p, the paragragh style</p>
</body>
</html>
```

Hint

The browser settings on your computer may show you different fonts to those shown here.

You will notice that your webpage has changed from this to this.

The page content has not changed but the styles applied to the page are very different. Notice that the font face, sizes, colours and alignment have all been specified in the stylesheet. This stylesheet is a poor example because it contains too many variations. If you change the markup to attach STYLE2.CSS to the page rather than STYLE1.CSS, you should see something like this.

This is the same webpage again, but with the slightly improved stylesheet STYLE2.CSS, which has a background colour defined in the stylesheet. You will discover how to create and amend these stylesheets in Section 15.5.

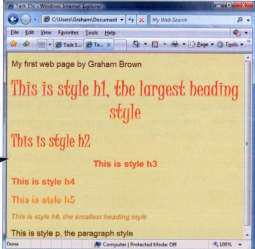

Reminder

In this book:

HTML markup is in blue text.

A stylesheet is in red text.

15.5   Creating a cascading stylesheet

It is very easy to create a cascading stylesheet in your text editor. The structure of a .css file has a few very simple rules. Stylesheets do not have tags in them as they are not a markup language. Each style has a style name which is called a selector. The selector is followed by curly brackets {}. Inside these curly brackets go the property for the style, followed by a colon and the property's value. For example, if you want to set the text in style h1 to be centre aligned it would appear like this. (Note the American spelling of 'center'.)

```
h1  {text-align: center}
```

Each style can have a number of properties and values. If there is more than one property then each property is followed by a semi-colon. For example if you want to set the text in style h1 to be centre aligned, 16 points high and bold it would appear like this.

```
h1  {text-align: center;
     font-size: 16pt;
     font-weight: bold}
```

If a value within a style contains more than one word, it must be placed in speech marks like this.

```
h2  {font-family: "Times New Roman", serif}
```

Stylesheets are saved with a .css format (in a similar way to saving in .htm format) from the text editor.

Font families

Individual fonts can be specified, but these are not always available in all browsers, so there are a number of **generic font families**, including **serif** and **sans serif** fonts, that can also be used. These include 'serif', 'sans-serif', 'cursive', 'fantasy' and 'monospace', which has proportional spacing. The generic font family must always be listed after the other preferred font/s. The **font-family** property must contain a hyphen. In the example above, the **font-family** is set so that the browser will look at the list of fonts installed in the machine, and will try to find Times New Roman first (it is in speech marks in the stylesheet because there are spaces in the font name); if it cannot find it, it will find any generic serif font that is available.

> **Hint**
>
> A serif font is one which has small lines or strokes (called serifs) at the ends of characters like this:
>
>
>
> A font that does not contain serifs is known as a sans serif font.

> **Hint**
>
> Any number of spaces can be placed between the style name and the opening bracket. This does not change how the browser interprets the markup, but sometimes makes it easier for us to read the markup.

> **Task 15d**
>
> Open a copy of the webpage that you saved in Task 15c. Create a new stylesheet called SERIF.CSS that sets all the styles as generic serif fonts. Apply this stylesheet to your webpage. View the webpage in your browser.
>
> Change the generic settings in the stylesheet to a different generic font style. Save the stylesheet with a new name. Try all the generic style settings to see what each one looks like.

Select the folder called Task 15d in your **Documents** window. Copy the webpage you saved in Task 15c into this folder and rename the file as Task_15d.htm. Open this file in your text editor and in your web browser. Edit the title of the webpage so it becomes Task 15d. To attach the stylesheet to the webpage you must edit the third line of the markup so that it becomes:

```
<link rel="stylesheet" type="text/css" href="serif.css">
```

Save the webpage. You are going to create the stylesheet by opening a second copy of the text editor. Enter the following style definitions into it.

Carefully verify your stylesheet by checking this original document with your typed copy. Save the file using the filename SERIF.CSS. Refresh your browser so that you can see the effects that this has on the webpage.

```
h1    {font-family: serif}
h2    {font-family: serif}
h3    {font family: serif}
h4    {font family: serif}
h5    {font family: serif}
h6    {font family: serif}
p     {font family: serif}
```

Grouping style definitions

As all the styles have the same values for the **font-family** property, you can group all of the styles together and change the value only once. This stylesheet can be simplified to this single line.

Edit it and save it so that it replaces the old version.

```
h1,h2,h3,h4,h5,h6,p        {font-family: serif}
```

Refresh the browser to check that it still works.

Edit this stylesheet so that it sets the **font-family** to 'sans-serif'. Save this file using the filename SANS-SERIF.CSS. Change the markup in the HTML to link to this file and save this webpage. Repeat this process for each of the other generic font families.

Font size

Font size can be specified by setting absolute values, by setting values relative to each other, or a mixture of both.

Absolute values can be used to set the number of **points** or **picas** or the number of **pixels** high for each character. If point sizes are used, there are 72 points to an inch, so a 28 point font will be about 1 centimetre tall. This will not be affected by the size or resolution of the monitor. The sizes specified are set as numbers with 'pt' to show it is in points, for example an 18 point font is written as 18pt. Some webpages are created using the measurement in picas, which is abbreviated as 'pc' and is the equivalent of 12 points, so a 2 pica font size would the same as a 24 point font. A pixel is one dot on a computer monitor. This means that pages will appear differently depending upon the size and resolution of the monitor used. For older style monitors, 1 pixel was often about the same size as 1 point, but full high definition (HD) monitors now mean that characters appear much smaller on these devices. The abbreviation for pixels is 'px'. Other absolute values include 'in' to show the measurement in inches, 'cm' for centimetres or 'mm' for millimetres.

Task 15e

Open a copy of the webpage and stylesheet that you saved in Task 15d. Edit this stylesheet so that style h1 is 36 points high, h2 is 24 points, h3 18 points, h4 16 points, h5 14 points, h6 12 points and the paragraph style is 12 points high.
Change these settings to try and get similar results using the settings for pixels (the number will depend upon your monitor display settings), picas, inches, centimetres and millimetres.

Because all of the font settings are different in this case, it is more sensible to keep all of the settings for each style together. It is possible to produce a stylesheet that gives these results like this.

Although this works, it would be easier to edit if all of the settings for each style definition are together like this.

```
h1,h2,h3,h4,h5,h6,p    {font-family: serif}
h1    {font-size: 36pt}
h2    {font-size: 24pt}
h3    {font-size: 18pt}
h4    {font-size: 16pt}
h5    {font-size: 14pt}
h6    {font-size: 12pt}
p     {font-size: 10pt}
```

```
h1    {font-family: serif; font-size: 36pt}
h2    {font-family: serif; font-size: 24pt}
h3    {font-family: serif; font-size: 18pt}
h4    {font-family: serif; font-size: 16pt}
h5    {font-family: serif; font-size: 14pt}
h6    {font-family: serif; font-size: 12pt}
p     {font-family: serif; font-size: 10pt}
```

Amend the markup for the webpage to link to the new stylesheet (SIZE.CSS) and save this in your Task 15e folder. Save the new stylesheet as SIZE.CSS in the same folder. Refresh your browser so that you can see the effect that this has on the webpage. Use trial and error to try and get similar results with the other absolute size settings.

Relative values are often based upon previously defined values for the fonts, as defined by the default browser settings. Two values are show using the abbreviations 'em' and 'ex'. 1 em is the same as the current font size, 2 em is twice the current font size, etc. This can be useful as this automatically selects the default fonts set by the user in other stylesheets or by the browser. 1 ex is about half the height of the current font size and is the measured height of the letter 'x'.

Task 15f

Open a copy of the webpage and stylesheet that you saved in Task 15e. Edit the stylesheet so that the paragraph style is 16 points high. Set style h1 so that it is 3 em, h2 is 2 em, h3 1.5 em, h4 3 ex, h5 2 ex and h6 so that it is 1.5 ex.

Open the webpage saved in Task 15e and edit this to attach the stylesheet SIZE2.CSS to it. Save this as Task_15f.htm in the folder Task_5f. Open the stylesheet SIZE.CSS and edit it so that it changes the font sizes like this. Save this stylesheet as SIZE2.CSS. View the webpage with this stylesheet attached. Notice the difference in the em and ex sizes.

Other relative values frequently used in cascading stylesheets are **percentage** values, for example setting the font size to 200 per cent would force the font to be twice the size of the current setting. Using percentage

```
p     {font-family: serif; font-size: 16pt}
h1    {font-family: serif; font-size: 3em}
h2    {font-family: serif; font-size: 2em}
h3    {font-family: serif; font-size: 1.5em}
h4    {font-family: serif; font-size: 3ex}
h5    {font-family: serif; font-size: 2ex}
h6    {font-family: serif; font-size: 1.5ex}
```

values allows you more flexibility in the relative sizes of the fonts, which can be very useful if classes are used. You will meet these later in this section. There is also a set of pre-defined relative sizes that can be used. These are: 'xx-small', 'x-small', 'small', 'medium', 'large', 'x-large' and 'xx-large'. Other acceptable relative values are 'smaller' and 'larger', which can be very useful if defining different classes within a style.

Task 15g

Open a copy of the webpage and stylesheet that you saved in Task 15f. Edit this stylesheet so that style h1 is xx-large, h2 is x-large, h3 is large, h4 is medium, h5 is small, h6 is x-small and the paragraph style is xx-small.

Open the webpage saved in Task 15f and edit this so that the stylesheet SIZE3.CSS is attached to it. Save this as Task 15g.htm. Open the stylesheet SIZE.CSS and edit this so that it changes the font sizes like this. Save this stylesheet as SIZE3.CSS. View the webpage with this stylesheet attached.

```
h1    {font-family: serif; font-size: xx-large}
h2    {font-family: serif; font-size: x-large}
h3    {font-family: serif; font-size: large}
h4    {font-family: serif; font-size: medium}
h5    {font-family: serif; font-size: small}
h6    {font-family: serif; font-size: x-small}
p     {font-family: serif; font-size: xx-small}
```

Aligning text

Hint

For centre aligned text, note the American spelling for center.

A font style (or class within a style) can be aligned in one of four different ways. You can use the **text-align** property to format text so that it is left aligned, centre aligned, right aligned or fully justified, as shown in this sample stylesheet.

```
h1    {text-align: left}
h2    {text-align: center}
h3    {text-align: right}
h4    {text-align: justify}
```

Task 15h

Open the file you saved in Task 15b. Add a new title 'Aligning text' in style h1. Change the word 'second' to read 'third'.

Set the heading style h1 to be centre aligned. Set style h2 to be right aligned. Set style p to be left aligned. Place a horizontal line below the title 'Aligning text'.

Place additional blank lines before the title at the top of the page and after the horizontal line.

Open the webpage saved in Task 15b and edit this by attaching a new stylesheet called ALIGN.CSS. Add the title 'Aligning text' in style h1. Change the word 'second' in the paragraph style so that it becomes 'third'. Save this as Task_15h.htm in your Task_15h folder.

Create a new stylesheet like this called ALIGN.CSS.

```
h1    {text-align: center}
h2    {text-align: right}
h3    {text-align: left}
```

Hint

Line breaks should not be used to split a paragraph into two. Each paragraph should have its own style definition.

Set h1 to be centre aligned, h2 right aligned and p to be left aligned. Save this stylesheet. Check that this works and that the styles have been applied correctly like this.

To place a horizontal line below the title you use the horizontal rule tag. This is one of the few single tags that are used in HTML. It does not have an open tag and a close tag. The tag appears like this.

```
<hr>
```

Aligning text

My third webpage by Graham Brown

Text can be enhanced in different ways. Here are some of those ways.

Text can be made **bold**

Text can be made *italic*

Text cannot be underlined in later versions of html because it looks like the text is a hyperlink

Text can be superscripted like x^3

Text can be subscripted like H_2

To insert a blank line before the title, move to the correct position in the markup and insert a line break tag. Again this is a single tag and appears like this.

`<br>`

This tag must appear within a style, for example between the **<h1>** and **</h1>** tags, or between the **<p>** and **</p>** tags. Place another line break below the horizontal rule. Save the webpage again. The markup and page should look like this.

Hint

The carriage returns within the HTML have no effect on the layout of the webpage.

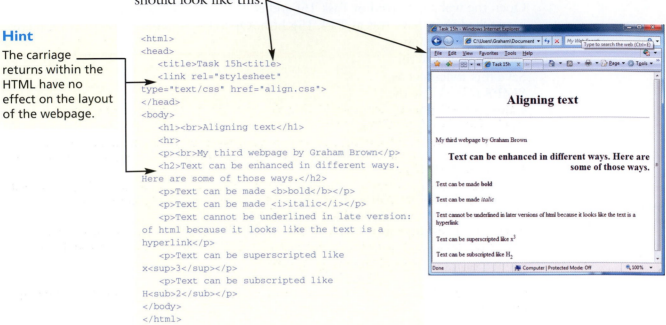

```
<html>
<head>
    <title>Task 15h<title>
    <link rel="stylesheet"
type="text/css" href="align.css">
</head>
<body>
    <h1><br>Aligning text</h1>
    <hr>
    <p><br>My third webpage by Graham Brown</p>
    <h2>Text can be enhanced in different ways.
Here are some of those ways.</h2>
    <p>Text can be made <b>bold</b></p>
    <p>Text can be made <i>italic</i></p>
    <p>Text cannot be underlined in late version:
of html because it looks like the text is a
hyperlink</p>
    <p>Text can be superscripted like
x<sup>3</sup></p>
    <p>Text can be subscripted like
H<sub>2</sub></p>
</body>
</html>
```

Enhancing text within a stylesheet

You are going to use some similar techniques to those used for Task 15b. This time the enhancements will apply to the whole style (or class of style as you will see later in this chapter). Each of the enhancements uses a different property setting. The default value for all three enhancements is normal. To get bold text, set the **font-weight** property to 'bold', like this.

To italicise text, set the **font-style** property to 'italic', like this.

To underline text, set the **text-decoration** property to 'underline', like this.

Hint

Although the underline command is no longer part of html, it can still be used by setting it within a style in the stylesheet.

```
h1    {font-weight: bold;
       font-style: italic;
       text-decoration: underline}
```

Task 15i

Create a new stylesheet called MYSTYLE1.CSS and attach this to the webpage called WEBPAGE2.HTM. This stylesheet will set style h1 to a bold, italic, 18 point font. If 'Times New Roman' is available the browser will use that, otherwise it will choose 'Times', but if this is not available any other serif font will be used. Make this text centre aligned.

Copy the file WEBPAGE2.HTM into your Task 15i folder. Open this file in your web browser and text editor. Enter this markup to create a new stylesheet called MYSTYLE1.CSS. Refresh this file in your web browser.

```
h1     {font-family: "Times
New Roman", Times, serif;
       font-size: 18pt;
       text-align: center;
       font-weight: bold;
       font-style: italic}
```

Activity 15b

Create a new stylesheet called MYSTYLE2.CSS and attach this to the webpage called WEBPAGE3.HTM. This stylesheet will set style:

- h1 as an italic, centre aligned, 24 point font. If 'Helvetica' is available the browser will use that, otherwise it will choose 'Arial Narrow' but if this is not available any other sans-serif font will be used.
- h2 as a bold, right aligned, 16 point font. If 'Courier Narrow' is available the browser will use that, otherwise it will choose 'Courier' but if this is not available any other proportional spaced font will be used.
- h3 as an underlined, left aligned, 16 point font. If 'Courier Narrow' is available the browser will use that, otherwise it will choose 'Courier' but if this is not available any other proportional spaced font will be used.
- p as a 14 point, left aligned, serif font.

Print evidence of your stylesheet and the browser view of the webpage with the stylesheet attached.

Using classes within a cascading stylesheet

Hint

Notice that each property and its value/s are on a new line. This makes it easier to read and check for mistakes.

You can define different classes which are sub-types within an element in a stylesheet. You can define a class in the stylesheet by using the . (dot or full stop) symbol. These are very useful for adding to or changing styles without defining completely new styles. For example, this stylesheet defines the style h1 in the normal way. It also defines a class that can be used with any style to change the colour and alignment of the style that it is applied to.

```
h1      {text-align: left}
.right  {color: blue;
         text-align: right}
```

Task 15j

Open the stylesheet called CLASS1.CSS and add a new class within this stylesheet that changes the default style to be right aligned and blue. Open the webpage called WEBPAGE4.HTM and apply this class to each line of text that starts with the word 'This'.

Copy the files CLASS1.CSS and WEBPAGE4.HTM into your Task 15j folder and rename WEBPAGE4.HTM as Task_15j.htm. Open these files in your text editor and the file Task_15j.htm in your web browser. Add this markup to the stylesheet and save this in cascading stylesheet (.css) format.

```
.right   {color: blue;
          text-align: right}
```

Enter the highlighted markup to the webpage to add a class sub-type to each line starting with the word 'This'. It should look like this.

```
<html>
<head>
  <title>Task 15j</title>
  <link rel>="stylesheet" type="text/css" href="class1.css">
</head>
<body>
  <h1>Task 15j</h1>
  <hr>
  <h1>Style h1 is a sans serif, 20 point, centre aligned font.</h1>
  <h1 class="right">This is the sub-type of h1 called .right</h1>
  <h2>Style h2 is a sans-serif, 14 point, left aligned font.</h2>
  <h2 class="right">This is the sub-type of h2 called .right</h2>
  <h3>Style h3 is a sans-serif, 12 point, left aligned font.</h3>
  <h3 class="right">This is the sub-type of h3 called .right</h3>
  <p>Style p is a serif, 10 point, left aligned font.</p>
  <p class="right">This is the sub-type of p called .right</p>
</body>
</html>
```

The screen should now look similar to this.

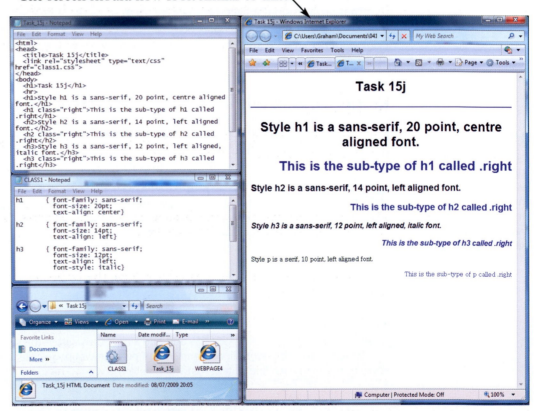

You can see from this printout that the original style definitions (except for the text alignment) have all been applied to the page. The text alignment and colour have been added to the styles using the class called 'right'.

Using comments in your markup

Comments can be used to annotate your markup. Each comment appears within a single tag. The exclamation mark followed by two hyphens (dashes) opens the comment and two hyphens close the comment. An example of comments in the markup looks like this.

```
<html>
<!-- This is a comment. Comments are not displayed in
the browser -->
<!-- Markup created by Graham Brown-->
<!-- This section defines the header of the webpage-->
<head>
```

15.6 Working with lists

You can include on a webpage either a numbered list, which is called an **ordered list**, or a bulleted list, which is called an **unordered list**. Bulleted (unordered) lists can also be nested (placed one inside the other) to give you more flexibility in the design of your webpages. Items to be placed in a list start with the markup **<li>** and close with **</li>**. These are used in the same way as the style definitions for headings (styles h1 to h6) and paragraph styles. Each item in the list must have the list tags around it. An example of an item placed in a list would look like this.

```
<li>This is one item from a bulleted or numbered list </li>
```

Numbered lists

Numbered lists are called ordered lists in HMTL. Place the tag **<ol>** at the start of the numbered list and the tag **</ol>** at the end.

> **Task 15k**
>
> Create a webpage containing the heading 'Fruit' and a numbered list for the following items: Apple, Orange, Pear, Banana and Lemon.

Enter this markup into your text editor. Save the webpage, which should look like this in your browser.

```
<html>
<!-- Task 15k by your name -->
<head>
   <title>Task 15k</title>
</head>
<body>
   <h1>Frlut</h1>
      <ol>
         <li> Apple </li>
         <li> Orange </li>
         <li> Pear </li>
         <li> Banana </li>
         <li> Lemon </li>
      </ol>
</body>
</html>
```

Bulleted lists

Bulleted lists are called unordered lists in HMTL. Place the tag **<ul>** at the start of the numbered list and the tag **</ul>** at the end.

Task 15l

Create a webpage containing the heading 'Colours' and a bulleted list for the following items: Red, Yellow, Blue, Green and Cyan.

Enter this markup into your text editor. Save the webpage, which should look like this in your browser.

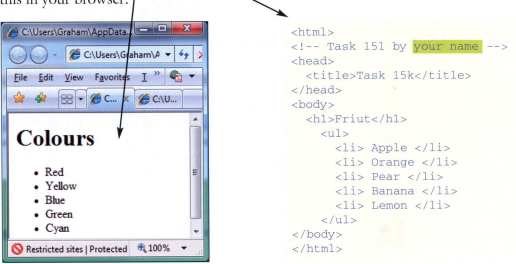

```
<html>
<!-- Task 15l by your name -->
<head>
   <title>Task 15k</title>
</head>
<body>
   <h1>Friut</h1>
     <ul>
        <li> Apple </li>
        <li> Orange </li>
        <li> Pear </li>
        <li> Banana </li>
        <li> Lemon </li>
     </ul>
</body>
</html>
```

Nested lists

Bulleted lists can be nested, by having sub-lists. These are created by placing one unordered list within another list.

Task 15m

Create a webpage containing the names of two resorts as a bulleted list. These resorts are: Ellmau in Austria and Sharm El Sheikh in Egypt. For each resort, list the main activities available.

Enter this markup into your web editor to create the primary list.

```
<html>
<!-- Task 15m by your name -->
<head>
   <title>Task 15km/title>
</head>
<body>
     <ul>
        <li> Ellmau </li>
        <li> Sharm El Sheikh </li>
     </ul>
</body>
</html>
```

After each resort, enter a new sub-list that contains the activities offered in each of these places. Note that the sub-list fits between the list item name and the close tag for that item. The finished markup will look like this.
Save the webpage, which should look like this in your browser.

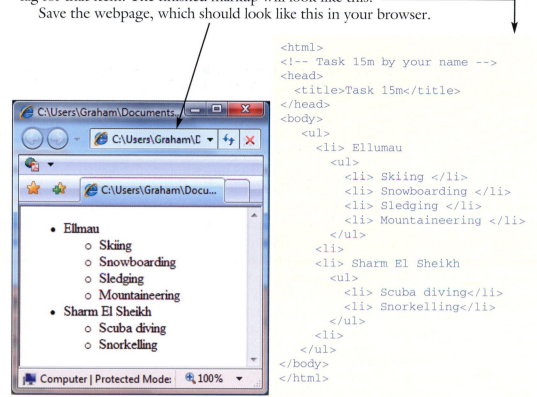

```
<html>
<!-- Task 15m by your name -->
<head>
  <title>Task 15m</title>
</head>
<body>
  <ul>
    <li> Ellumau
      <ul>
        <li> Skiing </li>
        <li> Snowboarding </li>
        <li> Sledging </li>
        <li> Mountaineering </li>
      </ul>
    <li>
    <li> Sharm El Sheikh
      <ul>
        <li> Scuba diving</li>
        <li> Snorkelling</li>
      </ul>
    <li>
  </ul>
</body>
</html>
```

Activity 15c

Create a new webpage containing the heading 'Winter sports', a brief introduction and an unordered list of the following winter sports: skiing, tobogganing and snowboarding. For each winter sport, make a sub-list of the items of clothing required. Set these sub-lists as unordered lists.
Print the webpage as viewed in your browser and as html.
Change these sub-lists to ordered lists. Again, print the webpage as viewed in your browser and as html.

15.7 Working with colour

Colour in HTML can be defined in two ways. One method is to use colour names, like red, green and blue within the html code. There are currently only 16 colour names accepted as web standards in HTML, CSS and by the World Wide Web Consortium (known as W3C) . These are: aqua, black, blue, fuchsia, gray (note the American spelling), green, lime, maroon, navy, olive, purple, red, silver, teal, white and yellow. Other colour names are, however, accepted by the major browsers and a table showing these colours and their names is included on the CD. This can be found on the webpage called COLOURCODES. You can open this webpage and use these colours in your own stylesheets attached to your webpages.

It is not always easy to remember the names of the colours, and many web designers prefer to use **hexadecimal** codes (often referred to as hex codes) to define the colour of text, backgrounds or objects. Hexadecimal is a counting system where counting is done in 16s rather than in the 10s used in the decimal system. Because we do not have sixteen different characters for numbers, we use letters and numbers as shown in Table 15.1.

Decimal	1	2	3	4	5	6	7	8	9	10	11	12	13	14	15	16	17	18	19	20	21	22	23	24	25	26	27	...
Hexadecimal	1	2	3	4	5	6	7	8	9	A	B	C	D	E	F	10	11	12	13	14	15	16	17	18	19	1A	1B	...

Decimal	...	152	153	154	155	156	157	158	159	160	161	162	163	164	165	166	167	168	169	170	171	172	...
Hexadecimal	...	98	99	9A	9B	9C	9D	9E	9F	A0	A1	A2	A3	A4	A5	A6	A7	A8	A9	AA	AB	AC	...

Table 15.1 The hexadecimal counting system

Hint

This table will help you work out which hex codes are useful in the practical examinations.

The largest number that can be stored in a single **byte** of information is the decimal number 255, which is FF in hexadecimal.

Each pixel (dot) on a monitor or projected onto a screen is made up of three different colours. The primary colours when using light (which is very different from the primary colours used in painting) are red, green and blue. You will notice that the initial letters are RGB, hence RGB monitors. Each of these colours can be off, partially on or fully on. In hexadecimal, if a colour is off it is set to 00 and if it is fully on it is set to FF. To create the colour for any pixel you must tell the computer how much red, green and blue light to show. This means that all colour codes have six characters, the first two being red, the next two green and the final two blue. This example is the hex code for red, as the red component is fully on (FF), the green component is off (00) and the blue component is also off (00).

color = #FF0000

All of the different combinations of red , green and blue allow more than 16 million different colours to be used. You do *not* need to learn the hex codes for the exam. Using a small number of values for each colour (like those shown in the table in the hint box) is more than enough.

Amount of light (colour)	Hex code	Example (red only)	Colour
Fully on	FF	FF0000	
3/4 on	C0	C00000	
1/2 on	80	800000	
1/4 on	40	400000	
off	00	000000	

The webpage COLOURCODES contains the hex codes (as well as the names) for the most popular colours. It is interesting to note that, working with light, mixing red and green gives yellow, green and blue gives cyan and mixing red and blue gives magenta. If all three colours are fully on, the result is white and no colours on gives black.

Task 15n

Create a new stylesheet called MYSTYLE3.CSS which sets the font styles:

- h1 to Times New Roman, or Times, or any serif font
- h1 to be 36 points high, black and centre aligned
- h2 to Arial, or Helvetica, or any sans-serif font
- h2 to be 24 points high, red and left aligned
- h3 to Arial, or Helvetica, or any sans-serif font
- h3 to be 18 points high, blue and right aligned
- p and li to Arial, or Helvetica, or any sans-serif font
- p and li to be 14 points high, dark blue, left aligned.

Open the webpage called WEBPAGE5.HTM and attach this stylesheet to it.

Copy the file WEBPAGE5.HTM into your Task 15n folder. Open this file in your text editor and in your web browser. Create a new stylesheet in a second copy of your text editor. For each style, add the font family, size and alignment as shown in previous sections.

The colour for each style is added using the color property and the value (note the American spelling of colour). For this example, the values will be in hexadecimal so that we can select from any of the 16 million available colours. You use the # symbol to tell the browser that the following six characters are hexadecimal. For h1 we will set the colour to black using #000000, h2 to red with #FF0000, h3 to blue with #0000FF and dark blue for the paragraph style with #000080. The final markup should look like this.

```
h1       {font-family: "Times New Roman", Times,serif;
          font-size; 36pt;
          text-align: center;
          color: #000000}
h2       {font-family: Arial,Helvetica,sans serif;
          font-size; 24pt;
          text-align: left;
          color: #FF0000}
h3       {font-family: Arial,Helvetica,sans serif;
          font-size; 18pt;
          text-align: right;
          color: #0000FF}
p,li     {font-family: Arial,Helvetica,sans serif;
          font-size; 14pt;
          text-align: left;
          color: #000080}
```

Save this with the filename MYSTYLE3.CSS. Add this markup to the head section of the webpage to attach your new stylesheet. Save your webpage and test it in your browser. The finished page

```
<title>Task 15n</title>
<link rel ="stylesheet" type="text/css" href
="mystyle3.css">
</head>
```

should look like this.

Style h1 is black

The paragraph style is a 14 point dark blue font.

Style h2 is red

Style h3 is blue

Task 15o

Using the webpage and stylesheet from Task 15n, add an extra stylesheet called MYSTYLE4.CSS that defines classes to change the text colour to red, yellow or green and adds enhancements like black bold and blue italic. Apply these styles in the webpage, so that each of the bulleted items has the correct colours and enhancements.
Set a khaki background to the webpage and make sure that all text is clearly visible.

Hint

Even though you may choose your own class names in the practical examinations, try to make them short and meaningful. Try to avoid using words that mean something in html, e.g. use 'rd' rather than 'red'.

Copy all the files from your Task 15n folder into the Task 15o folder. From the Task 15o folder, open the file MYSTYLE3.CSS in your text editor and the webpage in both the text editor and your web browser. In another copy of your text editor, create a new stylesheet called MYSTYLE4.CSS. In this stylesheet you are going to add classes. Some will change the font colours and some will add enhancements to make text bold or italic.

Like each style, each class is given a name. You will need to decide on the name for each class, which should be short but meaningful. In this example you can use the names 'rd' for the red class, 'yllw' for yellow, 'grn' for green, 'ital' for italic and blue, and 'bld' for the bold and black class. Create each class in your stylesheet. The final markup should look like this. Save this with the filename MYSTYLE4.CSS.

```
.rd        {color: #FF0000}
.yllw      {color: #FFFF00}
.grn       {color: #00FF00}
.ital      {font-style: italic;
            color: #0000FF}
.bld       {font-weight: bold;
            color: #000000}
```

Add this markup to the head section of the webpage to attach your new stylesheet.

```
<title>Task 15o</title>
<link rel="stylesheet" type=text/css"
 href="mystyle3.css">
<link rel="stylesheet" type=text/css"
 href="mystyle4.css">
</head>
```

Note that this stylesheet has been attached after the previous stylesheet, so if there were any clashes in style definitions, those in MYSTYLE4.CSS would take priority. These classes need adding to each style definition within the webpage. Edit the markup and save the webpage. The markup should look like this.

```
<ul>
   <li class = "rd">red</li>
   <li class = "yllw">yellow</li>
   <li class = "grn">green</li>
   <li>or left unchanged</li>
</ul>
<p>In fact any other colour could be used to enhance previously
defined text. Other enhancements could be added like having classes to
make parts of the work enhanced and coloured like:</p>
   <ul>
      <li class = "ital">blue and italic</li>
      <li class = "bld">black and bold</li>
      <li>or left unchanged</li>
```

The webpage will look similar to this.

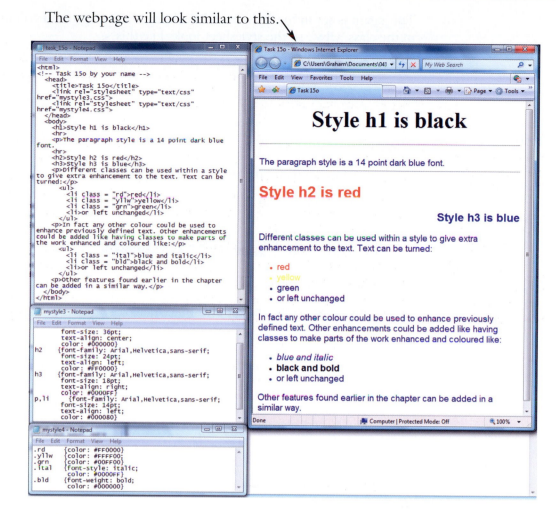

Background colour

Background colour can be added to many features of webpages, including the entire webpage, text on the page or, as you will see in Section 15.9, other objects like tables. In the original versions of HTML the colour was set in markup of the page rather than in a stylesheet, but many of the original commands have now been **deprecated** so all background colour settings are performed within the stylesheet.

The background colour for a page is set in the body style of the stylesheet. Edit the stylesheet MYSTYLE4.CSS to add the body style setting for the khaki (hex code #F0E68C) background like this.

```
body    {background-color: #F0E68C}
```

When you have applied this to the webpage, it is difficult to read the yellow text, so to make sure that all the text is fully visible, you are going to change the background colour of the yellow text to a contrasting colour.

extra enhancement to the text. Text can be turned:

- red
- yellow
- green
- or left unchanged

In fact any other colour could be used to enhance

This again is set in the stylesheet, by adding the background colour to the definition in the class 'yllw', so the stylesheet looks like this.

```
.rd      {color: #FF0000}
.yllw    {color: #FFFF00;background-color: #00008B}
.grn     {color: #00FF00}
.ital    {font-style: italic; color: #0000FF}
.bld     {font-weight: bold; color: #000000}
body     {background-color: #F0E68C}
```

The background colour has been applied with the yellow font colour like this.

extra enhancement to the text. Text can be turned:

- red
- yellow
- green
- or left unchanged

In fact any other colour could be used to enhance

Activity 15d
Create a webpage with a pale blue background that is about using colour in websites. Attach a stylesheet that defines classes to change the text colour to red, yellow, green, dark green, blue, dark blue or magenta. Have three different styles for the dark blue text, one for left aligned, one for centre and one for right. Apply these styles in the webpage, so that each colour is used appropriately.

15.8 Using hyperlinks

A **hyperlink** is a method of accessing another document or resource from your current application. Hyperlinks do not just relate to webpages: other applications software can also use them. Hyperlinks are often used to create menu options with webpages, using either text or images. When you select a hyperlink (usually by clicking the left mouse button), the hyperlink will perform an action. It may move your position within a page, open another page either locally or on the internet, or open your email editor so that you can send an email to a specified place or company.

Anchors

An anchor is a point of reference within a webpage. It is similar to a bookmark when using word-processing or desktop publishing software. If you create a webpage that will not fit in a single window, it is useful to use one anchor for each section of the webpage (or document), so the user can move to any section without having to scroll through the whole document. An anchor starts with an **<a>** tag and closes with a **</a>** tag. One common use of an anchor is to define the top of a page. This anchor is often called 'top' or 'start'. To create an anchor called 'top' enter this markup in the body section of the page. This anchor will work without any text between the open and close tags.

```
<body>
    <a name="top">Any content could appear here</a>
```

Hyperlinks within a webpage

Task 15p

Open the webpage WEBPAGE6.HTM and stylesheet STYLE3.CSS. Edit the webpage so that each new section contains an anchor. Use these anchors to create hyperlinks from the appropriate text in the first paragraph. Make the word 'top' in the last line a hyperlink to the top of the page. Make the words 'CIE website' a hyperlink to the website www.cie.org.uk and the words 'W3C website' a hyperlink to www.w3.org.

Copy the files WEBPAGE6.HTM and STYLE3.CSS into your Task 15p folder. Open the webpage in your text editor and in your web browser. Each section needs an anchor with a name. Each anchor name must be different. You should always choose short yet meaningful names for each anchor. For this webpage you will use the anchor names top, 15a, 15b, 15c, 15d, 15e and 15f as these relate directly to the sections within the webpage. It is sensible to place all the anchor names into the document before creating the hyperlinks to these anchor names. Each anchor name is created like this.

```
<h1><a name="top"></a>Chapter 15</h1>
```

You can see that the anchor tags are inside the tags defining the style for the text. The initial anchor tag contains the anchor name which is placed in speech marks. This name will be used in all hyperlinks to this point. Add the other anchors to the markup, one for each section of the document like this.

```
<hr>
<h2><a name="15a"></a>15a Understand what html is</h2>
<p>Many students sit the practical examinations without really
```

```
<hr>
<h2><a name="15b"></a>15b Problems with WYSIWYGs</h2>
<p>There are many well designed WYSIWYG packages on the market, some are
```

```
<hr>
<h2><a name="15c"></a>15c Use the correct terms</h2>
<p> Over the past few years, as the practical examinations have developed
```

Add anchors for 15d, 15e and 15f with similar markup. In the final sentence, find the word 'top'. This will be used to create a hyperlink to the anchor with the name top that you created earlier. The hyperlink is also created using an anchor. The two anchor tags are placed each side of the word top. The markup includes a hyperlink reference (the markup for this is href) and the name of the destination anchor. This anchor name is always inside speech marks and preceded by the # symbol like this.

```
<p>Back to the <a href="#top">top</a></p>
```

In the first paragraph find the text 'what is html'. Edit the markup for this text so that it creates a hyperlink to the anchor named 15a. It will look like this.

```
<h3>Here are practical tips for the exams, if you follow them you are
likely to increase your marks. First you need
know <a href="#15a">what is html? </a> Once you have a
sound understanding of html, it is worth
```

You need to add similar markup to the text 'WYSIWYGs', 'use the right terms', 'create and attach stylesheets', 'work with tables' and 'other resources'. The finished markup for this section should look like this.

```
<h1>Hints and tips for the practical examinations?</h1>
<h3>Here are practical tips for the exams, if you follow them you are
likely to increase your marks. First you need know <a href="#15a">what
is html?</a> Once you have a sound understanding of html, it is worth
considering the use of <a href="#15b">WYSIWYGs</a> and the potential
problems of using these packages. Make sure that you <a href="#15c">
use the right terms</a> to describe what you have done, are doing
or could be asked to do. Learn how to <a href="#15d">create and
attach stylesheets</a> to your webpages. Make sure that you can
<a href="#15e">work with tables</a>. These provide a fundamental
structure to webpages and seem to be replacing frames in many areas.
There are other methods of formatting layout including the use of
DIVs, but these are currently beyond the scope of this book. Look for
<a href="#15f">other resources</a> to help you prepare for the
practical examinations.</h3>
```

Now that the hyperlinks have been created, each one needs testing. Save the webpage and refresh your browser, then try each hyperlink in turn and make sure that it directs you to the correct place in the webpage. If the name that you have used in the hyperlink reference does not exist, your browser will go to the top of the page and the browser does not show you that there is an error.

Hyperlinks to other webpages

Hyperlinks can be created to another webpage stored locally, usually in the same folder as the current webpage, or to an external website on the internet. The markup for both of these links has the same syntax (structure). The only difference is the address of the webpage that the hyperlink is to go to. To complete task 15p, two hyperlinks need adding to external web addresses. These follow a similar format, with the URL for the web address appearing as the hyperlink. The markup for these two hyperlinks is shown overleaf.

```
<h2><a name="15f"></a>15f Other useful links</h2>
..<p>There are other places that can be used to gain valuable
information that may help. These include the
<a href="http://www.cie.org.uk">CIE website</a> and the
<a href="http://www.w3.org">W3C website</a>.</p>
    <p>Back to the <a href="#top">top</a></p>
```

Add these hyperlinks in to the last section of your markup and save your webpage. Test the hyperlinks to make sure they work as you expected.

References to pages stored in the same folder as your webpage just have an address without the URL. To link to a local file called 'next_page.htm', you would include a hyperlink reference like this.

```
<p><a name="next_page.htm">Click here for the next page</a>.<p>
```

Activity 15e

Open the webpage HTMLTIPS.HTM and stylesheet STYLE3.CSS. Replace the text 'YOUR NAME' with your name.
Edit the webpage so that each new section contains an anchor. Use these anchors to create hyperlinks from the appropriate text in the first section. Make the word 'top' in the last line a hyperlink to the top of the page.
Make the word 'CIE' a hyperlink to the website www.cie.org.uk, the words 'Hodder Education' a hyperlink to the website www.hoddereducation.co.uk and the text 'W3C' a hyperlink to www.w3.org.
Print the html view of this webpage.

Opening a webpage in a new browser window

When a webpage is opened, it may open in the current window or it may open in a new window. This is set using the **target attribute**. An attribute is something that is added to one of the markup commands to give further information/instructions to the browser. This attribute is part of the anchor and tells the browser which window to use for the webpage that you are going to open. The **target** attribute can either be set as a default setting in the head section of the markup, or as an individual setting for a hyperlink within the body section. If the **target** attribute is not used, the browser will decide where to open a webpage.

To set a target window for a single hyperlink, add the **target** attribute to the first anchor. Some **target** attributes have specific functions. If a target name of **_blank** is applied, this will open in a new target window. If **_self** is applied it will open in the current window. Other target names such as **_parent** and **_top** are reserved and perform different functions with **frames**, which are beyond the scope of this book. Any other target name that you use will open the specified webpage in a window with that target name if it exists, or open it in a new window with that target name.

Task 15q

Using the webpage and stylesheet from Task 15p, make the hyperlink to the W3C website open in the same window and the hyperlink to the CIE website open in a new target window called _cie.

Copy the file STYLE3.CSS and the webpage that you saved in Task15p from your Task 15p folder into your Task 15q folder. Open the webpage in your text editor and in your web browser. Edit the markup for the last two hyperlinks to include target windows like this.

```
<p>There are other places that can be used to gain valuable
information that may help. These include the <a
href="http://www.cie.org.uk" target="_cie">CIE website</a> and the <a
href="http://www.w3.org" target="_self">W3C website</a>.</p>
<p>Back to the <a href="#top">top</a></p>
```

Save your website and test the hyperlinks to make sure that they work as you expected.

Using a hyperlink to send an email message

Hyperlinks from webpages, other applications packages or documents can be used to open an email editor and prepare a message to be sent to another person or company. This is very useful in a website where you can set up your email address and subject line within the markup and instruct the browser to open the email editor and insert these details into a new message when the hyperlink is selected.

The format for this is very similar to the hyperlinks shown earlier in this section. In place of the URL or path of a webpage that is placed within the hyperlink reference of the anchor, the **mailto:** instruction is used. This is followed by the email address of the recipient. To include the subject line for the message, this is included by specifying **subject=** followed by the text for the subject line. All the hyperlink reference is enclosed within speech marks.

> ### Task 15r
> Create a new webpage that contains a hyperlink to prepare an email message to be sent to graham.a.brown@hotmail.co.uk with the subject line 'IGCSE Book'.

For this task you need to prepare a new markup in your text editor that contains this line.

```
<p><a href="mailto:graham.a.brown@hotmail.co.uk?subject=IGCSE%20Book">
Click here to contact us page</a></p>
```

Hint
Body text could also be added by adding &body=The%20 message%20here to the markup.

Save this in your Task 15r folder and try it in your browser. When you click on the hyperlink it will open your email editor, place the address in the **To:** section and the text 'IGCSE Book' in the **Subject:** line. Note how the space in the text 'IGCSE Book' has been replaced in the markup with '%20'. This is the hex value for the **ascii** character 32, which in the ascii code represents a space. There are no spaces inside the speech marks for the hyperlink reference.

15.9 Using tables

Hint

In the practical examinations, this planning stage will often be given to you in the question.

Tables are used to create the basic structure of many webpages. They are used to organise page layout and are often used in webpages even though they may not be visible. If you need to create a table within a webpage, it is always worth planning it on paper before starting to create the markup.

Task 15s

Create a new webpage that looks like this and has the caption 'Colours':

Red	36%
Green	23%
Blue	41%

Basic table structure

Hint

In the practical examinations it will be much easier to use WYSIWYG software to create your tables. This section is designed to ensure that you understand how to create and edit tables. You will need to understand the markup used to define tables, even if you decide to use a WYSIWYG package to develop your tables.

Tables in HTML always start with a **<table>** tag and end with **</table>**. Start by adding these tags in the body section of the markup like this. Everything between these tags will be included in the table, except for the caption. This is added using the **<caption>** and **</caption>** tags and allows you to display a caption (usually centre aligned) above the table. If a caption is used it must be the first html tag after the **<table>** tag.

Each table is split into rows. For this task, the table you need to create has three table rows. The tag for a table row is **<tr>**. Create the three blank rows between the caption and the end of the table like this.

Each table row will contain two cells of table data. Between each **<tr>** and **</tr>** tag place start table data **<td>** and end table data **</td>** tags like this. A table cell can contain text, images, other tables, lists, paragraphs, forms, horizontal rules, etc.

```
<html>
<!-- Task 15s by your name -->
<head>
  <title>Task 15s</title>
</head>
<body>
  <table>
  </table>
</body>
</html>
```

```
<body>
  <table>
    <caption>Colours</caption>
  </table>
</body>
</html>
```

```
<body>
  <table>
    <caption>Colours</caption>
    <tr>
      <td>
      </td>
      <td>
      </td>
    </tr>
    <tr>
      <td>
      </td>
      <td>
      </td>
    </tr>
    <tr>
      <td>
      </td>
      <td>
      </td>
    </tr>
  </table>
</body>
```

```
<body>
  <table>
    <caption>Colours</caption>
    <tr>
    </tr>
    <tr>
    </tr>
    <tr>
    </tr>
  </table>
</body>
```

The data can now be added to each cell like this.

Your table will look similar to this.

Colours

Red   36%

Green 23%

Blue   41%

Table borders

This table has been created but does not have a visible border. To show the table gridlines you must add a border. This is added as an attribute within the table tag which should be changed like this.

```
<body>
  <table border="1">
    <caption>Colours</caption>
```

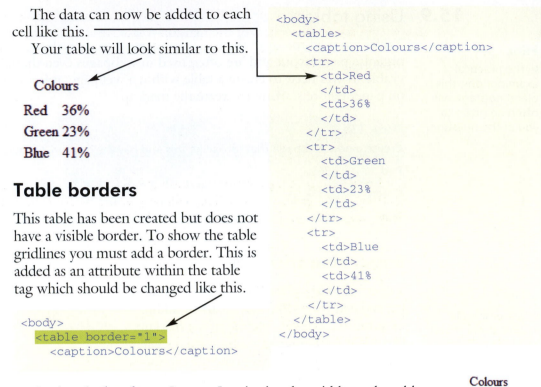

```
<body>
  <table>
    <caption>Colours</caption>
    <tr>
      <td>Red
      </td>
      <td>36%
      </td>
    </tr>
    <tr>
      <td>Green
      </td>
      <td>23%
      </td>
    </tr>
    <tr>
      <td>Blue
      </td>
      <td>41%
      </td>
    </tr>
  </table>
</body>
```

Setting the **border** to 1 sets a 1 point border width on the table like this.

Setting the **border** to 6 points looks like this.

Setting the **border** to 0 will hide the table border, yet allow the table to control the structure of the page.

Headers and footers in tables

Tables can have three sections: a header, a body section and a footer. These are defined using the **<thead>**, **<tbody>** and **<tfoot>** tags, and closed with **</thead>**, **</tbody>** and **</tfoot>** respectively.

Task 15t

Create a new webpage that looks like this and has the caption 'Fruit sales'. The colour codes you will need are #32879B for the header, #92CDDC for the footer and #B6DDE8 for the table body.

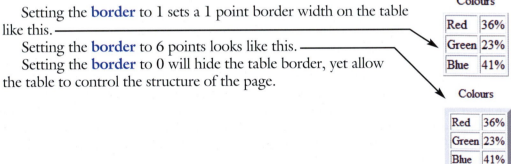

To create this webpage you need to first create the open table and close table tags within the body section of the markup. Place the caption tag between these in the same way that did when you completed Task 15s. The initial markup for this section of the markup should look like this.

```
<body>
  <table border="1">
    <caption>Fruit sales</caption>
  </table>
</body>
```

Before continuing with the markup it is worth planning the table using a hand-drawn sketch similar to this. This will help you work out the structure needed for the markup. For this table, you will need three sections to the table.

These three sections need creating next within the markup. The header section is created using the table head tags, with **<thead>** to start the section and **</thead>** to finish the section. The footer section uses the tags **<tfoot>** and **</tfoot>** and the body is defined with **<tbody>** and **</tbody>**. In HTML you must define the table header, footer and then body (in that order) if all three sections are to be included. Create the three sections within the table of your markup like this.

```
<body>
  <table border="1">
    <caption>Fruit sales</caption>
    <thead>
    </thead>
    <tfoot>
    </tfoot>
    <tbody>
    </tbody>
  </table>
</body>
```

Within each section add the correct number of table rows, using the notes you made on your sketch to help you.

You can add the table data sections to the footer and body of the table using the tags **<td>** and **</td>**. Do not use these tags in the table header. At each stage, save your webpage and check that the markup that you have written gives you the results that you expected.

In the table header, create heading cells (which are bold and centre aligned) using the tags **<th>** and **</th>** rather than the table data tags. These will set the column headings in heading style. Heading cells can be used inside the table body and table footer sections and are useful in the left column of a table if row headings are required.

Place the contents (in this case text) of the header section in the header cells and place the contents of the body and footer sections in the relevant cells. The finished markup and resulting table should look like this. ──────────────►

Fruit	Price
Apple	$1230
Orange	$780
Pear	$240
Banana	$4235
Lemon	$75
Total	$6560

Table styles using a stylesheet

You have created the table, but it does not yet look like the table shown in Task 15t. To format the sections of the header you will attach a stylesheet and add the formatting within the stylesheet. Add the stylesheet link to the head section of the markup like this.

```
<head>
  <title>Task 15t</title>
  <link rel="stylesheet"
    type="text/css"
    href="mystyle5.css">
</head>
```

You will now create a new stylesheet called MYSTYLE5.CSS. This stylesheet will have the style definitions for the whole table as well as the header, footer and body sections. As you are going to define some of the **table** attributes in the stylesheet it will be sensible to move the table border details into the stylesheet. Remove the **border="1"** attribute from the table tag in the markup. In your stylesheet, set the table attributes so that the **border-color** is black, the **border-style** is a solid line and the **border-width** is set to 1 pixel. ────────────────────────────►

```
<html>
<!-- Task 15t by your name -->
<head>
  <title>Task 15t</title>
</head>
<body>
  <table border="1">
    <caption>Fruit sales</caption>
    <thead>
      <tr>
        <th>Fruit</th>
        <th>Price</th>
      </tr>
    </thead>
    <tfoot>
      <tr>
        <td>Total</td>
        <td>$6560</td>
      </tr>
    </tfoot>
    <tbody>
      <tr>
        <td>Apple</td>
        <td>$1230</td>
      </tr>
      <tr>
        <td>Orange</td>
        <td>$780</td>
      </tr>
      <tr>
        <td>Pear</td>
        <td>$240</td>
      </tr>
      <tr>
        <td>Banana</td>
        <td>$4235</td>
      </tr>
      <tr>
        <td>Lemon</td>
        <td>$75</td>
      </tr>
    </tbody>
  </table>
</body>
</html>
```

```
table   {border-color: #000000; border-style: solid; border-width: 1px}
thead   {background-color: #32879B}
tfoot   {background-color: #92CDDC; color: #FF0000}
tbody   {background-color: #B6DDE8}
```

Set the **background-color** for each section of the table and the text **color** within the footer to red.

When this has been saved and is applied to the webpage the table will look like this.

Fruit sales	
Fruit	**Price**
Apple	$1230
Orange	$780
Pear	$240
Banana	$4235
Lemon	$75
Total	$6560

Formatting columns

The prices and heading in the right column need to be right aligned to match those in the question for the task, and the text in the left column needs to be left aligned (to override the centre align within the heading setting). You can set this in the markup for the page rather than the stylesheet. All of the cells in a column will be grouped together and have a style attribute set. In the case of the left column, this will be the alignment set to left and in the second column the alignment set to right.

These are set with tags for **<colgroup>** and **</colgroup>**. The colgroup tags always appear immediately after the caption but before the table header **<thead>** tag if it is used. The markup for this section looks like this. The table should then look like this.

```
<table>
    <caption>Fruit sales</caption>
        <colgroup align="left"></colgroup>
        <colgroup align="right"></colgroup>
    <thead>
```

Fruit sales	
Fruit	**Price**
Apple	$1230
Orange	$780
Pear	$240
Banana	$4235
Lemon	$75
Total	$6560

Formatting cells

This table still does not look exactly the same as that shown in the task. The ruled lines between the cells are not visible. To turn these on add to the table tag the **rules** attribute, with a value of 'all' to show ruled gridlines for all of the table.

```
<body>
    <table rules="all">
        <caption>Fruit sales</caption>
```

Although this sets the ruled gridlines within the table, they have not appeared the same as the border. This is beyond the scope of this book as the practical examinations are likely to require you to set the rules attribute to 'all' or 'none', although it is worth knowing that they could also be used to rule in 'rows', 'cols' or 'groups'. Try each of these settings and see how the table appears for each value.

Cell padding and **cell spacing** are used to improve the layout of a table. Cell padding is the amount of space between the contents of the cell (in this case text) and the cell border. In the table for Task 15t, you can see that there is no spacing around the text so the table looks crowded.

Fruit	**Price**
Apple	$1230
Orange	$780
Pear	$240
Banana	$4235
Lemon	$75
Total	$6560

By adding cell padding of 4 pixels to the table, you can make it appear like the one in the original task. To add cell padding insert this markup as a second attribute to the table tag. This has the effect of adding 4 pixels of whitespace between the text and the ruled gridlines of the cell like this. ——

Fruit	Price
Apple	$1230
Orange	$780
Pear	$240
Banana	$4235
Lemon	$75
Total	$6560

```
<body>
   <table rules="all" cellpadding="4px">
      <caption>Fruit sales</caption>
```

Save both your webpage and stylesheet.

Task 15u

Create a new webpage with a table that looks like this and has the caption 'Sales team'. Set the border to 5 points, the cell spacing to 5 points and the cell padding to 10 points.

Turtle Travel	Expenses		
	Lee	**Amir**	**Maxine**
Travel	$162.20	$285.75	$150.00
Hotel	$240.00	$182.40	$322.00
Food	$146.50	$102.10	$104.50

The background colour code that you will need is #548DD4. The image that you require is called TURTLE.JPG.

Plan the table using a hand-drawn sketch similar to this.

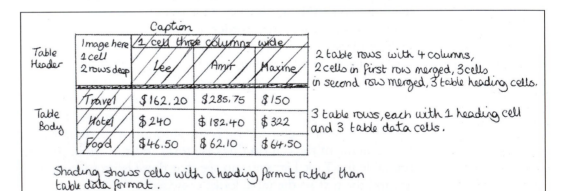

Create the basic markup as you did with Task 15t, starting with the table tags, the caption, the two sections of the table and then inserting the table rows. The markup so far will look like this.

The top row of the table header has only two cells. The first of these is a cell that covers two rows. For this you use a **rowspan** attribute to tell the browser this cell is going to span the two rows. The markup for this section will look like this.

```
<thead>
  <tr>
    <td rowspan="2">A</td>
    <th colspan="3">B</th>
  </tr>
```

The second cell in the top row is a cell that covers three columns. For this you use the **colspan** attribute to tell the browser that this cell is going to span three columns. This cell was identified in your sketch as a being a heading cell, so the **colspan** attribute is used within the table heading tag.

Using the sketch to work from, add the cells to each row of the table. In the body of the table, set the first cell of each row as a table heading and the next three cells as table data. This section of the table will look like this.

In the table tag near the top of the markup, add the attributes for the border, rules and **cellpadding**. Also, include the **cellspacing** attribute, which increases the spacing between each cell in the table. The markup for the table tag will look like this.

```
<body>
  <table border="5" rules="all"
  cellpadding="10px"
  cellspacing="5px">
    <caption>Sales team</caption>
```

The background colour cannot be added to the table tag so create a new stylesheet called MYSTYLE6.CSS and include the style definition like this. Save this stylesheet and attach this to your HTML markup.

```
<body>
  <table>
    <caption>Sales team</caption>
    <thead>
      <tr>
      </tr>
      <tr>
      </tr>
    </thead>
    <tbody>
      <tr>
      </tr>
      <tr>
      </tr>
      <tr>
      </tr>
    </tbody>
  </table>
</body>
```

```
      <th colspan="3">B</th>
    </tr>
    <tr>
      <th>C</th>
      <th>D</th>
      <th>E</th>
    </tr>
  </thead>
  <tbody>
    <tr>
      <th>F</th>
      <td>G</td>
      <td>H</td>
      <td>I</td>
    </tr>
    <tr>
      <th>J</th>
      <td>K</td>
      <td>L</td>
      <td>M</td>
    </tr>
    <tr>
      <th>N</th>
      <td>O</td>
      <td>P</td>
      <td>Q</td>
    </tr>
  </tbody>
</table>
</body>
</html>
```

```
table    {background-color: #548DD4}
```

Hint

When creating a new table like this, it is wise to add a single character as contents of the cell when you create it. In this case a single letter 'A' has been added to the top left cell, the letter 'B' to the next cell and so on. This is because some browsers, including *Internet Explorer* do not display a table cell without contents. By adding these single letters it allows you to test the table as you are creating it.

Enter all the text and currency values into the correct cells in the table. The webpage should look like this. This task is continued in the next section.

Sales team

A	Expenses		
	Lee	Amir	Maxine
Travel	$162.20	$285.75	$150.00
Hotel	$240.00	$182.40	$322.00
Food	$146.50	$102.10	$104.50

15.10 Using images

Images are frequently used on webpages, sometimes as a picture and sometimes in the form of icons that can be used for hyperlinks.

Inserting an image

To complete the webpage for Task 15u, you need to replace the letter 'A' in the top left cell of the table with the image TURTLE.JPG. To do this you have to tell the web browser the name of the **image source**, which should be stored in the same folder as your webpage. Make sure that you have copied the file TURTLE.JPG into your Task 15u folder. Add the following to the markup. As some browsers do not support graphics, you can tell the browser to replace the image with alternative text. This usually describes the image so that the user can still understand what is being shown, even though they cannot see the image. The markup will look like this.

```
<thead>
  <tr>
    <td rowspan="2"><img src="TURTLE.JPG" alt="Company Logo"></td>
    <th colspan="3">Expenses</th>
  </tr>
```

Where to store an image

Images must be stored in the same folder as the webpage. This is called the current folder. Notice in the markup shown above how the filename TURTLE.JPG is given as the image source. This does not contain any reference to which folder the image is stored. Because there is no absolute reference to a folder, the browser automatically looks in the current folder for the image. This means that if this webpage is opened on another computer, as long as the image is stored in the same folder as the webpage it will work properly. If an absolute reference had been used for a file, for example:

```
<img src="C:\My websites\My pictures\TURTLE.JPG"
alt="Company Logo"></td>
```

this would prevent the file being found unless the folders in all the computers were structured in this way. If the file TURLE.JPG is not in the current folder, the webpage will look like this. The image has been replaced by the text 'Company Logo' to tell the user what the missing image should be.

Sales team

⊠ Company Logo	Expenses		
	Lee	Amir	Maxine
Travel	$162.20	$285.75	$150.00
Hotel	$240.00	$182.40	$322.00
Food	$146.50	$102.10	$104.50

If the image file is stored in the current folder, this will be displayed.

Placing an image

Images are usually placed within tables. How an object (often an image or text) is viewed within a table cell will depend upon the alignment of the cells. The horizontal alignment has been covered earlier in the chapter using the **align** attribute, which can be applied to columns (as seen earlier), rows (to format all cells in that row), or individual cells in the table heading or table data tags.

Task 15v

Open the WEBPAGE7.HTM. In the top row, align the images in the second column to the top left of the cell, the third column to be centre aligned both vertically and horizontally, and the last column to be placed in the bottom right corner of the cell.

Copy the files WEBPAGE7.HTM, TURTLE.JPG and REMORA.JPG into your Task 15v folder. View the webpage in your browser.

You will edit the markup in the table data tags for the three images of a turtle in WEBPAGE7.HTM, adding new attributes to these tags to change the alignment in these cells. To align the image (or any other object) to the top of a cell of table data, use the valign attribute with the value set to top.

You can use the values of 'middle' or 'bottom' for this ⟶ `<td valign="top">` attribute to obtain these positions within the cell. The horizontal alignment is set using the **align** attribute, as seen in Task 15u.

For this task, apply the vertical alignment attributes to the table data tag as you did in Task 15t. Save the completed markup, which should look like that shown on the next page.

The finished webpage will look like this.

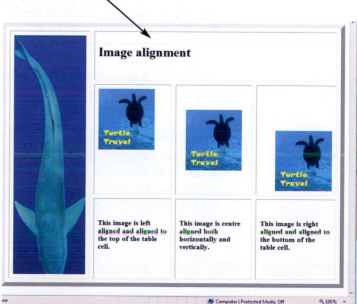

263

```
<html>
<!-- Task 15v by your name -->
<head>
  <title>Task 15v</title>
</head>
<body>
  <table width = "100%" border="10px" rules="all" cellpadding="10px"
cellspacing="10px">
    <tbody>
      <tr>
        <td rowspan="3"><img src="REMORA.JPG" alt="Remora"></td>
        <td colspan="3"><h1>Image alignment</h1></td>
      </tr>
      <tr>
        <td valign="top" align="left"><img src="TURTLE.JPG"
alt="Logo"></td>
        <td valign="middle" align="center"><img src="TURTLE.JPG"
alt="Logo"></td>
        <td valign="bottom" align="right"><img src="TURTLE.JPG"
alt="Logo"></td>
      </tr>
      <tr>
        <td><h3>This image is left aligned and aligned to the top of the
table cell.</h3></td>
        <td><h3>This image is centre aligned both horizontally and
vertically.</h3></td>
        <td><h3>This image is right aligned and aligned to the bottom of
the table cell.</h3></td>
      </tr>
    </tbody>
  </table>
</body>
</html>
```

Resizing an image

Images can be resized using two methods:
- The first method is to change the size of the displayed image in the markup. This is the easier of the two methods, but often uses large image files, which are slower to upload and can delay the display of a completed webpage.
- The second method is to physically resize the image in a graphics package and then save the new image. This method has the advantage of being able to reduce the file size of an image so that a webpage will be displayed more quickly. It has the disadvantage of using low resolution images, which can appear pixelated, particularly if you wish to enlarge them.

Task 15w

Open the webpage that you saved in Task 15v. Resize the image REMORA.JPG to a width of 80 pixels and maintain the aspect ratio. Use both methods to resize this image and compare the relative file sizes of the two images. Save both versions of your webpage. Make this image a hyperlink to the webpage REMORA.HTM.

Resizing an image in the markup

Copy the webpage and supporting files from Task 15v into your Task 15w folder. Also copy the file REMORA.HTM into your Task 15w folder.

To change the size of an image in the markup use either the **width** or **height** attributes within the image tag. For this question the **width** needs setting to 80 pixels. If you change the width of the image to 80 pixels and do not specify a height for the image, it will maintain its **aspect ratio**. This means that it will keep the same proportions. Sometimes you may be asked to distort an image to give a different effect within a webpage. This is done by specifying both **width** and **height** but not keeping the aspect ratio of the original image. Find the markup for the image REMORA.JPG which looks like this.

```
<tr>
    <td rowspan="3"><img src="REMORA.JPG" alt="Remora"></td>
    <td colspan="3"><h1>Image alignment</h1></td>
```

Add a new attribute to the image tag to specify the new width of the image, like this.

```
<tr>
  <td rowspan="3"><img src="REMORA.JPG" alt="Remora" width="80px"></td>
  <td colspan="3"><h1>Image alignment</h1></td>
```

The webpage will change from this to this.

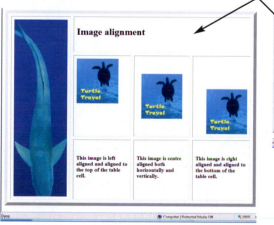

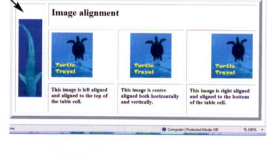

Although the vertical alignment of all three turtle images has not been changed in the markup, the effect is to make the images appear to have the same vertical alignment. This is because the row height has been reduced to fit with the new row height for the image of the remora.

Resizing an image in an external package

Open the image REMORA.JPG in your graphics manipulation package. In *Adobe Photoshop* images are resized using the **Image** menu, followed by the **Image Size...** option.

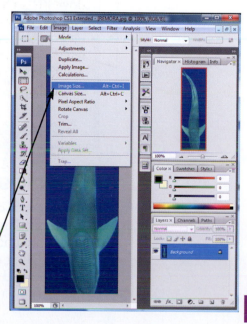

265

This opens the **Image Size** window. To set the image width to 80 pixels, change the value in the **Width:** box.

The image will maintain its aspect ratio as long as there is a tick in the **Constrain Proportions** box. To intentionally distort an image you would remove this tick and enter a height as well as a width for the image. Click on OK. This will alter the size of the image within the package like this.

To save the new image, select **File**, then **Save As...** and enter the new filename before clicking on Save. As this image will be saved in **JPEG** format, you are given options on the image quality that you require. These can be selected by typing a number between 1 and 12, using the slide bar, or selecting from the drop-down menu. 1 is the smallest file size that you can have, also gives the poorest quality images. 12 is the highest quality but results in large file sizes, which are much slower to download over the internet.

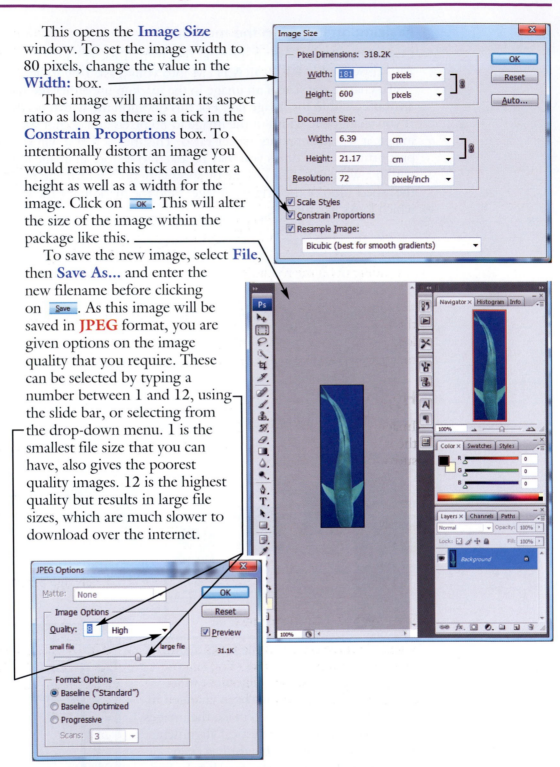

Resampling an image

This process of changing the image quality is called resampling. Images can be downsampled, meaning fewer pixels are used for the image, as you have just done by reducing the image quality. Images can also be upsampled by adding more pixels. Downsampling reduces the file size and therefore makes the webpage load more quickly. A good technique is to have a small, low resolution image (called a thumbnail) on a webpage. If the user wants to see more detail they can click on the image and a new window will open containing a high resolution version of the same image. The webpage needs amending so that the **width** attribute is no longer present, and the **source** attribute within the image tag points to the new filename.

```
<tr>
   <td rowspan="3"><img src="REMORA1.JPG" alt="Remora"></td>
   <td colspan="3"><h1>Image alignment</h1></td>
```

Save your amended webpage with a new filename. Now open the **Documents** window and navigate to the Task 15w folder. This folder contains the files saved during this task and shows you the difference in file sizes between the two methods. Your image sizes may vary from this, depending upon the resolution you selected when you saved the file. As can be seen here, in this case the new image should load in less than 60 per cent of the time the original will take.

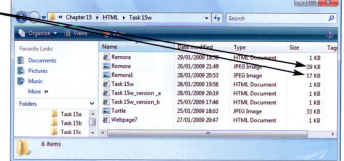

Hyperlinks from images

Images can be used as hyperlinks in the same way as text. To create a hyperlink to the webpage REMORA.HTM, add this hyperlink reference to an anchor surrounding the image tab.

```
<tr>
   <td rowspan="3">
      <a href="REMORA.HTM"><img src="REMORA1.JPG" alt="Remora"></a></td>
   <td colspan="3"><h1>Image alignment</h1></td>
```

This hyperlink will open the partially constructed webpage called REMORA.HTM.

File types for images

There are three common file types for images used in websites. These are **JPEG** files, **GIF** files or **PNG** files. You can use a graphics package like *Adobe Photoshop* to change images from one format to another by opening them and using **Save As...** to change the file format for the new image.

Printing webpages

You will be required to print different views of your webpages for the practical examinations. You must ensure that your name is included on the webpage before it is sent to the printer, in whichever view is specified. Printing the HTML view is frequently required, and even if you are using a WYSIWYG package you will need to open the webpage in a text editor to print the html. Browsers will often do this for you. In *Microsoft Internet Explorer* this is opened using **Page** and **View Source**.

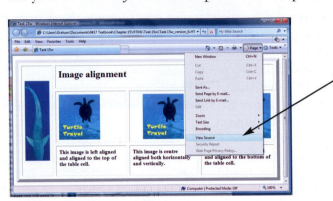

It is worth noting that the image above would not gain any credit in the practical examinations as there is nothing to identify the candidate on the printout. Browser views like this are acceptable, but you must ensure that, if you choose to use a WYSIWYG package, you test the webpage in a browser and not just within the package. Some products will display what appears to be the browser view, but is only a development tool and does not necessarily display the page as it should. Taking screenshots of your pages; using the <Print Screen> button on your keyboard to copy the screen contents into the clipboard, then pasting the clipboard into another package (usually a word processor) is a useful method of providing evidence of your work. If you have used stylesheets in your webpage make sure that you print evidence of these as well. It is more difficult to include your name in a stylesheet, so copying and pasting the stylesheet into a word-processed document containing your details is a good method of producing this evidence.

Activity 15f

Create a new webpage with a table that looks like this and has the caption 'Last week'. Set the border, cell spacing and cell padding to 4 pixels.

PTC Travel	Expenses			
	Anne	**Dan**	**Lisa**	**Udoka**
Petrol	$182.20	$185.75	$260.00	$322.00
Food	$80.00	$62.40	$54.00	$40.00
Hotel	$420.00	$382.10	$104.50	$260.00

The background colour code that you will need is #FFFF00. The image that you require is called PCTC.JPG. Print your webpage as html and as it is viewed in your browser.

CHAPTER 16

Presentation authoring

In this chapter you will learn how to:
- use a master slide to set up a presentation
- create presentation slides
- add and edit text
- insert an image
- create and add a chart to a slide
- insert other graphical features to a slide
- use transitions between slides
- animate objects on a slide
- save and print a presentation.

For this chapter you will need these source files from the CD:
- HTML.RTF
- POWERPOINT.RTF
- SLOGAN.JPG
- WEBSITE.JPG

16.1 What is a presentation?

A presentation is a series of slides used to give information to an audience. A presentation can be used in many different ways: to teach or inform as a visual aid in a lecture, or as a constant on-screen carousel giving information or advertising, for example in a shopping centre or mall. The media for delivery and type of presentation developed will depend upon the purpose of the presentation and the target audience. For example, you would design a presentation on road safety to a class of five-year-old children to be short (for a short attention span), have only a few simple words (as they cannot read fluently) and contain bright colourful moving images (to keep their attention). The medium for the delivery of this presentation would be using a multimedia projector and large screen.

It is important to understand all of this information before starting to design and develop the presentation, as different media will require different screen/page sizes. Most presentations will require a consistent colour scheme and consistently applied styles to all slides. In the practical examination, you will be given details of these colour schemes and styles.

16.2 Using the master slide

Task 16a

You are going to create and save a short presentation for IGCSE students telling them how to use *Microsoft PowerPoint*. The medium for delivery will be a multimedia projector.

Create a master slide with a pale yellow background on the right-hand side (about 1/4 of the width) with one vertical dark blue stripe as a border for the yellow background and two horizontal dark blue stripes. Each stripe should be 4 points wide. It should look like this.

A master slide allows you to design the layout of your slides before you start adding objects (like text or images) to the slides. It holds the information on colours, fonts, effects and the positioning of objects on the slides.

Open *PowerPoint* and select the **View** tab. Find the **Presentation Views** section and click on the **Slide Master** icon.

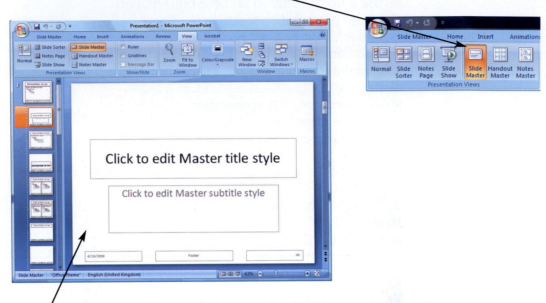

The display will change to this. The layout of a presentation will depend on the medium for its delivery. In this task, you are told that the medium for delivery will be a multimedia projector. To change the medium for delivery you must select the Slide Master tab and find the **Page Setup** section. Click on the **Page Setup** icon, which will open the **Page Setup** window.

Use the **Slides sized for:** drop-down list to select an **On-Screen Show**. You can also change the orientation of slides and handouts/notes pages in this window. When you have selected the settings, click on `OK`.

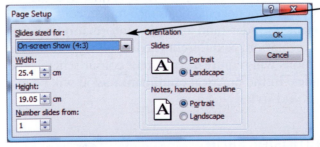

Delivery of a presentation with a multimedia projector may include the use of **audience notes** and/or **presenter notes**. Audience notes are paper copies of the slides of a presentation that are given to the audience so that they can take them away and refer to them after the presentation. These can be in different formats, with several slides on a page, or just one slide with space for the person to add their own notes. Presenter notes are a single printed copy of the slides from a presentation, with prompts and/or key facts that need to be told to the audience by the person delivering the presentation. These notes are not usually given to the audience. More information will be given on these later in this chapter.

When you look at the presentation, you will see a list of master slides will appear down the left side of the screen. You must select the **Office Theme Slide Master** at the top of the list.

Working in this master slide will affect all of the other master slides for each different style of page you may decide to use later. The master slide now appears like this.

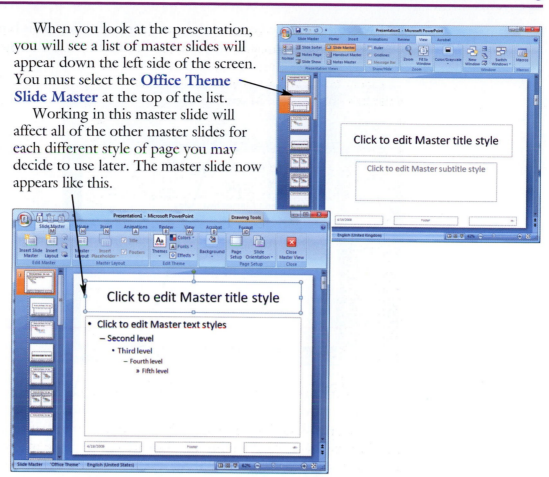

For this task, the master slide has to contain a number of lines and one filled area. You should start with the filled area. This will be created by placing a filled rectangle in the right place. However, this rectangle will cover some of the objects already on the slide, so these objects need resizing or moving out of the way first.

Select the title text box and use the drag handle to resize the text box.

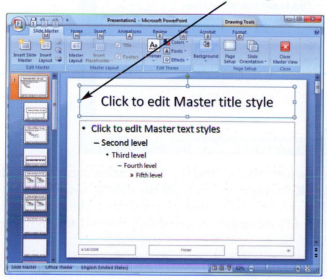

Repeat this for the body text box on the master slide. This box has also been made less deep using the lower drag handle, in order to create space to move the slide numbering.

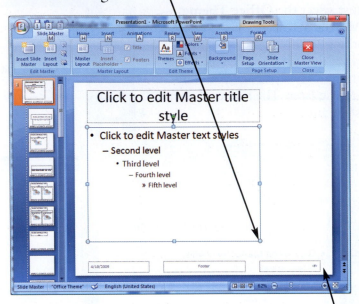

The text box containing the slide numbering is too small to resize, so this will need to be moved from the right-hand side. Drag the entire text box into the space created below the body text box.

The page layout should now look like this.

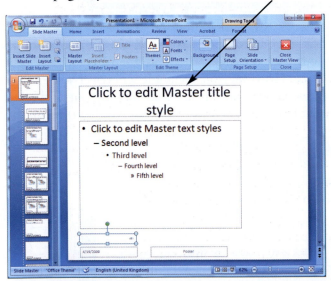

Select the **Insert** tab and find the **Illustrations** section. Click on the **Shapes** icon and select the **Rectangle** option from the drop-down menu.

Use the drag tool to drag a new rectangle that fills about a quarter of the slide. Make sure that this rectangle fits to the top, bottom and right edges of the slide and leaves no white space.

Hint

Many shapes like the rectangle can also be found in the **Drawing** section of the **Home** tab.

You now need to edit the appearance of the rectangle. Select the **Home** tab and find the **Drawing** section. Use the **Shape Fill** icon to select the fill colour and click on the **Shape Outline** icon, followed by **Weight** from the sub-menu. Select the **More Lines...** option to remove the border from the rectangle. This can be done by setting the width of the line to 0. The master slide should look like this.

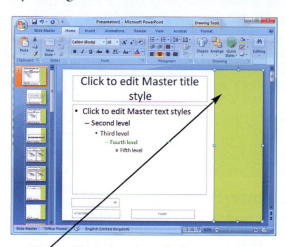

You will notice that all the other master slides (down the left-hand side of the window) now show the yellow background.

Next you need to add the three blue lines to the slide. Select the **Home** tab, then in the **Drawing** section select the **Shapes** icon and click on the **Line** option from the drop-down menu. Use the drag tool to draw a vertical line on the border between the yellow and white areas.

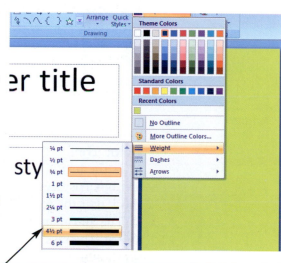

Use the **Shape Outline** icon to change the line colour to dark blue. The **Shape Outline** icon can also be used to change the line thickness. Select **Weight** and from the sub-menu select the line weight. For this task, the line weight should be 4 points. This option is not available from this menu so select the nearest weight available, in this case **4½**.

Right mouse click on the line and select **Format Shape...** from the drop-down menu. From the **Format Shape** window adjust the line **Width:** to **4 points**. Click on Close.

Repeat this process to add the two horizontal lines to the master slide, in the positions shown in the task. Save the presentation with the filename Ch_16_Task_16a.

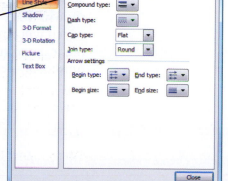

Task 16b

Open the presentation that you saved in Task 16a. Include the heading 'Using PowerPoint', left aligned in a dark blue, 60 point serif font above the blue line at the top of the master slide. Include an automated slide number in the bottom left of the footer.

Enter your name, centre aligned in the white area, at the bottom of the master slide. Use a black, 14 point, italic, serif font.

Place a clipart image of a computer or peripheral in the right-hand area. Crop and/or resize the image so that it fits within the yellow area and will not overlay the dark blue lines. Do not distort the image. Make sure that the image fills more than 50 per cent of the available space. Save your presentation.

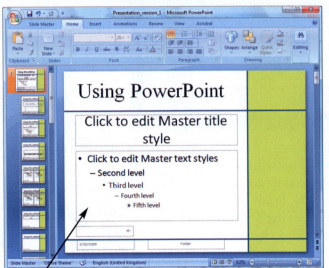

To include the heading, add a new text box in the top left section of the slide. This text box will replace the title text box, so move the title text box down the slide to below the blue line. Go to the **Insert** tab and click on the **Text Box** icon in the **Text** section. Drag out a new text box, select the **Home** tab and find the **Font** section. Set the font size to **60** points and select a serif font, e.g. Times New Roman.

Enter the text 'Using PowerPoint' into this text box. The window should now look like this. Highlight the text and set the font colour to dark blue, using the **Font Color** icon.

As the text is already left aligned, do not adjust the alignment. Notice how the text box has been aligned with the other objects on the slide so that the examiner can check that the text is left aligned.

The automated slide number is in the object moved from the right side of the footer. The task asks for this to be placed on the left in the footer. Resize this object (as shown previously) and change its alignment to left aligned by clicking on the **Align Text Left** icon in the **Paragraph** section under the **Home** tab. Drag the box into the bottom left corner. As the date is not required on all pages, this object can be deleted before moving the automated slide number.

Enlarge the automated footer so that it fills the width of the white space, as shown. Make sure that you enlarge the footer so that it overlaps the slide number, which will ensure that the examiner can see that the object is centre aligned. Change the text and the slide number to a black, 14 point, serif font, as described above. The finished footer area should look like this.

Although you have set the footer area of the master slide, you have not yet added your name to the footer, nor told *PowerPoint* to display the page numbers. To do this, select the **Insert** tab, then in the **Text** area click on the **Header and Footer** icon. This opens the **Header and Footer** window.

Tick the box for **Slide number** and the box for **Footer**. Move the cursor into the text box for **Footer** and type in your name. To set this on all slides, click on **Apply to All**.

Restore the full height of the body text box on the master slide using the drag handle. Now move down into each of the other master slides and resize all text boxes to ensure that they fit within the white space, for example from this to this.

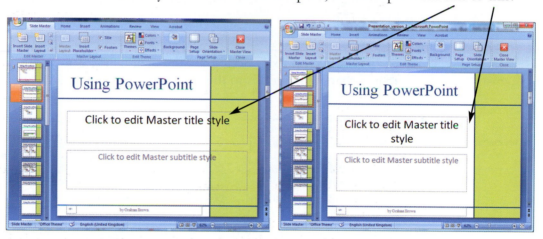

If the task required particular font styles or sizes for each of these objects, these can also be set in these master slides as described earlier.

Clipart images

To insert a clipart image, return to the **Office Theme Slide Master** and select the **Insert** tab. In the **Illustrations** section, click on the **Clip Art** icon to open the **Clip Art** pane.

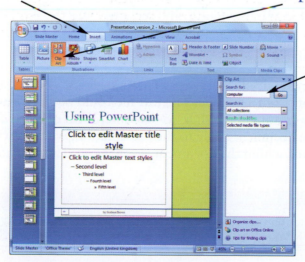

For this task you need to find an image of a computer, so enter **Computer** in the **Search for:** box and click on [Go]. (See Section 10.5 for further details on clip art options.)

This searches the clip art library and finds pictures that may match what you are searching for. Look through the images to find one that will fit well in the available space – remember that you can crop and resize the image, but cannot distort it. When you have chosen the image, click the left mouse button on it to select it. This places this clip art image onto the master slide. Move and resize it so that it fits into the correct area. To crop the image, select the image and click on the **Format** tab. In the **Size** section, click on the **Crop** icon.

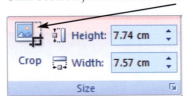

With the crop tool selected use the drag handles of the image to crop the edges so that it changes from this to this.

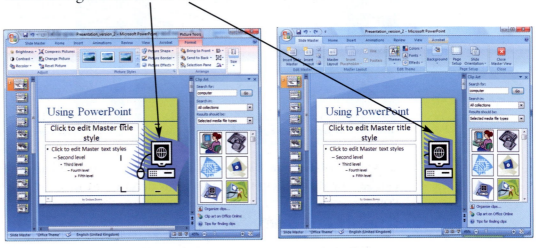

When the master slide is complete, select the **View** tab and in the **Presentation Views** section click on the icon for **Normal** page layout. Save your presentation.

16.3 Creating slides

There are two methods of creating presentation slides. The first method is to import the page contents from a text file. The text file could be stored in .txt or .rtf format. The method for creating these slides is the same. With rich text format, the styles saved within the document apply to the presentation, whereas with text format there are no styles saved within the document, so these need adding after the slides have been created.

Task 16c

Open the presentation that you saved in Task 16b. Import the file POWERPOINT.RTF, placing the text as slides in your presentation software. Save the presentation.

Open the presentation. Select the **Home** tab and in the **Slides** section select the drop-down menu from the **New Slide** option. Select **Slides from Outline...** near the bottom of this menu. Browse through your files until you locate the file POWERPOINT.RTF; click on this filename followed by Insert . This leaves the original title slide but adds five extra slides to the presentation. Save the presentation.

The second method used to create presentation slides is by inserting a new slide into an existing presentation.

Task 16d

Open the presentation that you saved in Task 16c. Insert a new slide between slides 4 and 5. This slide will contain the heading 'Ease of use', a chart and a bulleted list:

- 86% of students found it easy to use
- 120 students in the sample

Use this data to create a chart: Easy – 103, Difficult – 12, No response – 5. Show the percentage of students in each category.

On slide 1, add the heading 'Hints and tips' and add the subheading 'for IGCSE students'.

Set the following styles of text throughout the entire presentation:

- heading: dark blue, serif, left aligned, 40 point
- sub-heading: blue, sans serif, centre aligned, 30 point
- bulleted list: black, sans serif, left aligned, 24 point.

Save the presentation.

Open the presentation. Move into the left pane and select the **Slides** tab (if it is not already visible). Click the cursor between slides 4 and 5 so that it flashes as a horizontal line like this.

Select the **Home** tab and in the **Slides** section select the drop-down menu for **New Slide**. Look at the different slide layouts available from this menu and select the layout that matches the slide you are going to produce. This slide needs a small bulleted list and a chart, so the most appropriate slide type will be **Comparison**.

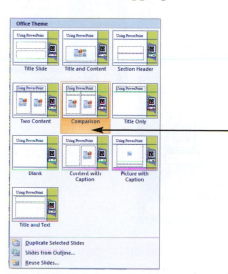

Although the option for 'Content with Caption' looks correct, it is more difficult to manipulate the caption box. Click once on this icon to get the new slide.

Delete both of the text boxes that say 'Click to add text'. These are not needed in this slide. To do this click on the line for the text box and press the < Backspace> or <Delete> key. Use the drag handles to edit the two larger objects below them to make them fit the available space. Move the title text box down, so it sits below the blue line. The slide will change from this to this.

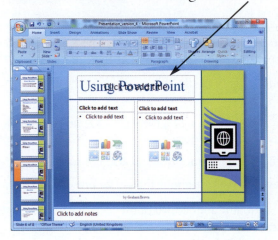

Click in the title text box and add the heading 'Ease of use'. Select the left object below the title. Click on the bulleted text 'Click to add text'. This will change this object into a text box. Type in the text '86% of students found it easy to use', <Return>, '120 students in the sample', so that it looks similar to this.

It is sensible to complete all the text parts of this task together and then add the chart at the end. Move onto slide 1. Add the heading 'Hints and tips' in the title text box. In the subheading text box add the text 'for IGCSE students' so that slide 1 looks like this.

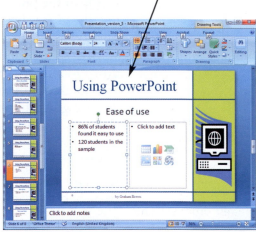

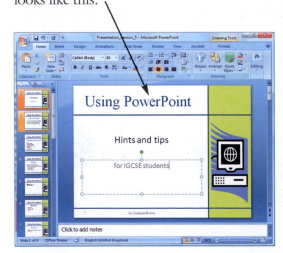

Select the **View** tab followed by **Slide Master** and select the **Office Theme Slide Master** (the top master slide). Highlight all the text in the heading (title) style and click the right mouse button to obtain a drop-down menu and miniature toolbar to allow you to edit the text style.

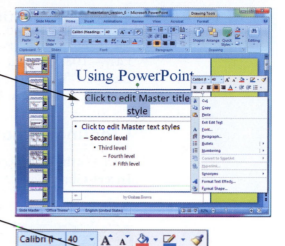

The heading style needs to be a dark blue, left aligned serif font; so select a serif font like Times New Roman, using the font list. Use the **Text Color** icon to select a dark blue colour and use the **Align Text Left** icon to change the text alignment. Use the drop-down list for the font size to change it to 40 points. The text box should now look like this.

Use a similar method to set the first level of the bulleted list, to a black sans serif, left aligned font (no changes needed for these parts), 24 points high. Adjust the font sizes for the other levels of bullet points so that they are smaller relative to this one.

The sub-heading style is not visible in this master slide, so you need to move into the master slide for the **Title Slide Layout** (the first master slide down).

In the master slide for the **Title Slide Layout**, highlight the text for the Master subtitle style and set this to a blue, sans serif, centre aligned, 30 point font. Use the same method as you did for the Master title style.

Move through each slide master in turn and edit any of the styles on other page layouts that need to be set.

Select the **View** tab and the **Normal** icon. Check each slide carefully to ensure that the styles that you have changed have been applied to each slide of the presentation. If they have not been

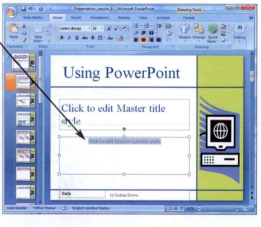

applied, you can right mouse click on the slide background (not on an object) and select **Reset Slide** from the drop-down menu to ensure that each slide matches the expected styles. You should not need to do this very often, but in this example, because you imported pre-defined styles into the presentation, added a new page and then set the styles, it may be necessary.

It is very important to make sure that all slides are consistent. A significant number of marks are lost in the practical examinations by students who assume that the software will format their slides correctly and do not check each slide carefully themselves.

This task is continued in the next section.

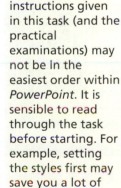

Hint

You may find it easier to define all the styles in the master slides before adding the contents to any of the slides. The instructions given in this task (and the practical examinations) may not be In the easiest order within *PowerPoint*. It is sensible to read through the task before starting. For example, setting the styles first may save you a lot of time later. Remember that the practical examinations are created for all platforms and many types of software.

16.4 Creating a chart

Move into slide 5. In the task you were instructed to 'use this data to create a chart: Easy – 103, Difficult – 12, No response – 5. Show the percentage of students in each category.' There are two ways of doing this: to create the chart within *PowerPoint*; or to create the chart in *Excel* and then copy and paste in onto the required slide.

Creating a chart in PowerPoint

Click on the chart icon in the unused object on this slide. This opens the **Insert Chart** window.

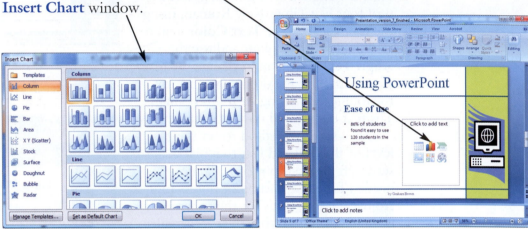

You must decide which type of chart is the most appropriate for the task. In this case, you are told to show the percentage of students in each category and there is a clue to the need for percentage values in the bullet points on the left of the slide. Because the chart needs to show percentage values (parts of a whole), a pie chart is the most appropriate type of chart. Select a simple pie chart from the available chart types and click on OK. This opens a default pie chart, but does not use the correct data. The slide should now look like this.

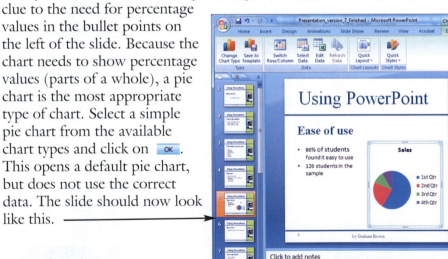

As you can see, the chart does not relate to the data for this task. Instead, it is about quarterly sales in a company. It may also open an *Excel* spreadsheet like this that contains the data. If this does not appear, select the **Design** tab under **Chart Tools**, find the **Data** section and click on the **Edit data** icon.

Move into cell B1 and replace the label 'Sales' with the word 'Students'. In cell A2, enter the text 'Easy' so that it replaces the existing text, in A3 type 'Difficult' and in A4 'No response'. Replace the sales figures in B2 with 103, in B3 with 12 and in B4 with 5. Delete the contents of cells A5 and B5. Drag the blue range marker using the drag handle so that it includes cells A1 to B4 only. It should now look like this.

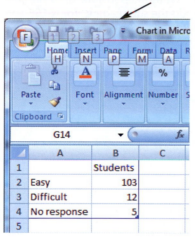

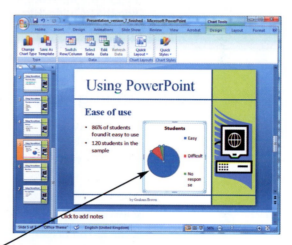

The slide now contains the correct chart. Close the spreadsheet containing the data.

Inserting a chart into PowerPoint

The second way of placing a chart into the slide is to create a chart in *Excel* and then insert this chart into the slide. This method is usually more flexible than the first method, as it allows you to create and edit the chart before adding it to the slide. Open *Excel* and enter the data into cells A1 to B3.

	A	B
1	Easy	103
2	Difficult	12
3	No response	5

Select the **Insert** tab, and in the **Charts** section click on **Pie Chart**. Manipulate and label the chart as shown in Section 14.8. Copy the chart and paste it into the slide. For this task you can paste it into slide 6. Resize both the chart and the text containing the bullet point so that they do not overlap. The completed slide will look like this.

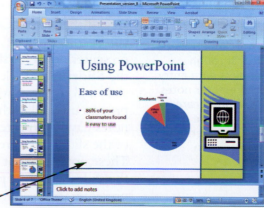

Activity 16a

You are going to create a short presentation for IGCSE students giving them hints on website authoring. The medium for delivery will be a multimedia projector.

Create a master slide with a green background at the top (about ⅛ of the height) and at the bottom of each slide (about 1⁄16 of the height) with a dark green horizontal line as a border between the white and green backgrounds. Add two vertical dark green lines to the left of the slide. Each line should be six points wide. It should look like this.

Include the heading 'HTML', right aligned in a black 40 point sans serif font at the top of the master slide (as shown above). Include an automated slide number in the green area to the left of the two vertical lines. Make this a 14 point black sans serif font. Include your name right aligned in the footer in the same style as the page numbering.

Set the following styles of text throughout the entire presentation:

- heading: black, sans serif, left aligned, 40 point, within the green 'header' section
- subheading: red, serif, centre aligned, 40 point
- bulleted list: dark green, serif, left aligned, 32 point
- level 2 bulleted list: dark green, serif, left aligned, 24 point.

Place a very small clipart image of a computer or peripheral in the bottom right corner of the white space. Crop and/or resize the image so that it fits. Do not distort the image. Import the file HTML.RTF, placing the text as slides in your presentation software. On slide 1, add the heading 'Hints and tips' and add the subheading 'for IGCSE and Level 2 students'. Use this data to create a chart: Text editor – 42, FrontPage – 37, Dreamweaver – 31. Show the percentage of students in each category. Insert this chart into slide 5 with the heading 'Percentage of users from the survey'.

16.5 Adding presenter notes

Task 16e

Open the presentation that you saved in Task 16d. Add the following presenter notes to the slides:

Slide 1: Welcome to this presentation giving you useful hints and tips on using *Microsoft PowerPoint* for your IGCSE practical examinations.

Slide 2: The presentation that you are watching is made using *PowerPoint*.

Slide 4: Hyperlinks can be used to give different paths or to open external websites or documents.

Slide 5: Graphs and charts can be added to enhance a presentation.

Hint

Take great care when entering presenter notes. A large number of marks are lost in the practical examinations each year through careless data entry in presenter notes. Take great care with the use of capital letters and punctuation.

Open the presentation that you saved in Task 16d. As you open the presentation in **Normal** view, it looks like this.

Move the cursor to the **Notes** area of the screen. Click the cursor into this box and type the presenter notes for slide 1. Use the **Slides** tab to select the next slide and continue with this process until all of the presenter notes have been entered. Not all of the slides have presenter notes. These notes will not appear on

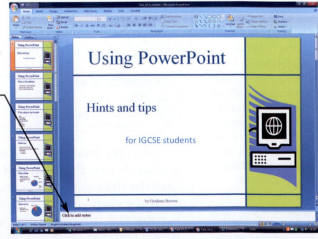

the slides when the presentation is run. You will learn how to print these so that the presenter can read from them in Section 16.9. Save the presentation.

16.6   Using images

Task 16f

Open the presentation that you saved in Task 16e. Add the image SLOGAN.JPG to the bottom of the final slide, above the blue line. Crop the image so that the red line and all contents below it are removed. Resize the image so that it fits about 1 centimetre from the left edge of the slide, 1 centimetre above the lower blue line and 1 centimetre to the left of the vertical blue line, maintaining its aspect ratio. Adjust the brightness and contrast of the image so that the background colour (pale yellow) is not visible.

In Task 16b, you inserted a new image from clip art into the master slide. For this task, you are going to insert an image given to you as a file.

Open the presentation saved in Task 16e and use the **Slides** tab to open slide 7. Select the **Insert** tab and then click on the **Picture** icon. This opens the **Insert Picture** window. Search through the files until you locate SLOGAN.JPG, select the file and click on to insert the image into the slide. Click the left mouse button on the image and from the **Format** tab select click on the **Crop** tool icon.

Hint

It is easier manipulate these objects if the ruler is showing. To select the ruler, select the **View** tab, find the **Show/Hide** section and click on the tick box for **Ruler**.

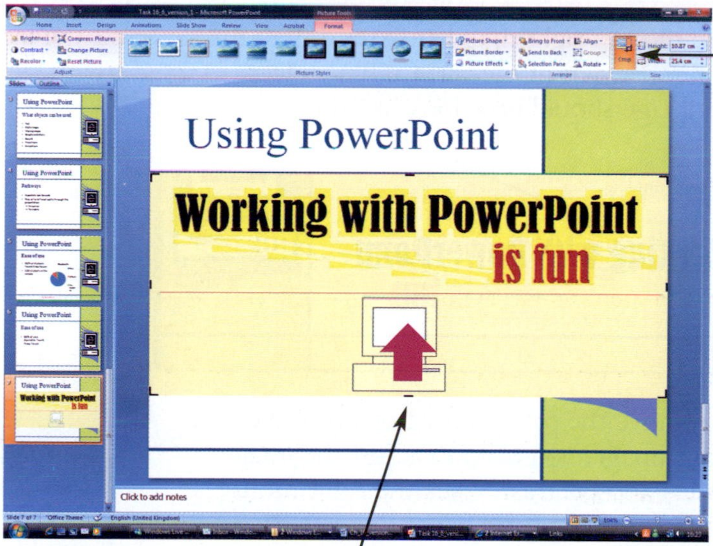

Drag the lower handle up the screen above the red line, but below the red text, to crop the image.

Click the left mouse button off the image then back on it and drag the image down so that the left and bottom edges are in the correct place on the slide.

Grab the top right drag handle and drag this to resize the image to the correct position to the left of the vertical blue line.

The image should now look like this.

To remove the pale yellow background colour from this image, you need to adjust the image brightness and contrast. Click the right mouse button on the image and select **Format Picture...** from the drop-down menu. This opens the **Format Picture** window. Select the **Picture** option from the left side of the window. Move the sliders for the **Brightness:** and **Contrast:**, so that the pale yellow background disappears but the other colours remain unaffected. These figures are found using trial and error: both settings change from 0% to a brightness of around 35% and a contrast of around 75%. When you have completed this, click on Close.

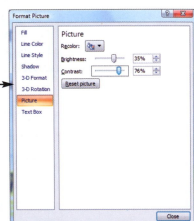

The slide should now look like this.

Notice how the red colour in the text has changed from its original dark red colour (see the previous page) to this shade of red. Save the presentation.

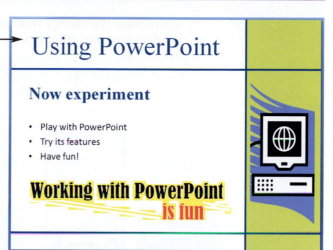

Task 16g

Open the presentation that you saved in Task 16f. Add:

● an arrow to slide 5 pointing from the first bullet point to the largest segment of the pie chart

● a callout box to slide 6 telling the reader that the image of a computer is placed on the master slide

● the text '© Microsoft' to the end of the first bullet point on slide 7 in a in a black, 12 point sans serif font

● a 6 point horizontal red line to slide 7, above the image you inserted in Task 16f.

Open the presentation and select slide 5 using the **Slides** tab. Select the **Insert** tab and click on the **Shapes** icon. This drop-down menu of available shapes will appear. Select an arrow to be included on the slide. Click the left mouse button where you want the arrow to start and drag the point of the arrow to the position that you want it to finish.

The finished slide should look like this.

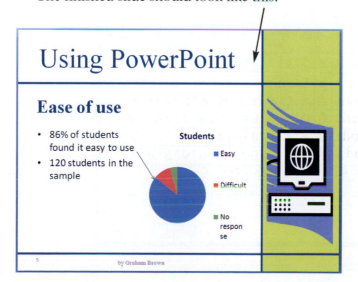

To place the callout box on slide 6, select slide 6 and again select the **Insert** tab and **Shapes** icon. This time select a callout box from the **Callouts** section of the drop-down menu. Click on the slide and drag the callout box to draw it. It is easier if you make the box too large and reduce the size later. When you have placed the box, grab and drag the yellow handle to move the point of the callout box so that it points to the image.

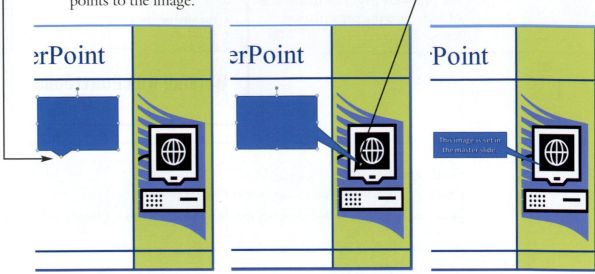

Type the text that you require into the callout box (you cannot see the cursor as you can with a text box) and then resize the callout box using the drag handles. It may look similar to this.

Select slide 7. To insert the copyright symbol, click the left mouse button to place the cursor after the 't' at the end of the first bullet point. Select the **Insert** tab and click on the **Symbol** icon. This opens the **Symbol** window. Scroll through the available list of symbols until you find the © symbol. Click on this symbol and then click on Insert followed by Close. Add the text 'Microsoft' after the symbol and highlight both the symbol and the new text. Set this to a black, 12 point sans serif font using the methods learned earlier in the chapter.

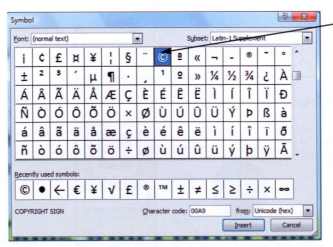

To insert the red line, select the **Insert** tab, then click on the **Shapes** icon and select a line. Drag the line horizontally across the page. Click the right mouse button on the line to open the **Format Shape** window. Use the **Line color** and **Line style** sections to change the colour and thickness of the line. The completed slide should look similar to this. Save the presentation.

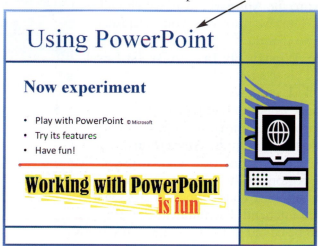

16.7 Transitions between slides

Task 16h

Open the presentation that you saved in Task 16g. Apply transitions between all slides in your presentation. In slide 3 animate all the bullets so that they appear one at a time.

The transitions between the slides are the methods used to introduce a new slide. This can be simply replacing the existing slide with a new slide or using a number of different features to change from one to another. All transitions are located in the tab.

Open the presentation. Select the **Animations** tab and find the **Transition to This Slide** section. Hold the mouse over each of the slide transitions to see the effect that it uses. There are more transitions available; you can use the scroll bar to see these.

Click on the icon to select the transition that you wish to use and then click on the **Apply To All** icon to apply the same transition to all slides. This task is continued in the next section.

16.8 Animation effects

Select slide 3 and highlight *only* the bulleted list. Select the **Animations** tab and find the **Animations** section on the left. Select the drop-down list next to the **Animate:** icon, which will look like this. The task instructed you to 'animate all the bullets so that they appear one at a time', so select **Fade**, **Wipe** or **Fly In** with **By 1st Level Paragraphs**. This sets the animation.

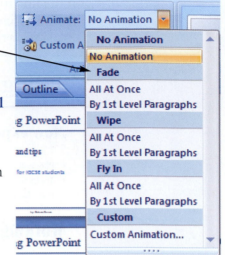

It is a good idea to have the **Custom Animation** pane open, so that when you need to show evidence of your animation effects these can be seen. To do this, still in the **Animations** tab, click on the **Custom Animation** icon. The button at the bottom of the **Custom Animation** pane allows you to test your animation and see if it works as you intended. Each individual animation can be edited in the **Custom Animation** pane by clicking on the item in the pane and clicking the right mouse button to obtain the options. The order of animation can also be changed by dragging the items up or down in the **Custom Animation** pane list. Save the presentation.

16.9 Saving and printing a presentation

As with all your work, make sure that you save your presentations regularly using the **Office** button and **Save**. To print evidence of your work, you must identify what types of printouts are required. Sometimes you will be expected to print only the slides, but more often you will need to print audience or presenter notes; for these printouts you will need to select the **Office** button and **Print**. To print evidence of the transitions and animations, screenshot evidence is the best method.

> **Task 16i**
>
> Open the presentation that you saved in Task 16h. Print your presentation showing:
>
> - only the slides
> - presenter notes
> - audience notes with three slides per page and space for the audience to make notes
> - evidence of the transitions between slides
> - evidence of the animations used on slide 3.

Printing slides

Select the **Office** button and **Print**, to open the Print window. In the **Print what:** drop-down list, select **Slides**. This will print only the slide/s content with no additional notes or space.

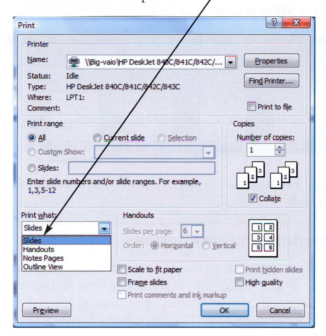

Printing presenter notes

In the **Print what:** section, select **Notes Pages**. This will print the content of the slides and the presenter notes that you typed in the **Notes** section for each slide.

Printing audience notes

In the **Print what:** section, select **Handouts**. This will give you several options to select from. The task asks for three slides per page, so in the **Slides per page** section, select the number 3 from the drop-down list. The small image to the right shows you what the printed pages will look like. In this case, the three slides are to the left and space to make notes on the right. This matches the requirements of the task.

You can click on Preview to check the printout is as you intended before printing or click on OK to print.

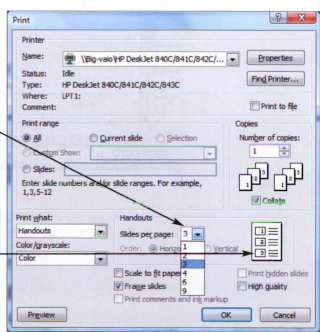

Printing evidence of slide transitions

Select the **View** tab and click on the icon for **Slide Sorter** view. Use the <Print Screen> key on your keyboard to copy this into the clipboard and paste the image into a word-processed document so that you can add your name and other details before sending it to the printer.

You can see from the **Slide Sorter** view the evidence that transitions have been added to each slide.

Printing evidence of animations

Select the **View** tab and click on the **Normal** icon to return to the **Normal** view of the slides. Select slide 3. Make sure that the **Custom Animation** pane is visible to the right of the slide. If it is not visible, open it using the **Animations** tab followed by the **Custom Animation** icon. Use the <Print Screen> key on your keyboard to copy this into the clipboard and paste the image into a word-processed document so that you can add your name and other details before sending it to the printer.

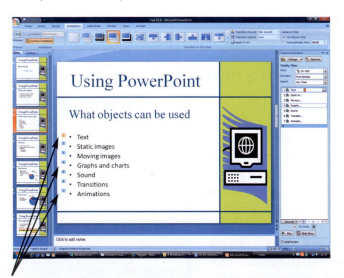

The numbering next to each bullet point shows that each bullet is animated separately from the others. Further detail about the animation of bullet point 1 can be seen in the **Custom Animation** pane. If the individual bullets are not visible, click on the icon in the **Custom Animation** pane to pull down the list.

Activity 16b

Open the presentation that you saved in Activity 16a.

Add the following presenter notes to the slides:

- Slide 1: Welcome to my presentation giving tips about website authoring using html.
- Slide 4: An intranet is internal within an organisation and is managed. The internet is global and is not managed.
- Slide 6: There are many other websites that can offer you help.

Place the image WEBSITE.JPG on the right side of slide 6. Crop this image so that only the crest and name are visible like this.

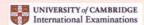

Add a red arrow, 3 points wide, from the text 'CIE website' to point to this image.

Apply transitions between all the slides in your presentation.

In slide 3 animate all the bullets so that they appear one at a time, in the order that they are in the list.

Print the presentation showing:

- presenter notes
- audience notes with six slides per page
- evidence of the transitions between slides
- evidence of the animations used on slide 3.

Index